DOROTHY DAY

and the

Catholic Worker

Cover photograph: Dorothy Day at her typewriter, 1970. (Bob Fitch photo)

THE CHRIST OF THE BREADLINES 1950

FRITZ EICHENBERG 1952

DOROTHY DAY
and the
Catholic Worker

by NANCY L. ROBERTS

State University of New York Press

ALBANY

To my parents,
Arthur and Doris Pellettier Roberts

Published by
State University of New York Press, Albany

For information, address State University of New York
Press, State University Plaza, Albany, N.Y., 12246

Library of Congress Cataloging in Publication Data
Roberts, Nancy L., 1954–
   Dorothy Day and the *Catholic Worker.*

   Based on the author's thesis (doctoral – Univ. of Minnesota).
   1. *Catholic Worker* – History.   2. Day, Dorothy, 1897-
3. Catholic Worker Movement – History.
I. Title
BX801.C369653R63   1984   282'.05   84-8492
ISBN 0-87395-938-8
ISBN 0-87395-939-6 (pbk.)

Contents

List of Illustrations

Preface

Sometime in the early Seventies when I was studying history at Swarthmore College, Moritz Fuchs, a priest in the diocese of Syracuse, introduced me to Dorothy Day and the *Catholic Worker*. For years he had kept her books in his lending library, and stacks of her paper in the back of his church in the farmlands of central New York. At a penny a copy, it had to be the best bargain on the reading rack. Easily it was the most impressive in appearance, with Fritz Eichenberg's wood engravings and Ade Bethune's drawings of worker-saints. It became apparent to me that historians of journalism have been slow to perceive the significance of the *Catholic Worker*, a remarkably long-lived, editorially consistent, and influential publication among the ranks of the advocacy press. And few have recognized how important the journalistic vocation was to Dorothy Day, who was a primary force behind the Catholic Worker movement and its paper.

I am deeply grateful to Edwin Emery, Sara Evans, and George Hage, my teachers at the University of Minnesota, who encouraged me and helped me define my interest in this subject. They have been models not only of intellectual achievement but of graciousness and good humor.

I also account my indebtedness to William D. Miller, Marquette University professor emeritus, the pioneering historian of the Catholic Worker movement. The collection of Dorothy Day's journals he is now editing will be yet another contribution to Catholic Worker history. I thank him in particular for sharing helpful information and responding to my questions.

Through association with Dorothy Day and the *Catholic Worker*, many have been inspired to strive to build a world "in which it will be easier for people to be good." Among them, I am especially grateful to Fritz Eichenberg, Ade Bethune, Joe and Mary Alice Zarrella, Monica and Tom Cornell, Florence Weinfurter, Nina Polcyn Moore, Frank Gorgen, Peggy Scherer, Sharon Wilson, Frank Donovan, and Lee LeCuyer, who patiently answered my questions about their experiences at the Worker. Thanks are also due Sister Peter Claver, the Rev. John J. Hugo of the Pittsburgh Diocese and Marc H. Ellis, Director of the Institute for Justice and Peace, Maryknoll School of Theology, who clarified certain points of Catholic Worker history.

It is a pleasure to thank Marquette University Library archivists Charles Elston and Phillip Runkel. They helped to make my research trips as fruitful as possible. Mr. Runkel, who specializes in the Catholic Worker-Dorothy Day Collection, was most generous with his time and expertise. He always responded swiftly and thoroughly to my many queries.

I would like to acknowledge financial assistance from the University of Minnesota that enabled me to complete this project in its original dissertation form, in a timely fashion: a Doctoral Dissertation Fellowship from the Graduate School, and the Ralph Casey Dissertation Award from the School of Journalism and Mass Communication. Thanks are also due my publisher, William D. Eastman, for his patient backing.

Special mention must be made of two colleagues for their helpful criticism. Prof. Michael True of Assumption College, Worcester, read selected chapters. Prof. Anne Klejment of the College of St. Thomas, St. Paul, a good friend and sister explorer of this area, read the entire manuscript and provided valuable commentary. (Her Catholic Worker index and bibliography will be published by Garland late in 1984.) Neither they nor anyone else but myself is responsible for any of the views or errors herein.

My husband Dodd Demas provided sympathetic support for this project, as he has for everything else I have attempted.

I owe a special debt to my father, who critiqued each chapter with the acumen of a seasoned English professor, the attentiveness only a parent could offer, and his characteristic zest. For more than thirty years, he and my mother have encouraged all my endeavors with a largesse of love, and it is to them that I dedicate this book.

Acknowledgements

The following have allowed the reproduction of their work, and their courtesy is gratefully acknowledged: artists Ade Bethune and Fritz Eichenberg; photographers William Carter, Bob Fitch, Ed Lettau, and Mottke Weissman; and the Dorothy Day-Catholic Worker Collection, Marquette University.

I: The Catholic Worker Movement

May 1, 1933: Massive crowds gathered ominously in world capitals. In Moscow, a million soldiers and workers—the largest May Day throng to date in the Soviet Union's history—surged through Red Square, flanked by a fearsome array of weaponry. They saluted Stalin and other government leaders who stood at the entrance to Lenin's monumental red granite tomb.[1] In Germany, the celebration was even more awesome. Bands played unceasingly all day in Berlin, while endless paraders sang "Horst Wessel" and other Nazi songs to honor their new chancellor, Adolf Hitler. A *New York Times* correspondent observed that "in all the world, never previously has there been anything to compare with this first Labor Day of the new Third Reich."[2] That evening, more than a million crowded Berlin's Tempelhof airfield to hear Hitler, while another million at home tuned in their radios.

In the United States, President Franklin Roosevelt had recently launched his "Hundred Days" emergency legislation to battle the Great Depression. The clouds of totalitarianism were already darkening the European sky, but most Americans, who were still reeling from economic disaster, paid scant attention—except in New York City's Union Square. There, May Day dawned balmy and bright on 50,000 leftists who gathered to hear speeches denouncing Hitler's fascism and advocating revolutionary social change. Late in the afternoon two Communist parades marching down Broadway overflowed into the Square, forming "a hot undulant sea of hats and sun-baked heads, over which floated a disordered array of banners, placards, and pennants."[3]

Seared in the minds of those in the crowd were memories of the previous winter, a season of nearly unmitigated despair. The Depression's lean fingers had at last gripped most Americans. Thousands of farms were foreclosed, and angry farmers dumped milk along the roadways rather than accept prices for it which did not cover transportation costs to processing plants. On the outskirts of cities, many without homes fashioned shelters of wooden crates, tar paper, old car bodies, or anything else they could glean. Quite a few sifted regularly through trash cans for scraps of edible food. Private charity and state and local welfare councils had exhausted their resources. The jobless felt they had nowhere to turn. Would Roosevelt's New Deal stem the tide of the republic's gravest economic crisis? None in that May Day crowd in Union Square or elsewhere could really say.

Into this surging throng, Dorothy Day and three young men sent by a priest to help her nervously ventured to sell the first edition of the *Catholic Worker* at a penny a copy. Doubtless some of the demonstrating Communists recognized Dorothy Day, for she had been part of the 1920s Greenwich Village avant-garde, and had long associated with Socialists, Wobblies, Communists, and other so-called "bohemians." Neither was her appearance soon forgotten. At thirty-five, she was tall and slender, with the high cheekbones and luminous slanting eyes of a Slavic beauty, though her ancestry was Scotch-Irish.

"Religion in Union Square! It was preposterous!" So Day later described the *Catholic Worker's* hostile reception among the Communists and Socialists that historic May Day.[4] For Catholics were generally understood to embrace an

Figure 1. Union Square readers of the *Catholic Worker*, about 1937. (Courtesy Dorothy Day-Catholic Worker Collection, Marquette University)

otherworldly spirituality that thwarted the development of a social conscience. And besides, Catholic clergy had often denounced the evils of Communism and Socialism from the pulpit.

But even though it bore the label "Catholic," this small tabloid was remarkably different from the rest of the religious press. It boldly proclaimed its purpose:

> To Our Readers
>
> For those who are sitting on park benches in the warm spring sunlight.
>
> For those who are huddling in shelters trying to escape the rain.
>
> For those who are walking the streets in the all but futile search for work.
>
> For those who think that there is no hope for the future, no recognition of their plight—this little paper is addressed.
>
> It is printed to call their attention to the fact that the Catholic Church has a social program—to let them know that there are men of God who are working not only for their spiritual, but for their material welfare.[5]

Indeed, the paper advocated something that to many seemed revolutionary at that time: the union of Catholicism with a concern for social justice, as Day and her co-founder Peter Maurin indicated in their very first editorial:

> It's time there was a Catholic paper printed for the unemployed.
>
> The fundamental aim of most radical sheets is the conversion of its readers to radicalism and atheism.
>
> Is it not possible to be radical and not atheist?
>
> Is it not possible to protest, to expose, to complain, to point out abuses and demand reforms without desiring the overthrow of religion?
>
> In an attempt to popularize and make known the encyclicals of the Popes in regard to social justice and the program put forth by the Church for the 'reconstruction of the social order,' this news sheet, *The Catholic Worker*, is started.[6]

Today, over half a century later, some 104,000 subscribers receive the tabloid-sized *Catholic Worker*. For more than fifty years, it has consistently prodded American consciences, holding to one price and typographical tradition, and hewing to one editorial line: the personalist, communitarian Christianity, voluntary poverty, pacifism, and nonviolent social justice activism that are the essence of the Catholic Worker movement co-founded by Day and Maurin. Written, edited, and produced largely by laypeople, it remains without official ties to the Roman Catholic Church. Today's *Catholic Worker* retains the densely printed columns that long-time readers have grown accustomed to. Striking illustrations by Fritz Eichenberg and Ade Bethune are commonly featured. Each issue includes chatty reports on the Catholic Worker "family" and columns by old-time members such as Deane Mowrer in a conversational, easygoing style. Articles of considerable intellectual depth also abound, on topics such as nonviolence, nuclear disarmament, tax resistance, United States involvement in Central America, the supernatural basis of moral values, and the relevance of Kierkegaard, Kropotkin, and Dostoevsky to Christianity.

Likened by Colman McCarthy to "a prowling animal outside the doors of our deaf and lazy institutions,"[7] the *Catholic Worker* has awakened Americans to the plight of the poor, and to other issues of social justice and peace. Jacques Maritain, Martin Buber, Lewis Mumford, James F. Powers, Maria Montessori, Claude McKay, William Everson (Brother Antoninus), Catherine de Hueck Doherty, Danilo Dolci, and the Revs. Daniel and Philip Berrigan are among the paper's contributors. Thomas Merton, also a *Catholic Worker* author, once acknowledged that he would not have become a Catholic—much less a Trappist monk—"if there were no *Catholic Worker*."[8]

And it was Michael Harrington's work as an editor of the paper in the early Fifties that formed the basis of his book, *The Other America*.[9] One of the first nationally recognized descriptions of poverty in our seemingly affluent nation, it commanded the attention of President John Kennedy and inspired his "war on poverty" (which was carried on by his successor, Lyndon Johnson).

Dwight Macdonald once aptly noted that the history of the *Catholic Worker* is as dependent on Dorothy Day as that of the FBI on J. Edgar Hoover. From the very beginning, the *Catholic Worker* was Dorothy Day's paper. She chose the news, wrote the copy, and composed the editorials. A gifted and tireless writer, over the course of her eighty-three years she wrote several books and more than a thousand articles, essays, and reviews. For several decades she produced a regular column which became the heart of the paper. Day's vintage pieces are still frequently reprinted in the *Catholic Worker*, where they continue to exert an uncommon power. Through her pen (or rickety typewriter, when one was available), Day touched thousands. Most of today's Catholic peace activists, including Fathers Daniel and Philip Berrigan, Thomas Cornell, Eileen Egan, James W. Douglass, James Forest, and Robert Ellsberg, have often acknowledged their debt to her relentless Christian witness. And the American Catholic bishops praised Dorothy Day's exemplary peace activism in their 1983 pastoral letter, which condemned the use of nuclear weapons as immoral. This represented a historic shift in their viewpoint.

Remarkably, over the years Day was consistently several decades ahead of the Catholic Church on social issues. A careful reading of her early *Catholic Worker* writings shows that she had formulated a social-activist theology of the laity that antedated Vatican II, to which that major Catholic council added only a systematic presentation.[10] Not surprisingly, David J. O'Brien, a Catholic historian, recently called Day "the most significant, interesting, and influential person in the history of American Catholicism." He judged her as having "exerted a tremendous influence on the maturing Catholic community."[11] In 1982, the *Nation* described her as "the closest thing there is to a twentieth-century American saint."[12]

But Dorothy Day's impact reaches far beyond the Catholic Left or even Catholicism. Through the Catholic Worker movement and its chief organ, the *Catholic Worker*, she challenged several generations of Americans—Catholics and non-Catholics—to scrutinize their commitment to social justice and peace.

Syndicated columnist Garry Wills, who derives much of his social thought from Catholic Worker philosophy, recently called Dorothy Day "one of the great figures of the twentieth century" whose "subterranean influence" made one say, after meeting her, " 'I've got to be better than I am.' "[13] The example of her life also inspired people abroad, particularly those engaged in peace activism. *Stimmen der Zeit*, the West German Catholic monthly, acknowledged as much in an article published shortly before Day's death.[14] In a recent interview, Petra Kelly, leader of West Germany's Green Party, praised the witness of "the nonviolent tradition" of Dorothy Day, placing her in the company of Mohandas Gandhi and Martin Luther King.[15]

After she died on the last day of the Church year — November 29, 1980 — Day's obituary appeared prominently in many major, mainstream publications, including the *New York Times, Washington Post, New York Review of Books, Nation, New Republic, Time, Newsweek, America,* and *Commonweal.* John Cogley, long-time religion editor for the *New York Times* who was responsible for updating Catholic obituaries, noted that years before Day's death, her obituary was clearly marked "Page One."[16] The *New York Times* ran it across five columns for two consecutive days, acknowledging Day's "seminal role in developing the social and economic thinking of a generation of American priests and laymen."[17] The *Washington Post* described her as a "towering figure in twentieth-century American radicalism."[18]

Dorothy Day's impact stemmed in part from the sincerity and seamlessness of her life. Inseparable from her formidable personal activism, her prose reflected her spritual purity. As she brought the poor to life on paper, she simultaneously fed and sheltered them, lived a life of the rudest voluntary poverty herself, and occasionally went to jail for her convictions. Such comprehensive commitment characterizes Catholic Workers. Peter Maurin, the French Catholic emigré whose ideas so inspired Day, gave everything he owned to the poor, gladly accepting whatever bed was his lot for the night, no matter how uncomfortable.

Maurin often remarked that the *Catholic Worker* is not just a journal of opinion, but a revolution, a movement, a way of life.[19] Dorothy Day often emphasized this point, adding with characteristic humor: "When our readers agree with us, they are Catholic Workers. When they disagree, they are readers of the *Catholic Worker*. It is a fluid situation."[20] The *Catholic Worker* cannot be separated from the Catholic Worker movement, which also includes farming communes and the nationwide Houses of Hospitality which shelter and feed the poor. Dwight Macdonald described the movement as a university, "constantly taking in freshmen and graduating seniors."[21] Another observer called it "an intellectual finishing school, offering courses in pacifism, Catholic radicalism, and works of mercy."[22]

Young people continue to flock to the Catholic Worker Houses of Hospitality and farms, embracing voluntary poverty as they minister to the destitute. After a few years of intense service they usually leave, often to marry and have children. Catholic Worker experiences have given many young volunteers interested in labor issues, politics, and pacifism a "springboard for professional work in their chosen field," as Dorothy Day has observed. In her travels about the country, she would often meet Catholic Worker "graduates" active in such fields as social work, editing, labor organizing and politics, teaching, writing, and nursing.[23] One famous alumnus is Eugene McCarthy, whom Day met years after his Catholic Worker days, on a train platform in Minnesota. The Senator laughed when he saw her and said, "You don't like me now, Dorothy, because I'm in politics." She told him that was "nonsense, because God puts people where they ought to be in life—although how far we go in that place is up to us."[24]

To understand the *Catholic Worker*, one must first examine the philosophy and programs of the Catholic Worker movement. Peter Maurin summarized them in a classic essay which has been reprinted many times in the *Catholic Worker*.

What the Catholic Worker Believes

The Catholic Worker believes
in the gentle personalism
of traditional Catholicism.
The Catholic Worker believes
in the personal obligation
of looking after
the needs of our brother.
The Catholic Worker believes
in the daily practice
of the Works of Mercy.
The Catholic Worker believes
in Houses of Hospitality
for the immediate relief
of those who are in need.
The Catholic Worker believes
in the establishment
of Farming Communes
where each one works
according to his ability
and gets
according to his need.
The Catholic Worker believes
in creating a new society
within the shell of the old
with the philosophy of the new,
which is not a new philosophy
but a very old philosophy
a philosophy so old
that it looks like new.[25]

Maurin's essay succinctly outlines the philosophical cornerstones of the Catholic Worker movement. They are: a communitarian Christianity, which stresses the necessity to live in community as Jesus did and the importance of individual action (personalism) to achieve social justice; pacifism and nonviolence; and voluntary poverty, which stems from a de-emphasis on material possessions. The movement's intellectual traditions are woven from a complex skein. Collectively, Catholic Worker ideas may seem very "radical," in the sense of "extreme." Especially during the Thirties and Forties, many judged a Catholic pacifist movement that tried to build a new earth as well as a heaven, as revolutionary indeed. Perhaps not surprisingly, the Federal Bureau of Investigation expended several hundred pages in trying to classify the type of subversion being practiced by Dorothy Day and her band of Catholic pacifists. The agents' thorough investigation even took them to *The Lives of the Saints* for background data — thus inadvertently enlisting the Catholic Worker movement in a spiritual work of mercy, instructing the ignorant. The file, which starts in 1940 and spans about thirty years, indicates that J. Edgar Hoover considered the Catholic Worker movement sufficiently threatening to deserve prosecution on grounds of sedition, and he recommended such action to the Attorney general on at least three different occasions. But his advice was not followed, and Day went free to continue what he viewed as "subversive" activities.[26]

But "radical" in the sense of "back to the roots" also accurately characterizes the Catholic Worker movement; for it is, after all, based on Christianity's most fundamental sources, the life and teachings of Jesus as revealed in the New Testament. Peter Maurin's statement that Catholic Worker ideas form "not a new philosophy, but a very old philosophy... so old that it looks like new," suggest this. And perhaps, as Anthony Novitsky has pointed out, the ideology of the Catholic Works movement — at least as developed by Peter Maurin — is not so much a product of the American Left or of liberal Catholicism as it is a product of reactionary European social Catholicism.[27]

Complex as their origins may be, inspiration for the ideas of the Catholic Worker movement can be traced to one major spring, the life and radical social teachings of Jesus, as recorded in the four Gospels of the New Testament. Two strong, additional influences are European in origin, reflecting the intellectual interests of Dorothy Day and Peter Maurin. One, transmitted by Maurin, is a body of thought produced by a group of Paris intellectuals immediately following World War I, which they called "Christian personalism." The French philosopher Emmanuel Mounier was the chief synthesizer of this idea, which stressed the importance of individual social action over broad, impersonal movements. In 1932 Mounier began to publish the articles of the Paris personalist group in his journal, *L'Esprit*, where they came to the attention of Maurin and directly inspired the personalist philosophy he presented to Dorothy Day in early 1933, shortly after they met. Indeed, Maurin admired *L'Esprit* as an ecumenical journal which promoted a just world, and he began to use it as an aid to his own teaching.[28]

The second European influence, also central to the Catholic Worker movement's personalist idea, is the philosophy of Jacques Maritain, who associated with the French group. An enthusiastic advocate for human rights and dignity, Maritain maintained personal contact with the *Catholic Worker* for many years. "Maritain meant a great deal to us in the early days of the *Catholic Worker* (and also today)," wrote a Catholic Worker veteran, Stanley Vishnewski, in 1964. He named Maritain as "the one philosopher who had the greatest influence on the thinking and actions of the Catholic Worker [movement]."[29]

The strong personalist influence of Nikolai Berdyaev on the Catholic Worker movement has also been widely acknowledged by historian William D. Miller and others. [30] The Russian emigré philosopher lived in Paris during the Thirties and Forties, where he associated with the other personalist thinkers. In *The Meaning of History*, Berdyaev articulated a personalist philosophy that is a direct source for the Catholic Worker movement's idea of personalism. He wrote:

> I would advocate… a profound integration of my historical destiny with that
> of mankind which is so intimately related to me. In the destiny of mankind I
> must recognize my own destiny, and in the latter that of history.[31]

Essentially, the personalism of Mounier, Maritain, Berdyaev, and the Catholic Worker movement emphasizes that change in society must begin with change in individuals. Each human being is thought to have a special, inviolable worth — and an equal responsibility for the welfare of others. Dorothy Day defined personalism as the most active form of personal responsibility. "If anyone comes to you hungry, you don't say to him, 'Be thou *filled*. Go be warm.' You go ahead and see to it that he does get what he needs. You're supposed to immediately reply to the need of that person." She constantly railed against "passing the buck," avoiding personal responsibility by referring the needy to "this agency or that," to the point that "so many charities… become referral agencies… and nothing is accomplished."[32] Thus Catholic Workers disavow "welfare" schemes, whether devised by church or by state. Their personalism is at odds with most forms of collectivism, which they believe too often glorify the group as "a sort of higher-order individual."[33] Because they stress personal accountability before state responsibility, they have sought neither incorporation as a nonprofit entity nor tax-exempt status. They disdain official rewards for performing the work they hold to be every human being's responsibility. Catholic Workers also decline state assistance on the grounds that "they who pay the piper call the tune."[34]

Another major influence on the movement's philosophy is the writings of the Russian novelist Fyodor Dostoevsky. Dorothy Day often acknowledged his profound influence on her life. The work of other Russian writers, such as Tolstoy and Gorky, also affected her deeply.[35] For Day, reading Dostoevsky was "a profound spiritual experience"[36] that "made me cling to a faith in God."[37] Dostoevsky's themes of love in action have become the heart of the Catholic Worker message. Throughout her life Day often quoted a passage from *The Brothers Karamazov* to describe the nature of the Catholic Worker movement:

> Love in action is a harsh and dreadful thing compared with love in dreams.
> Love in dreams is greedy for immediate action, rapidly performed and in the
> sight of all. Men will even give their lives if only the ordeal does not last long
> but is soon over, with all onlooking and applauding as though on the stage.
> But active love is labor and fortitude. ... just when you see with horror that in
> spite of all your efforts you are getting further from your goal instead of nearer
> to it — at that very moment... you will reach it and behold clearly the miracu-
> lous power of the Lord who has been all the time loving and mysteriously
> guiding you.[38]

Catholic Workers translate "love in action" into personalism, and into a communitarian Christianity. They denounce Marxism, nationalism, and capitalism
as dehumanizing collective systems, which rob the individual of dignity. Instead,
Catholic Workers advocate distributism to achieve a decentralized, simpler society based on cooperative, personalist sharing, in accordance with Christian
principles. In this new society, all "will be doing their own jobs in their own
sweet way" as they are simultaneously "working together in community,
sympathy, cooperation with fellow members of the Community toward a common goal."[39] In developing these ideas, the Catholic Worker movement draws
heavily upon the writings of Hilaire Belloc, G.K. Chesterton, Eric Gill, the Rev.
Vincent McNabb, and the English Dominicans.[40]

The primary source of the movement's emphasis on communitarianism,
however, is Christianity, which views all human beings as members of the same
spiritual family. In an early article, the *Catholic Worker* clarified the dogma of
the Mystical Body of Christ as the basis for the movement's communitarianism:
"Christ is the head and we are the members. The illnesses of injustice, prejudice,
class war, selfishness, greed, nationalism, and war weaken the Mystical Body
just as prayer and sacrifice of countless of the faithful strengthen it." The notion
of class war is precluded because all men and women, "the saint as well as the
sinner," are "members or potential members of the Mystical Body of Christ."[41]
Another way of expressing this might be the familiar Industrial Workers of the
World slogan, "An injury to one is an injury to all." Not surprisingly, given her
background as an early twentieth-century American radical, Dorothy Day occasionally quoted it.[42]

Besides personalism and Christian communitarianism, pacifism and nonviolence are fundamental to the Catholic Worker movement. Catholic Workers
refuse to use force against fellow members of the Mystical Body of Christ,
believing that "we are all members of one another."[43] Shunning coercion and
violence, Catholic Workers especially oppose government involvement in war
or preparations for war. Many have been jailed for refusing to register for the
draft. In a protest sent to Congress and President Franklin Roosevelt on the eve
of World War II, Catholic Workers articulated their opposition to conscription:

> We take our stand opposing conscription on the ground that in addition to
> imperilling man's natural and sacred rights, it constitutes an 'armed peace,' the

fallacy of which has been pointed out by Pope Pius XI. He said in regard to it, 'It is scarcely better than war itself, a condition which tends to exhaust national finances, to waste the flower of youth, to muddy and poison the very fountainheads of life, physical, intellectual, and moral.'[44]

Catholic Workers also refuse to pay income taxes that will be used to buy weapons, and to participate in civil preparedness exercises. Dorothy Day herself was jailed four times between 1955 and 1960 for refusing to comply with civil defense air raid drills.

In times of war, Catholic Workers have been conscientious objectors; America's first draft card burner to publicly violate the law was David Miller, a Catholic Worker who was subsequently jailed for this act. Catholic Workers believe that "Christ went beyond natural ethics and the Old Dispensation in the matter of force and war and taught nonviolence as a way of life."[45] Following Christ's example, they truly believe in turning the other cheek, believing that it is "much more meritorious to suffer conquest and persecution than to be responsible for the killing and maiming of anyone, let alone millions."[46] Furthermore, Catholic Workers believe there is no such thing as a "just war," in the modern world of massive armaments and nuclear weapons—if there ever was. They believe that if Christians and people of good will everywhere refuse to participate in war and to allow their governments to stockpile armaments, then war can no longer exist.

Catholic Workers reject the present social order, but they advocate that the revolution to be pursued in themselves and in society must be pacifist. "Otherwise it will proceed by force and use means that are evil and which will never be outgrown," resulting in monstrous tyranny.[47] To establish a new social order more in accord with Christian principles, in which there will be social justice for all, Catholic Workers advocate techniques of Gandhian noncooperation and nonviolent resistance to unjustified, coercive governmental authority.

Finally, Dorothy Day identified voluntary poverty as the "most fundamental and necessary plank" of the Catholic Worker movement. "I do feel strongly that we must put everything we have into the work in embracing voluntary poverty for ourselves," she maintained. "It is only when we do this that we can expect God to provide for us."[48] Day always distinguished between poverty freely chosen in community and a forced destitution without community. So concluded Marc H. Ellis, who spent a year at the Catholic Worker House of Hospitality in New York, St. Joseph's.[49] Voluntary poverty is the movement's response to the Gospel message which advocates a lessening attachment to the material goods of the world. Thus Catholic Workers live and work among the poor; they take their clothes from the same charity bins and eat the same food. Dorothy Day consistently set the example. The Rev. John J. Hugo of the Pittsburgh Diocese, Day's confessor for the last forty years of her life, expressed mild surprise at her long life (eighty-three years), given the rude food and shelter in the Houses of Hospitality that were Day's home during her life as a Catholic Worker.[50]

But of course voluntary poverty makes sense to Catholic Workers, for they view it as the only true path to personal freedom. The acceptance of voluntary poverty, Day has written, liberates people from fear, insecurity, and trivial concerns:

> Once we begin not to worry about what kind of house we are living in, what kind of clothes we are wearing, once we give up the stupid recreation of this world — we have time, which is priceless, to remember that we are our brother's keeper and that we must . . . try to build a better world.[51]

She often linked voluntary poverty directly with the Catholic Worker movement's Gospel nonviolence and pacifism, pointing out that one of "the great modern arguments" for detachment from material possessions is the modern economy's dependence on war preparation industries.[52] Everything one buys is taxed, she pointed out; so that in effect, one is "helping to support the state's preparations for war exactly to the extent of [one's] attachment to worldly things of whatever kind."[53]

Catholic Worker ideas are expressed in several practical applications or programs, among them Houses of Hospitality and farming communes. However, as many have observed and as Workers themselves freely admit, it can be misleading to use words such as "program" in connection with the movement. The Catholic Worker has never been an organization in the traditional sense. "Organization? We don't have any," Dorothy Day often remarked. "Certainly we are not a cooperative, not a settlement house, not a mission. We cannot be said to operate on a democratic basis." She often referred to the movement as a community of martyrs and saints; the martyrs were those who attempted to live with the saints.[54] Day further related how once when both an ex-soldier and an ex-Trappist were staying at St. Joseph's House of Hospitality in New York City, she asked each in turn how he found the Catholic Worker group. "The soldier said, 'It's just like the Army,' and the Trappist said, 'It's just like a Trappist monastery.' "[55] Ammon Hennacy, a *Catholic Worker* editor in the early Fifties, described the movement's organization as "truly anarchistic" in its lack of rules, by-laws, and a constitution. "There are," he wrote, "just about two unwritten rules here: (1) don't bring liquor in a bottle in the house . . . (2) we never call a cop."[56]

However, as another *Catholic Worker* editor noted, it is misleading to use the word "anarchist" in connection with the Catholic Worker movement, for it does have a degree of organizational structure.[57] Dorothy Day truly established a benevolent dictatorship as leader of the movement and editor of the paper. She herself preferred to use the terms "libertarian" or "decentralist" rather than "anarchic" to characterize the movement, because it is "diametrically opposed to the Marxist belief that through a dictatorship of the proletariat there would be a withering away of the state." While Day applauded Marxism's eventual goal of diminishing "Holy Mother the State" (her ironic term), she criticized the Soviet Union's use of force to achieve this end.[58]

Over the years, Catholic Worker programs have shown varying degrees of complexity, organization, and success. Participation in them has never been coerced, of course. Catholic Workers eschew official membership lists, constitutions, and policy meetings, relying instead upon the enthusiasm and dedication of those who choose to share their central ideas. Dorothy Day often acknowledged that such an approach expresses to many people "the folly of the cross."[59] But she always stressed that "success, as the world determines it, is not the criterion by which a movement should be judged." She counseled Catholic Workers to be ready to face "seeming failure." It is paramount, she wrote, to remain true to Catholic Worker values "even though the whole world go otherwise." Ultimately it would be for this, and not for the worldly success of their programs, that Catholic Workers would be asked by their God to make "a personal accounting."[60]

To the world, one of the Catholic Worker movement's most successful programs is the network of Houses of Hospitality. Since 1933, at least a hundred have appeared across the nation—no one knows exactly how many—and abroad. Today in the United States, they number about eighty.[61] In Boston, New York City, Syracuse, Atlanta, Chicago, Milwaukee, Minneapolis, Kansas City, Los Angeles, Winnipeg, and Montreal and elsewhere, Catholic Workers have rented storefronts, usually in the inner city, where they live in voluntary poverty as they feed and shelter the destitute, the unemployed, and the sick in body and mind. Here they practice "love in action," the physical and spiritual works of mercy (based on the Beatitudes, *Matthew 5: 3-12*), which may be summarized as:

> to feed the hungry; to give drink to the thirsty; to clothe the naked; to harbor the homeless; to ransom captives; to visit the sick; to bury the dead; to admonish sinners; to instruct the ignorant; to counsel the doubtful; to comfort the sorrowful; to bear wrongs patiently; to forgive injuries; to pray for the living and the dead.[62]

The original House of Hospitality, St. Joseph's, still maintains a vigorous presence in New York City from its present location at 36 East First Street. Nearby is Maryhouse at 55 East Third Street, a permanent residence for destitute women. Marc H. Ellis, who spent a year at St. Joseph's, described the daily soupmeal:

> Nine-thirty to eleven-fifteen . . . Anybody can come in for a bowl of hot home-made soup, bread and tea. Most soupmeal people come off the Bowery. They are homeless, sick, often beat-up, sometimes crazy and/or violent, mostly walking in a stupor. Twenty men sit at the tables, ten wait in seats against the wall, while forty sit in the basement on benches waiting for the first floor to empty. Often there are fights both at the table and in the basement. I have seen three knives drawn already.[63]

"The work is not without danger—this adventure of ours," Dorothy Day wrote. She added:

> We live on a warfront—class war, race war. Mental cases abound, drugged youth haunt our streets and doorstep. Not a week passes when there have not been knives drawn, a fist upraised, and the naked face of hate shown and the silence of bitterness and despair shattered by the crash of breaking crockery or glass, a chair overthrown.[64]

Figure 2. St. Joseph's House of Hospitality, 36 East First Street, New York City. (Photo by Ed Lettau, courtesy Dorothy Day-Catholic Worker Collection, Marquette University)

Of all the Catholic Worker Houses, St. Joseph's may be the most plagued by violence, since it stands on the fringe of the Bowery, where thousands of society's outcasts—disease-ridden alcoholics, junkies, the mentally unbalanced—wander homeless, without hope. But St. Joseph's and other Catholic Worker Houses around the country remain an alternative way of existing for the poor who come in for soup, especially in the recession of the early Eighties. "There are days," Day observed, "when suddenly there is laughter, scraps of conversation" among those in the soupline, and "one feels [they] have been wooed out of their misery for a moment by a sense of comradeship between the young people serving and those served."[65] Unlike their counterparts at the municipal shelters, Catholic Workers wear no uniforms. Nor do they carry clubs or guns. They do not preach at those they serve, nor do they require attendance at religious services in exchange for charity. Catholic Workers try to treat all visitors with dignity, even greeting them with a "good morning, sir" or "good morning, madam" at the door. Sometimes "it sounds absurd," Marc Ellis admitted. "But you would be surprised how many men and women come and comment to us on why, despite the fact that the food is far less substantial here, they prefer the Worker because they are treated like human beings and not herded like animals."[66]

The editorial offices of the *Catholic Worker* are located just upstairs at St. Joseph's, in modest, even dingy quarters. A small library contains books by Thomas Merton, Mohandas Gandhi, and other philosophers, as well as the lives of saints such as John of the Cross and Thérèse of Lisieux. Eight times a year, street people from St. Joseph's and Maryhouse help fold the 104,000 or so eight-page copies of the paper.

Besides Houses of Hospitality, the Catholic Worker movement has established farming communes, or "agronomic universities," as Peter Maurin called them. Their fundamental purpose is to enable both worker and scholar to share knowledge and to join in common physical labor on the land. Such joint activity is believed to break down barriers between people, encouraging community sharing and a cooperative society. The first farming commune was formed in 1936 near Easton, Pennsylvania. Typically, it sheltered about thirty people—"unemployed, invalids, strikers, children—all races, colors, denominations."[67] No one is sure of the exact total, but about fifteen Catholic Worker farming communes have existed at one time or another—near Upton, Massachusetts; Cape May, New Jersey; Tivoli, New York; Easton, Pennsylvania; Avon, Ohio; Detroit, Michigan; Rhineland, Missouri; and Aptos, California, among others. Peter Maurin Farm outside Marlboro, New York, remains the main Catholic Worker farm. It sometimes shelters Workers from the New York City residences. Other current farming communes include: Catholic Worker Farm, Sheep Ranch, California; Tom's Catholic Worker Farm, Gardner City, Colorado; Obonaudsawin Farm, Lexington, Michigan; Catholic Worker Farm, West Hamlin, West Virginia.[68]

The farming communes have not endured as long or as well as the Houses of Hospitality, perhaps because of Dorothy Day's insistence that need, rather than efficiency of workers, be the chief criterion in selecting guests. She freely acknowledged that some Catholic Worker farms were not true agronomic universities, but communities of need, of "wounded ones." She herself often thought of the Worker farms as "concentration camps of displaced people, all of whom want community, but at the same time want privacy. . . ."[69]

Besides feeding and sheltering the poor through the Houses of Hospitality and the farming communes, Catholic Workers place much emphasis upon nurturing the broad intellectual foundation of their movement. Like Lenin, they believe that "you cannot have a revolution without a theory of revolution." Dorothy Day cautioned, "If we do not keep indoctrinating, we lose the vision. And if we lose the vision, we become merely philanthropists, doling out palliatives."[70] In 1978, the *Catholic Worker* reaffirmed the movement's commitment to a strong intellectual basis:

> While we do not think the intellect is the center of human existence, still to 'love the Lord thy God with all thy mind' is part of the first great commandment.... Therefore, we must analyze carefully our concrete situation and consider 'what is to be done' in the light of Scripture and tradition.[71]

And so round-table discussions—still held on Friday evenings at St. Joseph's and many of the other Houses—are a prime part of the movement's program of study, discussion, and transmission of its ideas. Along with the Houses of Hospitality and the farming communes, they represent still another application of the movement's ideology. These discussions serve to "clarify thought," in Peter Maurin's words, providing a continuing intellectual foundation. Since the beginning, Catholic Workers have invited priests, Hindus, anarchists, and atheists to give lectures and discussions. Columbia University historians Parker Moon and Carlton Hayes, French philosopher Jacques Maritain, English historian Hilaire Belloc, and activist priests Daniel and Philip Berrigan are among those who have led "round-table" discussions. Topics have ranged from civil liberties to the history of pacifism, from tax resistance to the nature of salvation.[72]

The Catholic Worker movement's chief agent in publicizing its ideas remains the *Catholic Worker*. Offshoot publications have sprung into print, commonly from other Houses of Hospitality, in the United States and abroad. Examples include the *Chicago Catholic Worker*,[73] *Catholic Agitator* (Los Angeles), the Minneapolis *Catholic Worker*, the *Catholic Radical* (Milwaukee), *The Catholic Activist* (Rock Island, Ill.), *Shalom News* (Kansas City, Ks.), *On The Edge* (Detroit), *Agape* (Rochester, N.Y.), the first *Christian Front*, *The Sower*, the Melbourne, Australia *Catholic Worker*, the *Catholic Family Farmer* (Quebec), and the *Canadian Social Forum*. Perhaps because of the movement's stress on the intellectual diffusion of its message, especially through the written word, such local versions of the *Catholic Worker* surpass many other small publications in their unusually high quality. The *Catholic Agitator*, especially, has offered consistently excellent writing, photography, and graphics.

Despite inauspicious beginnings, the Catholic Worker movement and its primary newspaper, the New York-based *Catholic Worker*, have exerted a strong influence. And yet they are the products of two people whose backgrounds hardly qualified them, at least in the view of Church authorities, for such leadership. One was an ex-Socialist, a recent Catholic convert, a journalist; the other was a destitute, eccentric, French Catholic intellectual whose thick accent defied understanding. Together they achieved a success that neither could have alone.

S·BENEDICT·JOSEPH
Labre

ADE BETHUNE

II: Dorothy Day and Peter Maurin

A pair with more contrasting backgrounds would be difficult to find. Dorothy Day came from middle-class, Anglo-Saxon Protestant stock whose roots ran deep in American history. She was educated in the public schools of large American cities. Peter Maurin came from an old French peasant family, was raised in a rural area, and was educated completely within the Catholic tradition. His radicalism was born in the French Catholic social movements of the late nineteenth century and sustained by his reading; her radicalism was born in the secular Socialist, I.W.W., and Communist ferment of early twentieth-century America, and sustained by her writing and active demonstration. He favored a back-to-the-land solution to social problems; she was interested in urban labor problems and saw the strike as an instrument of social reform.[1]

Dorothy Day was born on November 8, 1897, in Bath Beach, Brooklyn, the third of Grace Satterlee and John I. Day's five children. Her vigorous ancestors included both workers and scholars. Day's Scotch-Irish newspaperman father belonged to a staid Cleveland, Tennessee, family of farmers and physicians whose rock-ribbed work ethic came directly from Calvinism. Her mother was from an equally established Marlboro, New York, family of merchants, craftspeople, whalers, and mill workers. The Satterlees belonged to the Episcopal Church.[2] Grace Satterlee Day was one of the first women trained as a stenographer; to her daughter, she was a graceful figure "in a high-collar blouse and long skirt, sitting on a stool." Later when Dorothy became interested in workers and labor movements, Mrs. Day described her own youthful work in a shirt factory in Poughkeepsie. But her view of "the workers" was less romantic than her daughter's.[3]

When Dorothy was six, the family moved to California — first to Berkeley, then to Oakland. She was an impressionable, reflective child who, even at that young age, often awoke at night feeling what she later called "the blackness and terror of non-being," a dread of "silence and loneliness." Her other childhood terror, she recalled, was an "awful and mysterious" apprehension of "Presence."[4] She was equally sensitive to human goodness. The San Francisco earthquake of 1906 made a deep impression on eight-year-old Dorothy. She marvelled at how the cataclysm lowered the usual human barriers, drawing out people's "warmth" and "kindliness."[5] Soon after, the Days moved to Chicago, where they lived in near-poverty as Mr. Day tried unsuccessfully to write fiction.

The Day home was Republican, conservatively American. Family life seems to have been fairly happy, although outward displays of affection were limited to the nightly austere kiss from Mrs. Day. She was the unifying force in the family, for her husband's relationships with his children were relatively remote. By her father's mandate, Dorothy led a very protected existence until she left for college. Having to work nights and sleep days, Mr. Day demanded an orderly, quiet family life with no visitors, blaring phonographs, or cussing. He wanted "to keep things as they were," believing that women and children belonged in the home; and he permitted no picture books, detective stories, or "trash" literature to disturb the domestic peace. He did allow the Bible, Scott, Hugo, Dickens, Stevenson, Cooper, and Poe, which the Day children read eagerly. Dorothy Day remembered sneaking romances and dime novels into the house to round out her reading.[6]

Religion was treated with respect in the Day household, but from a distance. Day has written that "the name of God was never mentioned, mother and father never went to church, none of us children had been baptized and to speak of the soul was to speak immodestly, uncovering what might better remain hidden."[7] Even in that milieu, young Dorothy's natural religious sensibility showed itself. As a child she attended an Episcopalian church alone, where she was deeply moved by the Psalms and formal prayers of the services.[8] And she never forgot Mrs. Barrett, the mother of one of her playmates, who gave Dorothy her "first impulse towards Catholicism." Watching the woman on her knees saying her daily prayers, Day felt "a warm burst of love" toward Mrs. Barrett that she would always remember. While still a child, Day recognized the "beauty and joy" in Mrs. Barrett's life that came from knowing God.[9] This was something Day's family had not taught her.

But she grew up knowing much about journalism. Her father, an itinerant sportswriter who helped found the Hialeah racetrack in Florida, was sports editor of Chicago's *Inter Ocean* and later became racing editor of New York's *Morning Telegraph*. He often incorporated Biblical and Shakespearean allusions into his columns. Occasionally he tried to write short stories or a novel, and he was extremely proud to have been published in the *Saturday Evening Post*. Not unexpectedly, by the time Dorothy was eleven, she and her siblings had already started to type out a little family newspaper. "We all liked to write," she recalled, "and I had been taught early to write personally, subjectively, about what I saw around me and what was being done.[10]

Like their father, her three brothers worked on newspapers all their adult lives.[11] Two had distinguished journalistic careers: Sam Houston Day became managing editor of the New York *Journal-American*; Donald Day was sports editor of the *Journal-American*, and eventually Baltic correspondent for the *Chicago Tribune*. When the young Donald began work on E.W. Scripps' experimental adless newspaper, Chicago's *Day Book*, he sent Dorothy the daily papers with his stories marked in them. Carl Sandburg was then one of the *Day Book*'s writers; and, Dorothy remembered, "This poet of the people sat on the copy desk and inspired my brother to look on the people as he did, with love and hope of great accomplishment." It was in Donald's stories that she learned of Eugene Debs, "a great and noble labor leader of inspired utterance."[12]

In public high school, Day read voluminously on her own. She was deeply moved by Dostoevsky and Tolstoy; she was intrigued by Kropotkin's *Memoirs of a Revolutionist*, "which especially brought to my mind the plight of the poor, of the workers. . . ." She read the life of one of the Haymarket anarchists, and was fascinated by the writings of another revolutionary anarchist, Vera Figner. She also immersed herself in the social novels of Jack London and Upton Sinclair. *The Jungle*, which exposed the meat-packing industry of Chicago and the West Side's slum poverty, made the most profound impression on her. No longer did Day wheel her beloved baby brother John to the park or lake, but explored firsthand the streets of the slaughterhouse section. She felt that "the very fact that *The Jungle* was about Chicago where I lived, whose streets I walked, made me feel that from then on my life was to be linked to theirs [the poor's], their interests to be mine; I had received a call, a vocation, a direction to my life."[13]

At sixteen, Day received a scholarship to attend the University of Illinois at Urbana. (Ironically, it was a Hearst scholarship—and Day was later to encourage *Catholic Worker* readers to boycott the Hearst newspapers.) Here she demonstrated her independent spirit. She smoked and uttered unladylike words such as "damn" and "hell," joined the Socialist Workers' Party, frequently skipped the classes she found boring—most, except English—and worked several jobs at once. She also apparently abandoned any religious sentiments she had held as a child.[14] Often she went without meals. She began writing columns for the town paper on space rates, and while her pieces which criticized the existing order never saw print, those criticizing the working conditions of the students did, and these sometimes got her into "hot water."[15] Many of her peers must have found the Chicagoan curious looking: tall and thin, she had a pale face with large, oddly slanting eyes whose shadows betrayed her lack of sleep.

Day soon joined a campus writers' club, and produced a story, probably for the campus newspaper, about her experience of going hungry.[16] She wrote with great zest of three days with no food but salted peanuts. The article brought her to the attention of Rayna Simons, a brilliant, wealthy student who encouraged Day to write, included her in her circle of literary friends, and helped her financially. Day found her sophomore year much brighter. She and her new companions attended lectures given by prominent Socialists and activists such as Rose Pastor Stokes and Scott Nearing, and listened to poets such as Edgar Lee Masters, Carl Sandburg, Vachel Lindsay, and John Masefield.

Dorothy and Rayna began to lose track of each other after college, but Dorothy was always immensely grateful for her friend's generosity. Rayna Simons Prohme eventually embraced Communism and became an agent for Mikhail Borodin in China, from where she smuggled Sun Yat-sen's widow to

Moscow in 1926. [17] Ultimately Dorothy Day trod a different path, one which combined the orthodox Catholicism of her mature years with the concern for the poor she had shown as a young secular radical. Certainly as an agnostic college student, she was "in love with the masses," as she put it,[18] and she asked difficult questions. "Why was so much done in remedying social evils instead of avoiding them in the first place?" she wondered. She questioned the justice of a system that allowed occupational diseases and sickness "which came from not enough food for the mother and her children." She was concerned about disabled workers who often received nought but charity for the rest of their suffering lives. "Where," she asked, "were the saints to try to change the social order, not just to minister to the slaves but to do away with slavery?"[19]

But Day did not search for a religious solution. When a professor she admired once remarked that the strong did not need religion, Day began to feel that she must ruthlessly cut it from her life. Deliberately, she hardened her heart against this "opiate of the people," afraid that it would impede her activism. "I wanted to have nothing to do," she later wrote, "with the religion of those whom I saw all about me."[20]

In June 1916, at the end of Day's sophomore year, her family moved to New York, where Mr. Day began to work for the *Morning Telegraph*. Homesick, Day joined them and began to search with difficulty for work on a newspaper. Her father, who vehemently opposed career women, let alone women in journalism, instructed his city editor friends to send her home with a lecture on women's proper place.[21] Because her father "had made it plain that no daughter of his was going to work and live at home,"[22] Day moved out and persuaded Chester Wright, editor of the Socialist *Call* and hardly a crony of her Republican father, to hire her as a reporter for five dollars a week. She lived on the cheap in a Cherry Street tenement, near the Manhattan Bridge on the Lower East Side, walking distance from the *Call* office on Pearl Street. Day covered strikes, pickets, marches to City Hall, community demands for housing, schools, and health care, and peace meetings.[23] She interviewed Leon Trotsky before he returned to Russia, and she heard many of the most stirring radical orators of the time: Alexander Berkman and Emma Goldman, the famous anarchists; Bill Haywood and Arturo Giovanitti of the I.W.W. She also heard Elizabeth Gurley Flynn, who was campaigning for the striking miners of the Mesabi Iron Range, and was "thrilled by her fire and vision."[24] (Later Gurley Flynn would regularly send blankets and old clothes to St. Joseph's House of Hospitality.[25] When she died in 1964, she left her tiny estate—clothing, books, apartment furnishings—to the Catholic Worker movement.[26]) Usually Day was far too busy at the *Call* to be an active Socialist. But on March 21, 1917, she joined with thousands at Madison Square Garden "in reliving the first days of the revolt in Russia. I felt the exultation, the joyous sense of the masses as they sang *Ei Euchnjem*, the workers' hymn of Russia."[27]

The snow in New York was gone by that April of 1917. America had just entered World War I. Day left the *Call* and joined a group of Columbia University students who were en route to Washington to protest the draft. When she returned, she joined the staff of the *Masses*, the most exciting little radical magazine of the day. Founded in 1911, the *Masses* was the first Socialist periodical to unite early twentieth century American cultural and political radicalism, and it did this with an unprecedented literary brilliance and aplomb.[28] Besides Max Eastman, who became editor in 1911, the stellar staff included writers Floyd Dell, Merrill Rogers, and John Reed, with artists Art Young, Hugo Gellert, Maurice Becker, and Boardman Robinson. The *Masses* office was located in the front part of a building facing Union Square; in the back half, Frank Harris edited *Pearson's*, a semi-Socialist muckraking magazine offering piquant literary gossip.[29]

At the *Masses*, Day was an assistant to Floyd Dell, who in his autobiography *Homecoming* recalled her as "an awkward and charming young enthusiast, with beautiful slanting eyes. . . . Dell recognized himself as the character "Hugh Brace" in Day's subsequent autobiographical novel, *The Eleventh Virgin*.[30] Eager to write that summer of 1917, Dell left for a cabin in New Jersey, leaving the nineteen-year-old Day, who had by now mastered make-up, in charge of editing the magazine. Day enjoyed living in a staff apartment on MacDougal Street that summer. Impatient to finish her work so she could go out into the streets and attend meetings, she sometimes returned the work of eminent poets with rejection slips that bore a single written word: "Sorry."[31]

Day joined many of the young leftist intellectuals in her set for picnics along the Palisades and spirited all-night discussions in taverns. She was as outspoken as the best of them and, when pressed, quick to take action on issues she considered important. Poet Claude McKay later recalled that when the editors of the *Masses* sat in Greenwich Village restaurants discussing radicalism and one of them, perhaps a Southerner, used the word "nigger," those at the table would feel embarrassed, but do nothing. Only Dorothy Day would rise and threaten to slap the face of the offender if the word were uttered again.[32]

Michael Gold (who became editor of the *New Masses* in 1926) admired Day's crusading spirit, and they saw much of each other that summer of 1917 and the next year. Day, Gold, and Maurice Becker would often stroll the streets of New York together. Savoring the struggles and joys of their youth, they would dally on park benches and dangle their feet off the ends of piers, singing revolutionary songs long into the starlit nights.[33] At one time Day was even engaged to Gold for a year, but being bourgeois in his attitude toward marriage, he decided she was too flighty to make a good wife and mother, although they maintained a lifelong friendship.[34] Later, after Day left her atheist common-law husband Forster Batterham, it was Gold who sympathetically supported Day's conversion to Catholicism, despite perceiving her sadness at having to make such profound changes in her way of life. Day observed that Gold "seemed to understand my misery and to sense that there had to be a price to pay, sometimes a heartbreaking price, in following one's vocation."[35]

About six months after Day joined the staff, the government suppressed the

Masses under the provisions of the 1917 Espionage Act. It was the August 1917 issue, one of the three that Day had almost single-handedly produced, that brought down the heavy hand of government censorship. But since her byline did not appear on any questionable articles in that issue, she was not named in the indictment. Eventually Day was subpoenaed as a witness for the state during the periodical's trial. Morris Hillquit, the Socialist-attorney, defended the *Masses* and he and Day labored together over the testimony.[36] "I was a bad witness for the state and a good one for the defense," was all she chose to recall.[37] Shortly after the *Masses* shut down, now unemployed, Day impulsively decided to accompany her friend Peggy Baird to Washington to picket the White House in support of women's suffrage. With the other demonstrators, she endured a thirty-day jail sentence in Occoquan, Virginia, experiencing oppression and despair firsthand.[38] It was the first of seven imprisonments for Day, but most of these would be for her pacifist convictions.

When she returned to New York, Day began to write for the *Liberator,* the successor to the *Masses*, edited by Max Eastman, his sister Crystal Eastman, and Floyd Dell. Now Day became part of the Greenwich Village literary and social avant-garde. She met Terry Carlin, an old Irish anarchist who had known the Haymarket martyrs. And she began to hang around the Provincetown Playhouse where young Eugene O'Neill was launching his career.

O'Neill, other writers, and actors from the Playhouse patronized the Hell Hole, a Village social center-saloon located on the corner of Sixth Avenue and West Fourth Street. In *The Exile's Return*, Malcolm Cowley described it as "tough and dirty; the proprietor kept a pig in the cellar and fed it scraps from the free-lunch counter. The boys in the back room were small-time gamblers and petty thieves." All the gangsters in the bar admired Dorothy Day, Cowley claimed, "because she could drink them under the table."[39] He probably exaggerated her alcoholic prowess, but she was certainly, with her cronies, a regular.

Day, O'Neill, Max Bodenheim the poet, and others would often stay up all night in the saloon, philosophizing. All shared an uncommon creativity that moved them to written expression: one, through plays; another, through poetry; and Day, through prose to foment social activism. She recalled sitting with O'Neill and Bodenheim and writing poems on the backs of old envelopes, each of the trio successively scrawling a verse.[40] It was also here on cold, bitter winter evenings that O'Neill in an alcoholic haze recited Francis Thompson's poem, "The Hound of Heaven," to Day. "Gene could recite all of it," she recalled, "and he used to sit there, looking dour and black, his head sunk on his chest...."[41] "The idea of this pursuit by the Hound of Heaven fascinated me," she later wrote. "The recurrence of it, the inevitableness of the outcome made me feel that sooner or later I would have to pause in the mad rush of living and remember my first beginning and my last end."[42]

Perhaps these were among her reflections when, after spending the night in a waterfront tavern, she would frequently stop at St. Joseph's Church on Sixth Avenue and kneel for the early-morning Mass. But first she would likely as not have accompanied the drunken O'Neill to his flophouse and seen that he was warmly covered. O'Neill found her strength of character especially attractive, but they were friends, nothing more. The playwright probably incorporated some elements of Dorothy Day's personality in the larger-than-life character of Josie in "A Moon for the Misbegotten."[43] In a three-page manuscript that she prepared some forty years later, entitled "Told in Context," Day recorded her opinion that religious questions defined O'Neill's life struggle.[44] She also remarked that she felt O'Neill's tragedies were inspired by a great love, by his searching for a forgiveness that he never found.[45] Years later, as the playwright lay dying, Day wired Richard Cardinal Cushing to ask that he try to see him.[46]

Day's other friends during her Greenwich Village life included John Dos Passos, Malcolm and Peggy Baird Cowley, Caroline Gordon, Allen Tate, Kenneth Burke, and Hart Crane. Liberal, radical, bohemian, they reminded Day of Samuel Johnson and his crowd, delving into literary and social controversy.[47] Several became life-long friends. Some thirty-five years later, in the early Fifties, Michael Harrington (then associate editor of the *Catholic Worker*) observed Allen Tate, Caroline Gordon, and Peggy Cowley turning up frequently at St. Joseph's House of Hospitality to visit their old companion. When Harrington was given a seersucker jacket of Tate's from the common store, he was "proud to wear the raiment of an established poet," even though it was several sizes too small.[48]

Day recalled that in the Twenties, many of her leftist friends used to say, "Dorothy's never going to be a good Communist. She's too religious."[49] Day was not yet a Catholic, but the New Testament, Thomas à Kempis' *The Imitation of Christ*, and the novels of Dostoevsky were all causing her to question the deeper meanings of her activism in secular social causes. By the end of 1917, she had come to value nonviolent solutions; in a review for the *Masses*, she praised Upton Sinclair's *King Coal* because it explicitly advocated such an approach.[50] In 1918, at the age of twenty, Day found her bohemian life rather purposeless, and she began nurse's training at King's County Hospital in Brooklyn. A compulsion to serve—fueled by the sufferings of a people at war—led her to this noble step. But she quit her training after only a year. It was not because she disliked the work, but because she had come to believe that journalism was her true calling.[51]

She wrote cryptically in her autobiography about the next few years. At the hospital Day had met a roughdrinking, macho newsman named Lionel Moise who had once worked with Ernest Hemingway on the *Kansas City Star*. Usually cautious, even prudish about "free love," she had a despairing affair with Moise, which ended when she became pregnant. She knew that if she had a child he would leave her, but despite the abortion she underwent the affair ended traumatically. Her biographer reports that she then married, apparently on the rebound, and in 1919 she and her 42-year-old husband, an unstable literary promoter named Barkeley Tobey, joined the exodus of the "lost generation" to Europe. Like many of her peers, Day began to write a novel, the obviously autobiographical *The Eleventh Virgin*.[52]

Day and Tobey were hardly compatible, and they soon separated. She returned to the United States in the summer of 1920 and spent the next two years living in Chicago slum rooming houses and holding nondescript jobs, among them modeling for artists and clerking for Montgomery Ward. An often-told but apocryphal story is that Day served as the model for Marcel Duchamps' painting, "Nude Descending a Staircase."[53] Day worked briefly during this time as secretary to Robert Minor, who edited the *Liberator* from Chicago. But she never joined the Communist Party, though her associates were once again radicals.

In Chicago in 1920 she went to jail again when police, concerned over the supposed Red menace, summarily raided the I.W.W. rooming house in which Day was comforting an acquaintance who had attempted suicide. After several days' imprisonment, the charges of prostitution against both women were dropped. Although Day's jail experience was sordid, she observed a generosity and community among the thieves, drug addicts, and prostitutes.[54] She always had a rare capacity to recognize signs of hope, however minute, in the midst of despair.

Out of jail and still unfulfilled by the course of her life, Day moved to New Orleans, where she wrote for the New Orleans *Item*. The paper had a sensational streak, and Day's first full-time assignment, which she hardly relished, was to get herself hired as a Canal Street taxi dancer and write stories about "the girls" there.

In the spring of 1924, Albert and Charles Boni, who were printing the works of many post-war authors, suddenly published the novel Day had written in Europe, *The Eleventh Virgin*. Perhaps attracted by its suggestive title, a Hollywood producer offered $5000 for the movie rights. Day's share was $2,500, a huge sum in those days. With the money, she returned happily to New York, and bought a cottage on Staten Island's Raritan Bay, among a colony of radicals and beachcombers. Now she renewed her ties with her old leftist and literary friends. A few months after the move, Day entered into a common-law marriage with Forster Batterham, a biologist whose guiding principle was a rationalist anarchism. Nature delighted him, but most humans and their unjust institutions did not. The next two years were happy ones for Day, although her mate, an individualistic loner, "had always rebelled against the institution of the family and the tyranny of love." He constantly reminded her that theirs was a comradeship, not a marriage.[55] Still, at first they found their life together to be satisfying. While Day wrote for the *New Masses* and contentedly gathered driftwood, Batterham fished in the bay. A picture from this period shows her at her typewriter by a window of the little cottage, her auburn hair bobbed with bangs in the style of the day.

With Batterham, Day felt the full measure of natural human happiness. A city girl, she learned to love the sound of the surf and the salt spray as much as he. The beach's serene and pristine beauty had a profound effect on her. "You hear things in your own silences," she would later remark about those days. Always contemplative, she sensed an enveloping creativity that called to her deepest self. And Dorothy Day found God. Some fifty years later, she would

FRITZ EICHENBERG © 1952

THE LONG LONELINESS 1952

recall that "The beauty of nature which includes the sound of waves, the sound of insects, the cicadas in the trees—all were part of my joy in nature that brought me to the Church."[56] But as she renewed her spirituality, Batterham grew distant. He found religion incomprehensible, even disturbing to discuss. "It was impossible to talk about religion or faith to him," she wrote. "A wall immediately separated us." In June 1926 when Day recognized the unmistakable signs of her pregnancy, she was delighted, for she had wondered for many years if she were capable of bearing a child. Doubtless she must have thought of the earlier life she had lost, and rejoiced in this opportunity for renewal.

Batterham was not pleased, for "his extreme individualism made him feel that he of all men should not be a father."[57] When Tamar Teresa was born in March 1927, Day felt such exuberance that she wrote an account of her experience which her old friend Mike Gold published in *New Masses*.[58] Later it appeared in leftist papers throughout the world.

As she gazed upon her newborn daughter, Day felt such joy and gratitude wash over her that she was eventually compelled to join the Catholic Church. As she explained,

> The final object of this love and gratitude was God. No human creature could receive or contain so vast a flood of love and joy as I felt after the birth of my child. With this came the need to worship, to adore. I had heard many say that they wanted to worship God in their own way and did not need a Church in which to praise Him. . . . But my very experience as a radical, my whole make-up, led me to want to associate myself with others, with the masses, in praising and adoring God.[59]

Now the Hound of Heaven haunted her more than ever, and Day faced a most difficult decision. Her husband was a man who spurned the idea of God as well as the sacrament of marriage. "To become a Catholic meant for me to give up a mate with whom I was much in love," she acknowledged, even though she "had known enough of love to know that a good healthy family life was as near to Heaven as one could get in this life." Eventually it came to "the simple question" of whether she "chose God or man." An excruciating tension developed between the couple. The executions of Sacco and Vanzetti on August 23, 1927, increased their own misery. Day and Batterham were deeply depressed by what they viewed as a grave injustice. For days, Batterham ate nothing and simply sat, "stupefied," in his boat. Finally, irritated by Day's religious leanings, he left.[60]

Day was baptized a Catholic on December 28, 1927, after a period of study and meditation. "It was not because I was tired of sex, satiated, disillusioned, that I turned to God," she explained to her bewildered radical friends. "It was because through a whole love, both physical and spiritual, I came to know God."[61] But conversion brought her no immediate joy; she had given up the man she deeply loved, and she still struggled with the tension between her commitment to social justice and her religious feelings. Day continued to oppose capitalism and imperialism as much as ever, yet here she was, "going over to the opposition," as she put it, for the Catholic Church was "lined up with property, with the wealthy, with the state, with capitalism, with all the forces of reaction."[62] Why, then, did she become a Catholic? Because it was the church of the poor, because she felt its continuity. "No matter how corrupt or rotten it became," she sensed its special feeling for humankind. And, "it had the mark of Jesus Christ on it."[63]

For the rest of her life, as a loyal Catholic traditionalist, Day sought to infuse Catholicism with the passionate concern for social justice that she had developed as a young American radical. But at first she wasn't quite sure how to go about this. Again she held a succession of jobs in a short time, including scriptwriting in Hollywood. The moral and social superficiality of such writing frustrated her, and she journeyed to Mexico City. She submitted a series of articles about the destitution and despair she saw around her to *Commonweal*, beginning a long relationship with this journal.

In 1932, over twelve million people were unemployed. Thousands could neither pay rent nor buy food in this time before unemployment insurance, welfare, and Social Security. Toward the end of that year, the thirty-five-year-old journalist found herself in Washington, D.C., covering the Communist-organized Unemployment Council's Hunger March for *Commonweal*, and a farmers' convention, composed of small farmers and tenant farmers from around the country, for *America*. The harsh realities of the Depression impressed her in a most dramatic way. Watching the "ragged horde" of marchers on the tree-lined streets of the capital, Day felt both joy and pride, and a certain bitterness. She had been a Catholic convert for five years, and she knew that she could write, protest, and arouse consciences. "But where," she asked, "was the Catholic leadership in the gathering of bands of men and women together, for the actual works of mercy that the comrades had always made part of their technique in reaching the workers?"[64] Two days later on December 8, the Feast of the Immaculate Conception, she went to the national shrine of that name at Catholic University. Lamenting the lack of social activism in the Catholic Church, she made an anguished prayer "that some way would open up for me to use what talents I possessed for my fellow workers, for the poor."[65]

When Day returned to New York she met Peter Maurin, whose spirit and ideas were to dominate the rest of her life. Indeed, she divided her life into two parts:

> The first twenty-five years were floundering years of joy and sorrow.... I did not know in what I believed, though I tried to serve a cause. Five years after I became a Catholic I met Peter Maurin.... he gave me 'a way of life and instruction'....[66]

At first glance, the fifty-five-year-old Maurin hardly looked imposing. Day saw before her a short, stocky "workingman" whose greying hair covered a "high, broad forehead." "Warm grey eyes" and a "wide, pleasant mouth" defined his weatherbeaten face. His shirt collar was dirty, she noticed, "but he had tried to dress up by wearing a tie and a suit which looked as though he had slept in it."[67] This was Peter Maurin, "as ragged and rugged as any of the marchers" she had just left in Washington.[68] He pronounced his name "Maw-rin," deliberately Anglicizing it. As usual, the pockets of his overcoat were stuffed with books and papers. But later, and for the rest of her life, Dorothy Day felt that Peter Maurin was a direct answer to her fervent prayer at the Shrine of the Immaculate Conception.[69]

When Peter Maurin died in 1949 at the age of 72, *Commonweal* observed that American Catholicism had "lost one of its most colorful figures."[70] *Time* pronounced the corpse's "castoff suit" and "donated grave" appropriate, for "during

Figure 3. Peter Maurin, 1941. (Courtesy Dorothy Day-Catholic Worker Collection, Marquette University)

his life, Peter Maurin had slept in no bed of his own and wore no suit that someone had not given away." But to his funeral in the poorest part of Lower Manhattan came priests from many orders and laypeople both rich and poor from all over the country. Francis Cardinal Spellman himself had sent his representative. Throughout the night before the funeral, *Time* reported, "they had come to the rickety storefront where the body lay, to say a prayer or touch their rosaries to the folded hands. For many of them were sure that Peter Maurin was a saint."[71] It was a fitting farewell to a man who had spent most of his life living and working in community, among the poor.

Aristide Peter Maurin was born in Languedoc, an ancient area of southern France, on May 9, 1877. He was the first child of a large farming family. When he was seven, his mother died after having borne five children (two of whom had died). His stepmother had nineteen more children.[72] Maurin often said that he was neither bourgeois nor proletariat: "I am a peasant. I have roots!"[73] Indeed the Maurin family had farmed the same land for over 1,500 years. At fourteen, Maurin entered a boarding school near Paris staffed by the Christian Brothers, then a teaching order for the poor. The school program was designed for farming children; at the same time that he was learning mathematical formulas, Maurin was being taught to hold a plow.[74]

In 1895 Maurin entered the Christian Brothers as a novice, remaining until 1903, while he taught in and near Paris. Though he was a Christian Brother, he was forced to serve as a soldier of the second class from November 14, 1898, to September 20, 1899. He detested the whole military system—the discipline for killing, the loss of individual dignity, the general lowering of moral standards. According to Maurin's brother Norbert, this year of forced military service marked the beginning of his interest in politics and the beginning of his advanced ideas on pacifism and social organization.[75]

On January 1, 1903, when his annual vows expired, Maurin left the Christian Brothers to join *Le Sillon* (The Furrow), a progressive Catholic movement led by Marc Sangnier. Unlike the well-established Catholic social movement *L'Action Française*, which desired a return to pre-French Revolution days, *Le Sillon* deplored the bourgeois attitude of the Church and advocated its involvement in the social and political problems of the day. Embracing a Tolstoyan pacifism, *Le Sillon* opposed nationalism and militarism. It was a decentralist movement, with no dues, rules, elections, or salaries. To Sangnier, the Russian revolutionaries of 1905 were "anarchists with a mystical and profound soul" who were disturbing Russia's "sweet dream" by spreading seeds of a "strange redemption."[76]

But Maurin grew disenchanted with *Le Sillon*, probably for several reasons. Sangnier's movement placed too little value on scholarship for the book-loving Maurin; and it tended to view itself as a crusade, with parades and rhetoric and sometimes violent encounters with its opposition.[77] The gentle Maurin was repelled by these sporadic, violent clashes.[78] For the next few years he worked at various jobs and continued to read widely. He was influenced by Peter Kropotkin, whose collection of articles entitled *Mutual Aid* had appeared in

1890. In this and in *Fields, Factories, and Workshops* (1913), Kropotkin offered a radical alternative to the prevailing Social Darwinism: an anarchism based on cooperation and common work. Kropotkin maintained that human beings survived not by ruthless struggle, but by cooperation; he felt manual labor could enrich intellectuals' experience. All his life Maurin expressed this idea in his emphasis on the unity of the worker and the scholar in common labor.[79] And certainly Maurin transmitted the thought of Kropotkin through the Catholic Worker movement's emphasis on restoring Christian communality.

Maurin was also influenced by the thought of French Catholic philosophers such as Leon Bloy, Charles Péguy, Emmanuel Mounier, and Jacques Maritain, and he synthesized many themes of the English decentralists and agrarians—Harold Robbins, Eric Gill, Hilaire Belloc, G.K. Chesterton, and the Rev. Vincent McNabb.

In 1909, when he was thirty-two, Maurin emigrated to Canada. He and a partner homesteaded somewhere on the frontier until the latter was killed while hunting. Then Maurin wandered about, working as a laborer in the Alberta wheat fields, digging ditches for the Canadian Pacific Railway, and quarrying stone in Ottawa. In 1911 he entered the United States, once more surviving on a variety of odd jobs—in a Pennsylvania coal mine; in a Kalamazoo sawmill; in a Chicago dry goods store. Once he even opened a language school in Chicago. Maurin's family sent a photograph of him from these days to Dorothy Day. In it he looks like a respectable, prosperous teacher of French.[80]

In 1925, at the age of forty-eight, he left Chicago for New York, where he apparently had a profound religious experience. Characteristically, he never discussed it in any great detail, but from then on his actions were quite different. He began to stop charging his students for lessons, telling them they could pay whatever they thought they were worth. No longer was Maurin stylishly dressed; instead, he had started to live as he would for the rest of his life—in voluntary poverty.

Catholic Workers treasure a rich store of tales about Maurin's humble demeanor. Dorothy Day recalled several instances when his unconventional attire created incidents of mistaken identity, each comic yet poignant. Once when Maurin went to address a Westchester County women's club, Day got a frantic call demanding to know why Maurin had not appeared. "Since I had put him on the train myself," she recounted, "I told them that he must be in the station." "There is only an old tramp sitting on one of the benches asleep," came the reply. Day assured them it had to be Maurin. And in 1939 when Maurin was invited to dinner at the home of Columbia University historian Carlton Hayes, Mrs. Hayes took one look at Maurin, decided he was the plumber, and ushered him into the basement. Too humble to protest, Maurin was still down there when Professor Hayes finally guessed his identity. Day told another tale of Maurin's going to speak at a Catholic Midwestern college. At the very sight of the ragged, eccentric Frenchman, the kindly brother at the door dispatched him into the kitchen for a good meal, "which Peter gratefully ate." As the time for his lecture approached and the "harassed fathers" were scouring the college, they finally found Maurin in the kitchen, indoctrinating whoever would listen.[81]

When the stock market plunged the masses into poverty, Maurin was working without pay at a Catholic camp for boys in Mount Tremper, New York, five miles from Woodstock. On weekends, he was given a few dollars to visit New York City, where he would stay in Uncle Sam's Bowery Hotel for fifty cents a night, read in the public library, and discourse with the radicals around Union Square. It was during these visits to New York that Maurin developed his "Easy Essay" style, with which he drove home his points—a combination of puns and simple, rhythmic, repetitive chantings of his ideas, punctuated by appropriate arm-waving. Maurin, as Dorothy Day put it, "fancied himself a troubador of God, going about the public squares and street corners indoctrinating his listeners by a singsong repetition, which certainly caught their attention."[82] His heavy French accent could be enchanting; his facial expressions were extraordinary.[83] Maurin's Easy Essays, printed in the *Catholic Worker* and in collections entitled *Catholic Radicalism: Phrased Essays for the Green Revolution* (1949), *The Green Revolution* (1949), and *Easy Essays* (1936, 1961, 1977)[84] are phrased paragraphs that reflect his ideas in the straightforward, concise manner of his speech. "Blowing the Dynamite," which has been reprinted many times in the *Catholic Worker*, is representative:

> Writing about the Catholic Church,
> a radical writer says:
> 'Rome will have to do more
> than to play a waiting game;
> she will have to use
> some of the dynamite
> inherent in her message.'
> To blow the dynamite
> of a message
> is the only way
> to make the message dynamic.
> If the Catholic Church
> is not today
> the dominant social dynamic force,
> it is because Catholic scholars
> have failed to blow the dynamite
> of the Church.
> Catholic scholars
> have taken the dynamite
> of the Church,
> have wrapped it up
> in nice phraseology,
> placed it in an hermetic container
> and sat on the lid.
> It is about time
> to blow the lid off
> so the Catholic Church
> may again become
> the dominant social dynamic force.[85]

In this, as in all his Easy Essays, the French philosopher never mentioned himself at all. What a contrast his single-minded, impersonal didacticism presents to Day's conversational, first-person style! Maurin may have drawn at least technically from the works of Péguy, who also wrote in short, phrased lines; undoubtedly, too, he was familiar with the meditations of St. Augustine, which also employ this technique of breaking up sentences into eye-catching phrases.[86] Such structure seemed to help people better grasp Maurin's ideas.

Nina Polcyn Moore, a long-time Catholic Worker who helped form a House of Hospitality in Milwaukee in October, 1937, remembered Maurin as a "nonstop communicator," a brilliant philosopher who had utterly no sense of dialogue. Maurin never engaged in small talk; his conversation was always sober and teacherly.[87] Another seasoned Catholic Worker characterized Maurin as irrepressible, "a walking idea, always speaking in the Easy Essay form, always indoctrinating."[88] "Peter could think of nothing he liked better," commented *Catholic Worker* illustrator Ade Bethune, "than to stand in the middle of Union Square and harangue people" with his ideas. She recalled that once during a hospital stay, Maurin proudly penned in "agitator" as his occupation on the patient chart. In the early Thirties when Bethune was a shy teen-ager just out of high school, Maurin decided she should speak on behalf of the Catholic Worker movement. "We will make you a public speaker," he repeated over and over, with fervor in his grey eyes. Every time Bethune declined, Maurin's face would assume a cast of sadness. "He thought my *dream* would be to go out into Union Square and start talking from a soapbox," the artist remembered, laughing.[89] Maurin was apparently immune to embarrassment. He once brought John Cogley of the *Chicago Catholic Worker* to the offices of the *New York Times* and told them that this was a promising young fellow they ought to hire. They did — about twenty-five years later.[90]

In 1932, Maurin was seeking a special person: someone who could promulgate his ideas on radical action based on Christian values. With sheaves of his Easy Essays always crammed into his pockets, he often visited the offices of Catholic publications, hoping to have his opinions published. One day George Shuster, then managing editor of *Commonweal*, suggested that Maurin contact Dorothy Day. The Frenchman immediately recognized her name, for he had read her articles in *Commonweal*, *America*, and *Sign*. And besides, as he later told her, a "red-headed Irish Communist in Union Square" had also highly recommended Day to him.[91]

So in December 1932, Maurin appeared at the door of the East Twelfth Street, New York apartment Day shared with her six-year-old daughter Tamar, brother John, and sister-in-law Tessa. Day soon discovered that Maurin was "one of those people who talked you deaf, dumb, and blind." Each time he met her, he began his conversation exactly where he had left off at the previous meeting, and only when she begged for rest did he stop — and that was not for long.[92] Always hoping for a stray apostle, Maurin approached the plumber, the landlord, and anyone else who happened to stop by.[93]

But he concentrated most of all on Dorothy Day. Maurin told her she needed a Catholic intellectual background, and he immediately began indoctrinating, assigning her spiritual classics to read, lecturing her on the history of the Church and the lives of the saints, showing her that her analysis of the social order could be turned into action. Recognizing that her vocation was journalism, he convinced her—with no difficulty—that she should start a newspaper to communicate the idea of social action rooted in Christian principles.

How did Maurin view Day? At first, perhaps as a modern-day Catherine of Siena who would be able to approach bishops and cardinals and have influence. But Day's idea was exactly the opposite: "I wanted to begin at the bottom," she wrote, "and I think my instinct was a right one."[94] Together, Day and Maurin succeeded where neither alone likely could have. Maurin became the movement's theoretician while Day, always practical, carried out his plan with a few of her own variations. Without Dorothy Day, Peter Maurin probably would have spent the rest of his life lecturing unceasingly to unhearing audiences in Union Square. And without Peter Maurin, Dorothy Day perhaps would never have discovered the life's work that would compel her for the next forty-eight years.

ADE BETHUNE

III: "Read the *Catholic Worker* Daily!"

During the winter of 1933, Dorothy Day painstakingly planned the first issue of the paper that would communicate the idea of radical social action based on Christian principles. The kitchen table of the four-room tenement she shared with her daughter, brother, and sister-in-law soon became her editorial headquarters. As she prayed and read the lives of the saints, she decided on the stories she would contribute to accompany Peter Maurin's essays and planned the makeup.[1]

But where would the money to publish come from?, Day asked her cofounder, who was increasingly making clear his role as theorist. "In the history of the saints, capital was raised by prayer," Maurin replied. "God sends you what you need when you need it."[2] In early spring, Day considered her financial resources. Two checks were due for her free-lance articles, and when she found she could have 2,500 copies of an eight-page tabloid printed for fifty-seven dollars by the Paulist Press, she decided to postpone the overdue rent, gas, and electric bills. Then the Paulist priest Joseph McSorley paid her generously for some research she had done for him; the pastor of a black Newark, New Jersey, church donated ten dollars; and a nun named Sister Peter Claver of the Missionary Servants of the Blessed Trinity, who would be a lifelong friend, passed on a dollar someone had just given to her.[3]

When the first *Catholic Worker* appeared on May 1, 1933, it addressed the day's leading concerns: the unemployed, the trade unions, the cooperatives. Stories described the exploitation of blacks in the South and the plight of sharecroppers, child labor in New York City, and a local strike over wages and hours. But Peter Maurin was not pleased. "Everybody's paper is nobody's paper," he declared; and departed for the boys' camp in Mount Tremper in upstate New York, where he had been a volunteer. Apparently he had envisioned a paper devoted exclusively to his essays, but Day had not even consulted him as to whether he liked the title that was given to his writings in the paper, "Easy Essays." Later she acknowledged that his confidence could easily seem like "conceit and vanity" to the casual observer.[4] But what especially disturbed Maurin was the paper's emphasis on strikes, wages, and labor conditions — instead of on his solution: a radical Christian personalism. This can be seen in the co-founders' gentle sparring over the name of the paper: Maurin wanted to call it the *Catholic Radical*, while Day, who after all had been a card-carrying Wobbly and Socialist, held out for the *Catholic Worker*. Perhaps the history of the paper would have been quite different if her wisdom had not prevailed.

When he returned from upstate New York, Maurin seemed different to Day. "Man proposes, woman disposes," was his only explanation of his absence. Day noticed that he seemed to regard her no longer as a Catherine of Siena, but rather "as an ex-Socialist, ex-I.W., ex-Communist, in whom he might find some concordance, some basis on which to build."[5] Characteristically, Maurin almost immediately pulled a spiritual classic out of his pocket and resumed his schooling of Day.

In the next issue the Frenchman explained that he did not wish to be an editor, for as such "it will be assumed that I sponsor or advocate any reform suggested in the pages of the *Catholic Worker*. I would rather definitely sign my own work."[6] He preferred to be an occasional contributor. And he proceeded to outline briefly his program of round-table discussions for clarification of thought, Houses of Hospitality, and farming communes, which, along with the paper, form the major elements of the Catholic Worker movement. But if Maurin thought his occasional contribution would be splashed across the pages, he was mistaken. Dorothy Day was in charge now, and she did not run his piece as the lead editorial, perhaps because, as she later admitted, she was "irked" at his exclusion of women in his description of a prototypical House of Hospitality.[7]

Later, quoting St. Augustine, Day mused of her editorship that "the bottle will still smell of the liquor it once held."[8] As a former radical journalist, she tended to view social ills in terms of urban-industrial class conflicts. And so the *Catholic Worker* in its early years reflected Day's keen interest in labor unions and strikes, and the fight for better wages and hours, as indeed it bore the distinctive stamp of her editorship throughout her life. To Maurin, it truly must have seemed to be "everybody's paper," while Day instinctively recognized the importance of crafting an appeal as universal as possible. Having inspired Day with his ideas, Maurin soon settled into a lesser role in the Catholic Worker movement, that of theoretician and "elder statesman." By necessity and by choice, Day carried on much of the practical work, including editing the *Catholic Worker*.

How did the co-founders view the paper's purpose? Maurin did not believe that journalists should merely report history, but make history by influencing the era in which they lived. They were to be propagandists and agitators—what he himself had always been. After all, as Maurin once told Day, he had started to write because he could not get enough people to listen to him.[9] Maurin defined good journalism in an early Easy Essay, using his typical brief, phrased lines to catch the eye:

To tell everybody
that a man died
leaving two million dollars
may be journalism,
but it is not
good journalism.
But to tell everybody
that the man died
leaving two million dollars
because he did not know
how to take them with him
by giving them to the poor
for Christ's sake
during his lifetime
is good journalism.
Good journalism
is to give the news
and the right comment
on the news.
The value of journalism
is the value of the comment
given with the news.

... The news is the occasion
for the journalist
to convey his thinking
to unthinking people.
Nothing can be done
without public opinion,
and the opinion of thinking people
who know how
to transmit their thinking
to unthinking people.[10]

Clearly this is advocacy journalism, in the fullest meaning defined by Everette Dennis and William Rivers in their classic work, *Other Voices: The New Journalism in America.* Central in advocacy journalism (which is represented by Gloria Steinem's work in *Ms.* and Pete Hamill's in the New York *Post* and *New York*), they write, is "to be involved, to be *engaged.*" Advocacy journalists participate in the events they cover. They "write with an unabashed commitment to particular points of view, casting their reporting of events along the lines of their beliefs."[11] Thus Dennis and Rivers distinguish advocacy journalism from the alternative journalism or "modern-day muckraking" which has characterized the *Village Voice, Cervi's Rocky Mountain Journal,* and the San Francisco *Bay Guardian.* The alternative journalist also presents the news subjectively, using "personal," "highly individualized expression," but with a more "middle-ground approach." The alternative journalist aims primarily to expose social, political, and economic abuses which the conventional press passes over.[12] By contrast, the advocacy journalist is totally committed to proselytizing for his or her cause.

Dorothy Day completely agreed with Peter Maurin's view of journalism, candidly avowing that the paper's purpose was "to influence the thought of its readers." Forthrightly espousing advocacy journalism, she wrote: "We are quite frankly propagandists for Catholic Action."[13] "None of the Catholic Workers has any news sense," she observed approvingly in 1942 in her paper. "They are not journalists, thank God—they are revolutionists. They don't see a feature story in the fact that someone in Boston contributed a tree to the House of Hospitality there."[14] As a journalistic advocate, Day's commitment to "spreading the word" was paramount. The *Catholic Worker*'s mission, she explained, was "to change public opinion, to indoctrinate, to set small groups to work here and there in different cities who will live a life of sacrifice, typifying the Catholic idea of personal responsibility." Don't worry about "numbers and organization," she cautioned, for "we are just beginning after all. . . ." Such was Catholic Worker anarchism, which has always shunned large, impersonal movements. Describing the effectiveness of one "lone man" in Butte, Montana, who distributed the paper to the miners as they exited the shafts, she stressed the power of personalism: that "one person can do a tremendous amount of boring from within."[15]

Day further defined good journalism as the reporting of *eyewitness* events, "not just taking the word of other papers and rewriting accounts." Catholic Workers (including the paper's reporters) were present at such affairs as strikes and picketing, she wrote, because "we think that lay apostles should bring their beliefs to the man in the street. . . ."[16] This is a clear call for activist reporting.

The roots of contemporary advocacy journalism run deep in American history, starting with the colonial pamphleteers and including nineteenth-century editors who wrote in a highly personalized style such as Edwin L. Godkin of the *Nation* and the New York *Post* and Horace Greeley of the New York *Tribune* and, to various degrees, turn-of-the-century muckrakers such as Lincoln Steffens, David Graham Phillips, and Ida Tarbell. But the development of such subjective journalism does not follow a smooth, uninterrupted path. For about a decade after World War I, it was objectivity—the facts unembellished by opinion or interpretation—which reigned as the American journalistic ideal. This came about partially as a reaction to the skepticism of late nineteenth and early twentieth-century thinkers such as Nietzsche and Freud, and to the experience of the persuasive power of both wartime propaganda and the growing field of public relations. Since reason was not to be trusted, the best the responsible journalist could do was report the facts, as even-handedly as possible.[17] But then about the time of the New Deal, according to Dennis and Rivers, the increasing intricacy of public affairs "made it difficult to confine reporting to the straitjacket of unelaborated fact." The complexities of American society proved so overwhelming as to require more interpretation in journalistic accounts. Washington reporters of that time say they can cite "the exact moment when the old journalism failed utterly"—April 19, 1933, the day when America went off the gold standard. The correspondents asked the White House to send an economist to explain the knotty implications of this change, but he was little help. The journalists were hardly successful at clarifying what he told them, but they "had committed themselves to explanatory journalism, an abrupt departure from the superficialities of who-what-when-where-why reporting."[18] The *Catholic Worker*, which appeared in 1933, might thus be viewed as part of this broad trend toward interpretive reporting.

But it was much more. Carey McWilliams has observed that reform journalism thrives in times of social crises.[19] Just as the muckrakers' exposés sprang into print when social and political abuses threatened Americans at the turn of the century, and the so-called "new journalism" appeared in the midst of the Sixties' social upheaval, the *Catholic Worker* began at the height of the human trauma visited by the Great Depression. Desperate for solutions, people were ready to look at radical sources, even one with the unlikely title of "Catholic Worker."

And Dorothy Day's paper did not disappoint them; it went far beyond interpretation into clear-cut advocacy. The upheaval of the Depression provided plenty of material for hard-hitting commentary. However, despite Peter Maurin's initial fears, muckraking articles on lynchings, sweatshops, and housing problems did not dominate the *Catholic Worker* of the Thirties, for merely reciting litanies of injustice has never been the paper's sole editorial concern. The *Catholic Worker* aims more to show life's positive side, as Day often made plain. "If a Catholic paper has any reason for existence," she wrote, it is to nurture and show evidence of the "spirit of faith," as well as "to enunciate the great truths of our religion" and to recite instances which show God's workings in everyday lives. "If we were the Devil," she once addressed the paper's detractors, "we wouldn't be interested in detailing evidences of the gifts of the Holy Spirit."[20]

And so the *Catholic Worker* emphasizes not injustices, but Christian methods of dealing with problems. When some early would-be contributors suggested "bitter drawings" for the paper, according to *Catholic Worker* illustrator Ade Bethune, Dorothy Day demurred. She did not like illustrations depicting the grim side of workers' lives, preferring to show them in positive settings, such as harvesting crops. "There's enough bitterness, anger and sarcasm in the world," Day told Bethune, "without emphasizing it."[21] Day clarified this perspective when she first explained the paper's stand on birth control in 1934. Rather than publish articles criticizing contraception, the *Catholic Worker* would "point out all that is being done to give free, or reasonably cheap care to mothers in the way of clinics and hospitals, prenatal and postnatal care." In this way, the paper would perform the "constructive" task of boosting "public opinion amongst doctors and mothers . . . for recognition of the need for more and better babies."[22] This emphasis on the positive remains current editorial policy, according to editor Peggy Scherer.[23]

Given the current controversy over contraception among Roman Catholics, the wisdom of Day's approach is apparent. Astutely, she maintained a broader editorial appeal by avoiding divisive politicization on many issues, those of both church and state. The *Catholic Worker* has tended to make its general point of view known, without expending excessive energy in the denunciation of the specific. Thus, while the paper has disagreed with many governmental policies over the years—especially in times of war—it has steadfastly resisted political partisanship since 1933. Catholic Worker personalism has never embraced mass politics as a means to achieve social change. Day clarified this in an early letter in which she acknowledged the "great deal of criticism" the paper got because it was not " 'for' any line of political action" in particular. "After all," she wrote, "we're just a paper, disseminating Catholic thought and as such can write about all these things without sponsoring them."[24] Politically independent, the paper stands ready to reveal the sources of any material it uses, as the editors first made plain in 1935 in response to a reader's question.[25]

The *Catholic Worker* is still tabloid-sized, usually four to eight or even twelve pages. Until the early Eighties, it was published monthly except for occasional combined issues (usually July-August and October-November). Sometimes other issues have been merged when money has been low. Today, the *Catholic Worker* publishes eight issues annually, usually combining the January and February, March and April, June and July, and October and November editions. This is partially to offset rising printing and postage costs. Even more, according to Frank Donovan, the Catholic Worker who handles the paper's financial matters, this is done to spare time for the editors to perform the works of mercy, an activity which they deem equally worthwhile.[26] As Dorothy Day once remarked, the *Catholic Worker* has "many writers and editors. But they are all so engaged in baking bread, making soup, begging from the market, not to speak of taking care of St. Joseph's House," she added, "that writing is always done at the last minute."[27]

The *Catholic Worker* has always been funded by faith, hope, and charity, as so many letters in the Catholic Worker Papers attest. For instance, in August 1934 the editors acknowledged that their new issue would be out by September 1, "provided we can finish paying off our printing bill by then." They also mentioned that the "lean summer months" had curtailed other important activities, such as the Workers' school (for study of Catholic Worker principles) and St. Joseph's House of Hospitality.[28]

To pay for the second issue of the *Catholic Worker*, Dorothy Day in a remarkable show of faith sold her typewriter.[29] It was an act quite characteristic of Catholic Workers, who have always done everything as informally and non-commercially as possible. For them, the profit motive does not exist, not even in fundraising. And certainly not in publishing. Dorothy Day shrewdly set the paper's price at a penny a copy, providing both proletarian appeal and an eventual trademark. Although the paper's price more than doubles with a subscription, which costs a quarter a year, subscriptions and street sales barely make a dent in the printing bill, which by December 1934 was at least $245 a month. By 1960 it cost at least one and a half cents to print each copy.[30] Frank Donovan recently provided some revealing statistics: By the early Seventies, it cost about $2,200 per issue to print the 80,000 or so copies. Today, the *Catholic Worker*'s printing bill for each issue of about 104,000 copies ranges from $4,000 to $5,000. Like everything else, postage costs have risen dramatically over the years. In the early Seventies, postage per issue (for about 80,000 copies) cost about $1,400; today it runs at least $6,000.[31] Renewal notices are never sent out; instead, the paper depends on its subscribers' good will (and good memories).

Despite hefty production and postage costs, many copies of the *Catholic Worker* are still distributed free. And advertising—what little the paper carries, usually that of other social justice groups—has never been a source of revenue. From its start, the *Catholic Worker* has eschewed paid advertising, only exchanging an ad occasionally at the request of another party.[32] Such a decidedly uncapitalistic approach comes from Catholic Workers' belief that money is not a neutral commodity. They regard the source of their financial support, like everything else, as a matter of principle. Therefore, not only do they refuse paid advertising in the *Catholic Worker*, they do not solicit foundation grants. They accept neither state assistance, nor stocks and bonds. Dorothy Day asked neither church nor state for financial aid, explaining on one occasion that "Cardinal Spellman did not ask us to undertake this work, nor did the Mayor of New York."[33] Furthermore, Catholic Workers do not bank on interest, for like the early Christians they stress the duty of charity and take a nonmaterialistic view of human service. This is why in 1960 they returned nearly $3,600 to the City of New York, the interest on the delayed-sale payment for their Chrystie Street House of Hospitality which the City bought to augment the subway.[34]

Consistently advocating decentralism in both the United States government and in its own establishment, the Catholic Worker movement is not incorporated as a legal entity. This means it receives no tax breaks for its charity nor bequests. But this never deterred Dorothy Day from her principles. Yes, she acknowledged, many of her "organization-minded friends" pointed out the loss in funds such a policy assured. But she always told them, "It is better that we remain poor and dependent on the small contributions of those who can send a dollar now and then. That keeps us humble." And besides, she added, "you don't need to be incorporated to wash a man's feet."[35]

Still, Day's free-lancing income could not sustain the *Catholic Worker* for long. To raise funds for the paper and the movement, she always prayed to its patron saint, Joseph, as she urged others to do. "Pray and God will pay the printer," she often said.[36] And she appealed primarily to individuals, to those who had indicated their interest by subscribing to the paper. Each spring and fall, she usually wrote an eloquent appeal which was printed in the paper and also mailed to others interested in the work. Priests and nuns often sent in checks, and sometimes bishops; but most of the money filtered into the office in small amounts from individuals, often on the verge of destitution themselves, who had been touched by Day's depictions of hope and despair on the Lower East Side. Three years before her death, scores of appeals behind her, Day still retained her ability to evoke a strong response with such moving words as these:

We are all poor in one way or another, in soul, mind, and body, in exterior or
interior goods. Yet even the widow gave her mite and the little boy his loaves
and fishes, and the Lord will see to it that they are multiplied to cover our
needs. . . . We are a family, not an institution, in atmosphere, and so we address
ourselves especially to families, who have all the woes of insecurity, sin, sickness,
and death, side by side with all the joys of family.[37]

Typical of many, a college student who admired Day's writing and work sent in
ten dollars, explaining that Day's articles were "the most beautiful pieces I have
ever read." She went on:

You seem so very happy and peaceful, although I am sure your life is one of
constant hardship.

I would like to help a little. . . . Someday, I hope, I will have just a little
portion of the love, strength, and courage which marks the Catholic Workers.
But for now all I can give is this and my prayers.[38]

The Catholic Worker Papers brim with letters from humble souls such as one
elderly woman, who donated money in memory of her "good pastor." She
wrote, "Although I am old and poor, I am sheltered and may God shower you
with His choicest blessings for the work you are doing for His aged poor, and
may He bless your work abundantly."[39]

However, Catholic Worker finances have always been tenuous. In the words
of Dorothy Day, "There is never anything left."[40] She described a "good" month
during the Thirties:

Looking back to last Christmas when we were so poor that we had to skip our
January edition, we praise the Lord and all His saints for the abundance this
year. Christmas cards came to us enclosing money and little by little the bills
were paid. The telephone was almost shut off but wasn't quite, the electric man
came around to deprive us of light, but didn't (there had been an offering
through the mail), there were a few meals of beans, and then a basket of food
came in; and we were preparing to put off the January edition until late in the
month when a generous check came in from a priest.[41]

And with more than forty years of survival behind the *Catholic Worker*, Day in
the June 1975 issue still could reflect, "How we pay our bills I do not know. God
knows." She then quoted Scripture: "If we 'sow sparingly we will reap sparingly';
so when we are in need we become more generous and serve an even richer
soup to an ever growing line."[42]

Putting out the paper is no less informal than fundraising. Day described
keeping a pot of stew (I.W.W. style) and a pot of coffee going on the coal range in
the kitchen, just before the paper went to press. As she and her editors worked
from early morning until midnight, all who came in were fed.[43] Joseph Zarrella,
a Catholic Worker since the early Thirties, remembers the long, busy hours
before the paper went to press. "How I loved those days," he said. "We'd
proofread, do the headlines and everything else way into the wee hours."[44]

For many years when the papers returned from the printer's, students, Catho-

Figure 4. Preparing newspapers for mailing, 1962. (Photo by William Carter, courtesy Dorothy Day-Catholic Worker Collection, Marquette University)

lic Workers, and street people at St. Joseph's helped fold, address, and apply stickers to them, tying bundles together according to cities and states.[45] In the first few years no machines lightened this burden, both from lack of money and from Day's desire to give as many as possible an opportunity to share in the work, according to Stanley Vishnewski, one of Day's earliest (and lifelong) recruits. He described the camaraderie of common labor, how he and the others sang as they worked on the paper—mostly Gregorian chants and folk songs. A passer-by, Vishnewski wrote, "might well have thought that a religious revival was taking place—and he would have been right."[46] Some aspects of this scene are scarcely different today. Each bundle contains two hundred-fifty newspapers, which must be transported from the truck (rented for the day) to the second floor. Forming a line, Catholic Workers and street people, perhaps having just finished their soupmeal, pass the bundles from hand to hand. The work becomes even more taxing when the exhausted drop out, and each person remaining then has to ascend an increasing number of stairs. Although there may be many available helpers, not even the gentlest requests are made for assistance; all is personal initiative only.[47]

But the *Catholic Worker* departed significantly from tradition when it purchased, in the fall of 1983, an Apple IIe microcomputer. Although the paper's most recent addressograph machine (which stenciled mailing labels) was only four years old, it was rapidly becoming obsolete because so many of its former users had turned to computerized systems. Soon it was impossible to find parts for the machine, and monthly breakdowns became common. According to *Catholic Worker* associate editor Katharine Temple, three choices then emerged: Either handwrite more than half a million addresses a year "(an improbable feat, even for devotees of manual labor); use a small computer; or stop the paper. There was no other alternative."[48] With great ambivalence, the *Catholic Worker* plunged into modern technology. Some felt that Dorothy Day was turning over in her pine coffin. They compared the computer to the videogame, viewing both as frivolous distractions from more significant aspects of life. "Just as money—dollars and cents—cannot be divorced from capitalism," Temple observed, "so this home computer or that little video game cannot be divorced from our enslavement to technology." She summarized the dilemma presented by the computer: Peter Maurin taught Catholic Workers the value of decentralization, but "What does it mean if his ideas have caught on enough that our mailing list is too big to cope with? We can computerize or go under. Either way, the computer wins as yet another tradition is technically steam-rollered or absorbed."[49] And the issue remains controversial around the *Catholic Worker* office.

"Not only was the *Worker* not ready for the computer age," said Lee LeCuyer, a veteran of St. Joseph's House of Hospitality, "the computer age was not ready for the *Worker*." None of the standard mailing list computer programs were appropriate for the intricate sorting that the paper requires (especially to package bundle orders to comply with postal regulations). LeCuyer, a graduate of St. John's College in Annapolis who had originally opposed the acquisition of a computer on moral grounds, found himself fine-tuning a program to meet the paper's needs. "We've always tried to involve street people in the mailing and labelling work, in a kind of sheltered workshop," he said. "But computers are frightening to many people. In a way ours is making things more difficult, yet easier. There are a lot of trade-offs."

Today the paper's labels are more legible and many other aspects of the mailing process have been made more efficient. While the computer reduces the total amount of work, LeCuyer observed, it focuses more work on the individual who has computer expertise, making for a more distinct division of labor. The person who can operate the computer for the six to eight hours a day that may be required (once the old stencil mailing list is transferred and updated) will not likely be spared to serve on the soupline. Some Catholic Workers are wary of creating such circumstances. LeCuyer mentioned a more overriding issue they now face: "supporting a new form of technology now only available to the rich," thereby helping "to increase the gap between rich and poor."[50] No doubt the computer's value, both practical and philosophical, will continue to be debated.

Figure 5. Folding newspapers at St. Joseph's, 1966. (Photo by Ed Lettau, courtesy Dorothy Day-Catholic Worker Collection, Marquette University)

But so far the computer is an anomaly. Most things Catholic Workers do are still informal and unstructured, from folding the paper and labelling, tying, and bagging the bundle orders, to replying to readers' many letters. Dorothy Day personally answered much of the mail that arrived, often hauling it around in a large sack on her travels, for precious spare moments.[51] Street people also answered the mail, occasionally with disastrous results. More than once, Day had to make peace with offended readers whose letters had been curtly answered by Edward J. Breen, a choleric journalist who lived and died at St. Joseph's in the early Thirties. She apologized at length to one particularly disgruntled correspondent:

> Your letter certainly was a scorcher, and I can't say as I blame you. . . .
>
> It's this way: our office here is made up of the lame, the halt and the blind, mentally as well as physically. And it was one of the lame, halt and blind ones that answered you on the pious and snippy card. . . .
>
> He is our cross, specially sent by God, so we treasure him. He is sixty-five years old, an ex-newspaper man who used to work on the Boston, Washington, and New York papers, lunched with Coolidge, and so forth. He got out of a job when the old [New York] *World* went under, landed in the Municipal Lodging House where he slept in the largest bedroom in the world, 1,700 men there, and eventually found his way to us. He has been with us the past year. All summer he was sick, having had two strokes and he had to be nursed like a baby.
>
> And he's not just a nice sweet old man by any means. He's a hellion. He roars at us from morning to night and doesn't agree with a single stand we take. Occasionally, when he is bellowing for some work to do, we give him letters to acknowledge, and yours went to him. . . .[52]

Day's letter indicates how unlike a traditional newspaper office the *Catholic Worker*'s is. And her personal approach, emphasized by her personal writing style, is consonant with the movement's personalism. Day viewed each subscriber as a significant individual, and she tried to find time to answer as many letters as possible, sometimes at great length.[53] She insisted that the donor of the smallest sum be thanked, even when the cost of the thank-you letter exceeded the donation.[54] Day's reply also illustrates the *Catholic Worker*'s utter refusal to compromise its principles in order to achieve a smoother-running editorial operation. Despite Breen's apoplectic, racist outbursts and general trouble-making, she refused to evict him. "We can't put him in a home," she decided. "There is no place but the city home on Welfare Island and they'd kill him there. He's living with us, and he'll probably die with us, so that's that."[55]

This steadfast commitment to its principles despite the cost has characterized the *Catholic Worker* throughout its more than five decades of history. The paper has shown such consistency particularly in its unswerving advocacy of pacifist principles despite popular opposition, especially during the Spanish Civil War and World War II, when thousands of subscribers cancelled the paper and *Catholic Worker* salespeople were even beaten in the streets. And it has always refused paid advertising and preserved its below-cost penny price, hardly practical measures but consistent with its no-profit motive.

As an advocacy publication, the *Catholic Worker*'s goal is to get the word out, not to make money, and circulation practices reflect this. Especially at first, the paper was often given away free. "If you find you cannot sell the papers, I would advise distributing them free," Day instructed a bundle recipient in 1934. She said that many would undoubtedly not wish to buy what they viewed as "a radical sheet." But continual contributions from priests and others in the wealthier parishes enabled the *Catholic Worker* to be generous with its copies, and so she advised him to "have no scruples in disposing of them as best you can."[56] Day herself mailed the paper to academicians, editors, book reviewers, heads of Catholic organizations, priests, bishops, and nuns, and requested their comments.[57] "If we reach one or two thinking people, they will do a great deal to leaven the lump," she reasoned.[58]

And so in the hope of reaching that one or two, Catholic Workers have continued to leave the paper on subways, in restrooms, and on park benches. Clergy, especially, are encouraged to distribute the *Catholic Worker* in the churches. In the paper's first few years, some received a few more copies than they had anticipated. In 1934 the Rt. Rev. Msgr. Leo G. Fink of Allentown, Pennsylvania, was sent one hundred-fifty copies in answer to his order for "at least one hundred." The editors admitted interpreting his words "liberally," but assured him that "they can be profitably disposed of in your section."[59]

In its street sales, the *Catholic Worker* occasionally leaned toward the colorful in order to command attention. Stanley Vishnewski and "Big Dan" Orr, the paper's "chief-of-the-streets" in the Thirties, sold the *Catholic Worker* from a wagon driven by a horse they christened "Catholic Action."[60] Big Dan's favorite ploy was to approach a Communist hawking the *Daily Worker* and shout, "Read the *Catholic Worker* daily!" Once when he saw Dorothy Day approaching, he modified his shout to: "*Catholic Worker*, romance on every page!" Day acknowledged the duo's role in soliciting thousands of subscriptions in the Thirties.[61]

Encouraging letters and donations soon deluged the *Catholic Worker* office. An admiring priest in Alberta, Canada, even offered to send a quarter of moose to the *Catholic Worker* office, which the editors had to decline for storage reasons.[62] Before long there were sufficient funds to rent the barbershop below Day's East Fifteenth Street apartment as an office. A 1934 letter from the editors acknowledging a donation summarized the paper's early, spirited response:

> Your letter really thrilled us, especially coming as it did within a few days of a very laudatory one from the head of the Catholic Evidence work in Australia, who wants to start a similar paper there; a wonderful article syndicated in some of the Catholic papers in Germany on our work; a package of books and pamphlets from Father Gemelli, the Italian Franciscan who, we're told, is a very dear friend of the Holy Father [Pope Pius XI]; and a flood of queries from Mexico, Canada, and other distant parts, when our July issue was late in reaching subscribers there. We're tremendously awed by the significance attached to the *Catholic Worker* seemingly all over the world.[63]

The paper's circulation growth was impressive. Starting with 2,500 copies in May 1933, it reached 20,000 in November 1933. By March 1934, circulation climbed to 25,000. A year later, it was 65,000. It continued to rise during most of the Thirties; by May 1935 it stood at 110,000; by May 1938, 190,000; and then by 1940 on the eve of World War II, about 120,000.[64] The *Catholic Worker* never fully recovered from the massive loss of readership caused by its pacifist stand during World War II, but today the circulation has stabilized at about 104,000.

Readers have informed Dorothy Day of their discovery of the *Catholic Worker* in dentists' offices, five miles underground in a coal mine that stretched out under the Atlantic Ocean off Nova Scotia, even under a mattress in a cheap hotel in Tampico. A seminarian in Rome received his repaired shoes wrapped in a copy of the *Catholic Worker*.[65] Dorothy Day found the paper in the library of the American Export ship she boarded in Italy, en route to New York from the Second Vatican Council in 1965. Perhaps rightfully she could ask, "What need do we have of a circulation manager?"[66] Even at the height of its circulation just before World War II, the paper continued to operate in a very casual, informal manner, just as it does today. "A great many of our friends urge us to put our paper on a business-like basis," Day admitted. "But this isn't a business; it's a movement." She continued:

> And we don't know anything about business around here, anyway. Well-meaning friends say, 'But people get tired of appeals.' We don't believe it. Probably most of our friends live as we do, from day to day and from hand to mouth, and as they get, they are willing to give. So we shall continue to appeal and we know that the paper will go on.[67]

The *Catholic Worker* has never undertaken an audience poll, nor have social scientists demographically profiled its readers. But certain conclusions can be reached about its audience, from study of the letters to the editor in the Catholic Worker Papers, and from other sources.

The paper has always had a strong following among nuns, brothers, priests, and some bishops, many of whom send donations regularly. Indeed, it was a nun and two priests who helped finance the first issue. When Father Theodore Hesburgh, president of Notre Dame University, presented Day with the prestigious Laetare Medal as an outstanding American Catholic in 1972, he summarized the longstanding admiration of many clergy and religious for her when he said, "Dorothy Day has been comforting the afflicted and afflicting the comfortable all her life."

College students and academicians have also been stalwart subscribers over the years, some joining the movement as a "finishing school" in works of mercy. Abigail McCarthy (later to become a *Commonweal* columnist and book author) was among the first, selling the paper to striking Ford plant workers in St. Paul during her studies at the College of St. Catherine there. Young people gravitated to the *Catholic Worker* offices during the Vietnam War, as the pacifism that Day had advocated for many decades became respectable and even popular.

Of course, the *Catholic Worker* is widely read by Catholic peace and social justice activists. Dorothy Day is recognized as the inspiration behind the Association of Catholic Trade Unionists; John Cogley and Thomas Merton; the Le Moyne College pacifist David Miller, first to go to prison for burning his draft card in protest against the Vietnam War; and Daniel and Philip Berrigan, the brother priests who have also been imprisoned for their opposition to war.[68]

But no matter what their church affiliation, many involved in promoting social justice and pacifism read the *Catholic Worker*. The paper's Quaker artist, Fritz Eichenberg, has declared his conviction that "the Catholic Worker... should be an example for Friends in general, to convey the spirit of poverty and unconditional devotion to nonviolence that most Friends profess but not many live up to." Day "stood for everything I thought would make this world a better place," he has said.[69] Ruth Kilpack, the editor of the international Quaker magazine, *Friends Journal*, recently remarked: "I know of no other paper that has so pricked my conscience, renewing my faith in humanity."[70] An Episcopalian bishop, Ausim Pardue, wrote to Dorothy Day in gratitude for the "spirit of Christ" he found "on every page" of her paper. He said he hoped to interest his own clergy in the *Catholic Worker*. "I don't know that you could ever convert me to becoming a Roman Catholic," he wrote, "but if I keep reading your paper I may possibly become a real Christian."[71] And a Methodist pastor commented that "The regular event of the arrival of the *Catholic Worker* is always like a visit from a friend who moves with freedom and fearless abandon to follow the direction of Christ."[72] The *Catholic Worker* also appeals to non-Christian religious leaders, such as a Buddhist who told Day that he found the paper "very interesting indeed and good.... We can see you are doing good work and as Buddhists, with palms placed together we salute you for this."[73]

Writers and editors of small literary and opinion magazines and of many larger publications such as *Newsweek, New Republic, New York Times, Washington Post, The Progressive, Commonweal, America*, and *Christian Century* have long read the *Catholic Worker*.[74] Many of them, such as James O'Gara, editor of *Commonweal*, and John Cogley, former *Commonweal* editor and *New York Times* religion editor, have been associated with the Catholic Worker movement and the *Catholic Worker*.

And the *Catholic Worker* has been no stranger to major writers such as Aldous Huxley, who affixed to his contribution this note to Dorothy Day:

> In this Age of Organized Noise—noise on the ear-drums, noise in the mind, intellect, feelings, and imagination, noise in the clamorous and constantly stimulated desire—anybody who does something for Silence, as you are doing, is performing a real act of charity.[75]

Among these different groups—clergy and religious, college students and academicians, writers and editors—are found many intellectuals, of course. With only this audience, the *Catholic Worker* might be said to be elite indeed. But relatively larger is the group of everyday people (including many with little education)—blue- and pink-collar workers, retirees, and their families—who also read the paper avidly. More often they are Catholics, but not necessarily. And while wealthy readers may send in donations from time to time, such as the high executive in a large New York investment house who contributed generously in the early years,[76] the average reader's station is far more humble, judging by the *Catholic Worker*'s correspondence files. Often readers would write to tell Day personally how much they admired her journalism and efforts for the poor. "The deep warm glow I get when I read of your tremendous efforts will probably never get me to pray," one admitted, "but I can do penance for the sins of the world and I can give alms—a little out of my earnings."[77]

After reading the paper, ordinary people would often write letters to Day and describe their own circumstances in very personal terms, as one widow did:

> Until the first Friday of Our Lady's Month of May, I had a very good husband, not well for seven years, but a convert and a very fine man, who felt very bad that I had to make the living, as he was unable to work. On Thanksgiving night he fell here in the kitchen (sober) he wasn't a drinking man. Gangrene set in his leg....he suffered terribly for 5½ months—and now since he's gone I'm scared to death of the future. I can't understand it....still I pray all day for him....I can't forget you for a moment... so I am enclosing two ($2.00) dollars, and ask you to pray for my dear husband's soul....
>
> Now here I am writing you all about my troubles as if you haven't enough of your own to worry you....Please pray for me.[78]

A G.I. sent in a dollar, all that he had, and mentioned that he was "thinking that possibly when I get out I might head for New York and work with you. If I do or if I don't my everyday living will be influenced by the example Catholic Workers give."[79] His letter and many others like it illuminate several important aspects of the *Catholic Worker*'s relationship with its audience. Because the editors have always doled out soup, swept the floor, and put out the paper simultaneously, they are remarkably in touch with those less fortunate about whom they write. They truly live the example to which the soldier referred. By their voluntary poverty—they receive no salaries but room, board, and clothing—they are even closer to the street people. The *Catholic Worker* offices are upstairs at St. Joseph's, a stone's throw from the Bowery, not hermetically sealed in a Madison Avenue skyscraper. "But where does the staff begin and where does it leave off?" Dorothy Day aptly described the situation. "Since the Catholic Worker is also a movement, our editors and writers cook, clean, and wash dishes." She summarized the rest of their duties:

> They tend the sick, chauffeur the ailing to hospitals, and clean vermin-ridden apartments; sometimes they decorate, carve, paint, play the guitar, and all of them join together in singing Compline, the evening prayer of the Church, which brings the day to a close.[80]

It has been this way since the beginning. As early as November of 1933, just six months after the paper's start, an observer remarked in *Commonweal*:

> The editorial staff has the advantage of constant contact with those for whom it writes. Their habits of thought, their needs, their dilemmas, their duties, and most important, their essentially fine instincts are carefully studied, and on the basis of this knowledge, editorial and news policies are developed.[81]

The paper's content reflects this unusually intimate relationship with readers.

Over the years, *Catholic Worker* editors have kept further in touch with their audience through the many letters to the editor they encourage and regularly receive, and through visits by readers—some of whom become workers in the Houses of Hospitality and farming communes. The paper has always stressed the importance of reader participation, as in this early editorial, which asserted: "The *Catholic Worker* is interested in hearing what the Catholic layman has to say. It offers itself as a mouthpiece."[82] And from the first, the response has been quite spirited, as an early *Catholic Worker* article reported:

> Estimating very modestly, we have received at least 18,250 letters during the last year from farms, villages, and cities, from workers and scholars. We have received visits from priests and laymen from Italy, Spain, Belgium, Germany, Switzerland, France, China, South Africa, Mexico, and probably other places we cannot recall now.... [83]

The "Letters" column is a routine *Catholic Worker* feature, often about a page—one-eighth of the total edition. Letters from famous readers such as Thomas Merton have been printed alongside those from average citizens, reflecting the dual content of the paper in general. The Catholic Workers Papers include many editorial manuscripts and correspondence which indicate only the slightest editing of letters to the editors, usually merely to cut the longest ones to a printable length.

Besides intellectuals and workers, another group of *Catholic Worker* readers, those such as Evelyn Waugh, gives a passive, non-ideological support, much as they would support the Red Cross, Salvation Army, or other charitable group. Waugh always made his occasional checks payable to "Dorothy Day's Soup Kitchen," apparently not recognizing the Catholic Worker movement as anything other than a movement that had to do with feeding people.[84] Another non-ideological reader was a New York advertising copywriter, who wrote Dorothy Day that her paper had "become a valuable part of my life." He elaborated:

> I'm not a Catholic, not a pacifist.... I can't... envision our *entire* society transformed and still able to function. Nevertheless, the paper is a constant reminder (1) that commitment is still possible and valuable in this age of disillusionment with causes and (2) that it's possible for man to be better than most of us are willing to admit.[85]

Such a testimonial—from an advertising copywriter to the editor of a paper at odds with capitalism—says a great deal about the success of the broad appeal Day cultivated so carefully.

Today's *Catholic Worker* looks not much different from the earliest issues, with the same packed columns and distinctive illustrations by Fritz Eichenberg and

Ade Bethune. Atop page one, two brawny workers, one white, one black (at the suggestion of an early reader) hold pick and shovel and clasp hands, while Christ approvingly embraces them. This image has become a *Catholic Worker* emblem. Reflecting the twofold nature of the movement, as well as the audience, content alternates between the chatty (reports on the Catholic Worker family) and the intellectually sophisticated. Dorothy Day's conversational column, "On Pilgrimage," has been a regular, popular feature nearly from the beginning, and even after Dorothy Day's death it is often reprinted. Also regularly featured are Peter Maurin's Easy Essays, reprinted so frequently since his death in 1949 that new readers sometimes believe he is still living.

From its start the paper has been distinguished by a personalized writing style that focuses on the details of people's lives and is presented with the warm, appealing quality of small talk. Conversational and unpretentious, the *Catholic Worker* is a personalist newspaper expressing a personalist movement. This is especially true of Dorothy Day's writings. Her supreme talent was the ability to link the everyday and the ultimate, to cut through abstractions to reach grassroots Christianity. All her life she was committed to addressing plain, ordinary working men and women who are Catholic or who respond to Christian social justice. Her friend Robert Coles has explained that

> she never wanted to lose contact with these people; never wanted to lead them,
> either, or tell them they were being tricked, duped, fooled—and so, by
> implication, tell them they were dumb or gullible; never wanted to look upon
> herself as knowing, as 'mature' and 'responsible,' an example to the benighted,
> illusion-saddled 'masses' who need to be uplifted by their betters.[86]

This orientation determines the *Catholic Worker*'s dual content: serious, even academic essays are presented alongside down-home, people-oriented articles and reports from the Catholic Worker family. The paper's personalism grows from the movement's special, twofold nature, which is characterized by a simultaneous concern with the works of mercy and with ultimate spiritual questions. We are part of *this* world, too, the Catholic Worker movement asserts, and so it does not purge religion of all concern for the things of this world. Rather, it tries to combine religious hope and betterment on earth, by advocating radical social reconstruction based on the Gospels. This "schizoid" content, as Dwight Macdonald once called it, also results directly from Dorothy Day's recognition of the importance of an editorial appeal as wide as possible, from her wish to reach both scholar and worker. With a proletarian name, front-page emblem, and price, with down-to-earth, conversational articles, the *Catholic Worker* also includes sophisticated spiritual and social essays, with knowledgeable references to Church sources, such as papal encyclicals and the lives of the saints.

For more than fifty years, the Catholic Worker movement has addressed many social issues through its paper. The major ones include labor relations, racism, anti-Semitism, militarism and conscription, Communism, the excesses of capitalism, voluntary poverty, and most prominently, pacifism. Although the paper initially emphasized strikes and labor relations, pacifism soon emerged as its most dominant issue. This is because pacifism intersects with nearly every issue, especially voluntary poverty. Since entire modern economies are based on preparation for war, it is "very difficult to avoid contributing to the war (misnamed 'defense') effort," Dorothy Day has written.[87] The *Catholic Worker* also links racial justice with pacifism. War would be impossible, it asserts, if all believed in the complete equality of humankind as part of the Mystical Body of Christ.

One who reads just a few random issues can gain a fairly representative understanding of the *Catholic Worker*'s editorial content, because it has been so consistent for so long. To appraise the paper's subject matter more systematically, however, an analysis of content was undertaken. The design was to select an issue from each season for every third year, 1933-1981 inclusive. Staggering the months provided a look at a complete twelve-month year every three years, which produces a more representative sample. For example, the issues examined for the years 1942, 1945, and 1948 together constitute a complete, twelve-month year: 1942 — December, March, June, September; 1945 — January, April, July-August, October; 1948 — February, May, July-August, November. This selection sequence sometimes varied, since occasionally the *Catholic Worker* combined two issues, and (rarely) skipped an issue. This study evaluated all appeals (often boxed notices, smaller than regular articles), and all articles, most of which are longer than 1,000 words. Only short (usually one-paragraph), boxed notices of meetings were excluded. With only an illustration or two on each page, the *Catholic Worker* can accommodate as many as six lengthy articles in its eight to twelve tabloid-sized pages. The total number of items examined was 1,184, which averages to about seventeen per issue. The tables at the end of this chapter summarize the findings.

Besides appeals, types of items included reports from the Catholic Worker family in various Houses of Hospitality and farming communes; religious poetry; essays that are primarily spiritual; and essays on a variety of social issues. The latter were divided into several categories according to subject matter: those primarily on the topic of pacifism (pro); those opposing capitalism, the wage system, the welfare state, and supporting labor (these themes were almost always combined); those opposing the lynching of blacks in the Thirties, and/or more subtle manifestations of racism; those supporting family life; and so on. Because so many issues in the *Catholic Worker* are interrelated, it is difficult to isolate essays that are devoted entirely to one social issue. Therefore, in each case, one issue was judged predominant and the article categorized accordingly. Also, the "social essays" are never entirely secular; they always link action on earth to the next world, but they can be distinguished from the essays that are primarily spiritual-devotional.

Some themes, such as those supporting pacifism, often enjoyed full coverage in separate, individual articles; but not the personalist theme. Instead it pervades many different articles on various subjects throughout many *Catholic*

Worker issues. This is also true of the theme of voluntary poverty, which might seem to have been assigned a low priority over the years, since it represents only two percent of the total sample. The interrelationship between the *Catholic Worker* themes explains this apparent lack of coverage.

Some essays are comprehensive, undertaking a discussion of the complete Catholic Worker philosophy. They appear more often in the first few years, when the *Catholic Worker* was building its following. Although they appear less frequently as the years progress, such essays remain a *Catholic Worker* staple, especially at anniversaries—fifteenth, twentieth, twenty-fifth, and so on. Examples include "Catholic Worker Celebrates 3rd Birthday; A Restatement of C.W. Aims and Ideals" (May 1936) and "Aims and Purposes" in the May 1983 fiftieth-anniversary issue. There are many others.[88] Together, the many anniversary articles, each one restating Catholic Worker philosophy and purposes, underscore the most important finding of this study: The *Catholic Worker*'s singular editorial consistency from 1933 through 1981. It has never wavered from the point of view it presented in its first issues, although its emphasis may have changed here and there. In part, this is accomplished by the occasional reprinting of earlier articles; some of the anniversary pieces that outline the movement's comprehensive philosophy are themselves reprints from earlier *Catholic Worker* issues. One who reads current issues of the paper will be impressed by their similarity to those of more than half a century ago. Today, the *Catholic Worker* still stands for absolute pacifism and a radical social reconstruction based on the Gospels. Such editorial consistency, for so long, is a rare phenomenon in American journalism history.

Dorothy Day's contributions have been frequently featured. The sample included forty-eight columns by Day, constituting 4.05 percent of the total sample. Her signed articles (which have been counted elsewhere on the basis of their content) number thirty-one, or 2.61 percent of the sample. The category of appeals—forty-two or 3.54 percent of all content—includes notices dealing with both outside charities and the Catholic Worker movement. Day wrote most of the in-house appeals, which appeared once or twice a year. In this sample, the appeals actually signed by Day number nine, or .76 percent of all content. Thus the total number of columns, articles, and appeals bearing Dorothy Day's by-line in this sample is eighty-eight, or about 7.43 percent of the total. Clearly, she was a very steady contributor. But nearly impossible to document is the number of unsigned articles that she contributed, which would probably increase the total significantly.

This analysis of content also traces the development and frequency of editorial issues; for example, strikes and labor issues dominated the first issues. As the Thirties went on, pacifism increasingly emerged as an important theme in the *Catholic Worker*. The highest percentage of all 1,184 items analyzed—14.02 percent or one hundred sixty-six items—was devoted to the theme of pacifism. If the anti-conscription items are included, pacifism jumps to nearly sixteen percent of the entire sample, one hundred eighty-eight items. The pacifist theme emerged strongly during the paper's first decade, from two items in the 1933 sample, to eighteen in the 1942 sample. Although pacifist items eclipsed labor items in frequency, the latter have also been prominent. One hundred twenty-three items (10.38 percent of the total) dealt with the issues of labor and capitalism. These items appeared most frequently in the Depression years— twenty-six in the 1933 sample, thirteen in the 1936 sample, eighteen in the 1939 sample—when the *Catholic Worker* sought to address the great mass of unemployed workers.

This analysis also shows which themes have appeared chiefly in response to the events of the day. These are articles of very limited, specific scope in time. Only one article in the entire study dealt with Sacco and Vanzetti. Not surprisingly, it appeared in 1936, when their trial still commanded substantial interest. Likewise, articles denouncing Nazism and anti-Semitism were more common during the Thirties. (The apparent infrequency of such articles is explained in part by the editorial policy which emphasized the positive; also, this theme was sometimes combined with others, and thus difficult to isolate.) Likewise, articles denouncing McCarthyism and redbaiting appeared in the early Fifties, when those issues were most salient. The anti-conscription theme was especially frequent during the World War II and Vietnam years, in response to contemporary events.

Reports from sites of injustice, a *Catholic Worker* staple, are comparatively information-packed accounts of topics such as the plight of migrant workers, and iniquity in prisons, factories and slums, both at home and in countries such as Biafra and El Salvador. There are also follow-up reports, sometimes positive, of efforts to solve social problems. Although the *Catholic Worker* deals with current issues in the news, it does not seek to rival the fact-filled reportage of either traditional news publications or muckraking journals. "We are not giving you news such as you get in your daily paper," Dorothy Day remarked on occasion. "We are giving you ideas as to Catholic Action."[89] The *Catholic Worker* aims to interpret, educate, and advocate.

Finally, spiritual content—poetry, prayers, essays—has been routinely featured since 1933, totaling one hundred thirty-three items (11.23 percent of the total examined). This comparatively high percentage attests to the paper's strong base of Christianity. Devotional essays, poetry, and prayers have been regularly printed for their own sake, without any explicit connection to the temporal concerns of the movement, although certainly Dorothy Day was not unaware that such copy made the paper seem more "Catholic." The amount of spiritual content has remained fairly stable throughout the *Catholic Worker*'s history.

Just as the editorial content and the penny price have remained consistent, so have the graphics and makeup. The pair of workers clasping hands next to Christ remains the paper's front-page emblem, along with the words "a cent a copy" (changed in 1933 from "a penny a copy" at the suggestion of a radical Irishman who disliked the English undertone). Three-thousand-word articles are common, so the columns have always been densely printed. Occasional

startling headlines have been employed as eye-catchers throughout the history
of the paper, such as "Forget Pearl Harbor" during World War II when
"Remember Pearl Harbor" was a popular song.[90] Other examples, all but one
on the front page, include: "Breeding Frankensteins," "Puerto Rican Families
Dispossess Rats," " 'Yes, I am a Radical!' — Peter Maurin," "National Biscuit
Sweats Workers to Sell Dividends," and "Feed the Poor — Starve the Bankers."[91]
In an editorial entitled "The Opium of the People?" Dorothy Day admitted
that she sought to shock people into reading articles, by that and similar
headlines. She explained that she had adopted a technique used by Peter Maurin,
"who liked to shock people into attention" by using "some startling statement to
call attention to a truth which has become so familiar that it is no longer dynamic."[92]

No doubt some readers find the stark wood engravings and drawings of Fritz
Eichenberg and Ade Bethune startling. These are not idealized portraits of
Christ, His Mother, and the Saints. Rather, Christ is shown working in a carpen-
ter shop; Mary is wielding a broom; and St. Joseph is busy at his sawbench.
Likewise, worker-saints are depicted, such as St. Crispin the shoemaker, St.
Peter the fisherman, and St. Paul writing in prisons, walking the roads and
indoctrinating St. Timothy. Like its articles, the *Catholic Worker*'s art is power-
fully personalist, fusing the divine with the human. Both God and men and
women are united in everyday manual labor.

Adelaide de Bethune was a young Belgian just out of New York's Cathedral
High School for Girls, when she began to illustrate for the *Catholic Worker* late in
1933. She had been sent by the editor of *Liturgical Arts* magazine, and soon
discovered that "Dorothy's *Catholic Worker* provided the perfect forum" for the
type of pictures she wished to create.[93] Fifty years later, Bethune can clearly
recollect her first encounter with Day, which had humorous aspects. The bash-
ful nineteen-year-old high school graduate had dragged two large paper bags
crammed with clothes for the poor into St. Joseph's. "I must have looked forlorn,"
Bethune recalls, for "suddenly a tall, lanky lady approached me and said, 'Are
these your things? I'm awfully sorry — we have no room.' " It was Dorothy Day,
and she had mistaken Bethune for what would later be called a "bag lady."[94]
With much encouragement from Day, Bethune was soon drawing a series of
saints in modern dress. Her illustrations added lively, indispensable visual
interest to the *Worker*. One of her most famous portraits is that of St. Joseph,
rendered with the striking bold lines that are Bethune's signature. To her, St.
Joseph's trade, carpentry, was especially symbolic: "the primal artistic occupation,
using wood, tools, and imagination for the service of human beings."[95]

Perhaps through a printer's mistake (no one is quite sure why), Adelaide de
Bethune's name was spelled "Ade Bethune" in the paper, which it has ever since
remained. Not only did she draw for the *Catholic Worker*, she also allowed her
work to be reprinted in papers all over the world, Catholic and non-Catholic.
Today she is a nationally recognized liturgical artist, architect, and designer
based in Newport, Rhode Island. "Pictures," she has written, "should not be
made to gratify the senses. Their purpose is to inform our mind by their mean-

ing and arrangement."[96] This is consistent with the serious purpose of her own life; the Bethune family, after emigrating to the United States at the close of World War I, exemplified manual labor and the love of neighbor "to the highest degree," according to Dorothy Day.[97] However, despite stressing her art's didacticism, Bethune has always disdained "substance expressed in an amateurish way. I always sought to delineate the message with the best technique I could muster," she recently remarked. "There is no question that Dorothy's influence also greatly shaped the content and substance of my work," she added.[98]

FRITZ EICHENBERG © 1951

THE LORD'S SUPPER 1951

Quaker artist and author Fritz Eichenberg began to contribute wood engravings to the *Catholic Worker* in 1950. Now 83 years old, he is the foremost living master of wood engraving, and his work is seen in galleries and museums around the world. Born in Cologne, Germany, he studied and worked as a lithographer there and in Leipzig and Berlin, before moving to the United States in 1933, as Hitler was coming to power. He has taught at the New School for Social Research, the Pratt Graphic Arts Center (as founder and director) and the University of Rhode Island (as Art Department chairman). He lives just a few miles away from Bethune in Peace Dale, Rhode Island. Over the past six decades, Eichenberg has illustrated more than one hundred books by authors with whom he feels a special spiritual kinship, including most of the Russian classics by Dostoevsky, Pushkin and and Tolstoy, works by Goethe and Shakespeare, Emily Brontë's *Wuthering Heights* and Charlotte Brontë's *Jane Eyre*. Masterly blendings of subtlety and power, many of his engravings have become emblems, in some cases better remembered than the literary texts they illustrate. One thinks, for example, of Eichenberg's portrayal of the distraught Heathcliff brooding under a windswept tree, a forceful image of agitation and loss.

Eichenberg met Day in 1949 at a conference on religious publishing at the Quaker retreat center Pendle Hill, near Philadelphia. The two pacifists discovered a mutual reverence for Dostoevsky's novels; Day remembered seeing Eichenberg's illustrations in *Crime and Punishment*. She told the Quaker artist of the personalist art she desired for the *Catholic Worker*. He remembers that "she wanted something emotional, something that would touch people through images, as she was trying to do through words, and something that would communicate the spirit of the Catholic Worker to people who perhaps could not read the articles."[99] Eichenberg describes his initial efforts for the *Catholic Worker* as "rather timid. To me, the Catholic religion was unexplored territory."[100] So the always-practical Day promptly handed him a book of the lives of the saints, and at her urging he began to study her favorites. His engravings of Catherine of Siena and Teresa of Avila have become *Catholic Worker* classics, as have his many illustrations of St. Francis (whom Eichenberg had admired as a "universal" saint long before his conversion from Judaism to Quakerism in the Thirties). As an unpaid staff artist, he went on to create several distinctive versions of "The Peaceable Kingdom" (based on the work by Quaker artist Edward Hicks) and "Christ on the Breadline," perhaps the most emblematic of his hundred-plus *Catholic Worker* illustrations. The print pictures Christ as one of the skid-row unfortunates, desperate for a daily crust of bread at St. Joseph's House of Hospitality. These and other images capture the vision of the Catholic Worker movement, a world charged with the presence of divine love. Today wherever he goes, Eichenberg is recognized by people who know his work from the pages of Dorothy Day's paper. Like Ade Bethune's, his *Catholic Worker* art has been taped to the walls of coal miners' homes in West Virginia, farmworkers' shacks in California, and many other dwellings both humble and grandiose.

Reflecting the *Catholic Worker*'s simultaneous concern with the everyday and the ultimate, its writers include both famous philosophers and authors, and ordinary people. Catholic Workers around the country and abroad often send in accounts of their Houses of Hospitality and farming communes, which are published either in the letters column or separately. Reader participation is encouraged, resulting in a regular and lively letters column. Some of the best-known correspondents include Mother Theresa of Calcutta, who greatly admired Dorothy Day,[101] Thomas Merton,[102] and Jacques Maritain.[103] Many of the renowned letter-writers have also contributed long essays to the *Catholic Worker* on various themes from pacifism to labor relations. The paper has also reprinted the work of notable authors whom Day admired, such as the muckraking journalist I.F. Stone.[104]

Reprinted and quoted material has also included papal encyclicals, writings of the saints, and writings of cardinals, bishops, and priests. But the paper has always kept a careful balance of articles by illustrious personalities — enough to ensure quality and appeal, but never enough to overwhelm the average reader. Day was acutely aware of this tenuous balance. One entry in her diary reads: "Press day — late again but good issue.... Too long center article by Merton. After all we are a layman's paper — for workers, not men of letters."[105] Former *Catholic Worker* editor Thomas Cornell recalls that the October 1962 issue brought Day's wrath upon him, for it contained pieces by three priests. "This is a layman's paper!" Day bawled him out. "What are you trying to do, let them (the priests) take over? You're too impressed by clerical authority!" She reminded him that laypeople should have the lead in secular matters.[106]

Day especially encouraged laypeople — readers — to be writers.[107] When Mary Jo Weiler of Jamestown, North Dakota, sent Day an encouraging letter in 1935, Day recruited her, writing in a personal note: "We wish that you would consider yourself one of our correspondents and send us news of what is happening among the farmers of North Dakota."[108] For it was Dorothy Day, more than any other, who set the tone of the *Catholic Worker*. Her roles of editor and publisher took her from recruiting the paper's writers and readers, to shaping its content, appearance, and distribution. She herself was an able writer whose warm but unsentimental prose evoked the deepest response.

Summary of Sample

Type of Item	Total Number, 1933-1981	Percentages of Total Content,
Appeals	42	3.54
Reviews (book, film, play, press)	95	8.02
Reports from C.W. Houses and Farms	215	18.15

continued on next page

CONTRIBUTIONS BY DOROTHY DAY

Dorothy Day's Appeals	9	.76
(counted in "Appeals" category above)		
Dorothy Day's Columns	48	4.05
Dorothy Day's Signed Articles	31	2.61
(counted in other categories)		
Total of (signed) Contributions		
by Dorothy Day	88	7.43
Peter Maurin's Essays	40	3.37
Reports from Sites of Injustice	149	12.58

PRIMARILY SPIRITUAL CONTENT

Essays	63	5.32
Poetry	42	3.54
Prayers	28	2.36
Total Spiritual Content	133	11.23

ESSAYS

Comprehensive C.W. Philosophy	27	2.28
and Programs		
Pro-Agriculture & Farm Communes	26	2.20
Opposing Nazism, Anti-Semitism	9	.76
Opposing Capital Punishment	1	.08
Opposing Capitalism; Pro-Labor	123	10.38
Opposing Communism	7	.59

Pacifist Content (Essays)
Pro-Peace

166	14.02	
Opposing Militarism & Conscription	22	1.85
Total Pacifist Content	188	15.87
Pro-Family	5	.42
Opposing Racism	45	3.80
Opposing McCarthyism	4	.33
Pro-Papal Authority	6	.50
Pro-Voluntary Poverty	20	1.68
In Support of Sacco & Vanzetti	1	.08

TOTAL NUMBER OF ITEMS = 1184

SAMPLE DATES	Appeals	Book, Film, Play, Press Reviews	Reports from C.W. Houses and Farms	Dorothy Day's Columns	Dorothy Day's Signed Articles	Peter Maurin's Essays	Reports from Sites of Injustice
1933 (Dec., May, Sept., June-July)	5	2	5	0	4	2	8
1936 (Jan., April, July, Oct.)	1	4	9	2	1	6	19
1939 (Feb., May, July-Aug., Nov.)	5	3	19	4	0	9	9
1942 (Dec., March, Sept., June)	0	4	16	3	0	3	6
1945 (Jan., April, July-Aug., Oct.)	0	6	7	2	0	3	7
1948 (Feb., May, July-Aug., Nov.)	3	2	9	4	2	2	8
1951 (Dec., March, June, Sept.)	7	12	12	4	2	1	5
1954 (Jan., April, July-Aug., Oct.)	3	10	12	2	6	1	9
1957 (Feb., May, July-Aug., Nov.)	3	11	8	4	3	5	14
1960 (Dec., March, June, Sept.)	3	4	12	4	2	3	16

Year							
1963 (Jan., April, July-Aug., Oct.)	3	4	14	3	0	0	3
1966 (Feb., May, July-Aug., Oct.-Nov.)	3	4	10	2	2	1	5
1969 (Feb., March-April, June, Sept.)	2	7	13	3	2	1	6
1972 (Jan., March-April, July-Aug., Oct.-Nov.)	2	4	19	3	1	1	13
1975 (Feb., May, July-Aug., Oct.-Nov.)	1	7	22	4	3	1	13
1978 (Dec., March-April, June, Sept.)	0	7	11	4	0	0	2
1981 (Jan.-Feb., April, June-July, Oct.-Nov.)	1	4	17	0	3	1	6

SAMPLE DATES	Primarily Spiritual Content		
	Essays	Poetry	Prayers
1933 (Dec., May, Sept., June-July)	6	0	0
1936 (Jan., April, July, Oct.)	7	0	8
1939 (Feb., May, July-Aug., Nov.)	2	1	2
1942 (Dec., March, Sept., June)	9	2	4
1945 (Jan., April, July-Aug., Oct.)	3	6	1
1948 (Feb., May, July-Aug., Nov.)	3	5	0
1951 (Dec., March, June, Sept.)	4	1	1
1954 (Jan., April, July-Aug., Oct.)	4	4	2
1957 (Feb., May, July-Aug., Nov.)	2	4	1
1960 (Dec., March, June, Sept.)	1	6	1
1963 (Jan., April, July-Aug., Oct.)	3	4	2
1966 (Feb., May, July-Aug., Oct.-Nov.)	2	4	0
1969 (Feb., March-April, June, Sept.)	4	1	2
1972 (Jan., March-April, July-Aug., Oct.-Nov.)	0	0	0
1975 (Feb., May, July-Aug., Oct.-Nov.)	6	0	0
1978 (Dec., March-April, June, Sept.)	6	1	1
1981 (Jan.-Feb., April, June-July, Oct.-Nov.)	1	3	3

ESSAY THEMES

SAMPLE DATES	Pro-Peace	Opp. Militarism & Conscription	Pro-Family	Opp. Racism	Opp. McCarthyism	Pro-Papal Authority	Pro-Vol. Poverty	In Support of Sacco & Vanzetti
1933	2	0	0	13	0	1	1	0
1936	13	0	1	7	0	0	1	1
1939	8	1	0	1	0	1	1	0
1942	18	4	0	6	0	0	1	0
1945	13	0	2	6	0	1	1	0
1948	10	2	0	1	0	0	1	0
1951	6	0	0	1	0	1	1	0
1954	6	0	0	1	2	0	0	0
1957	12	0	0	1	2	0	0	0
1960	9	0	0	2	0	1	2	0
1963	12	2	0	2	0	1	2	0
1966	7	4	2	4	0	0	2	0
1969	6	1	0	0	0	0	0	0
1972	10	1	0	0	0	0	0	0
1975	13	3	0	0	0	0	3	0
1978	12	3	0	0	0	0	3	0
1981	9	1	0	0	0	0	1	0

ESSAY THEMES

SAMPLE DATES	Comprehensive C.W. Philosophy and Programs	Pro-Agriculture & Farm Communes	Opposing Nazism, Anti-Semitism	Opposing Capital Punishment	Opposing Capitalism; Pro-labor	Opposing Communism
1933	4	5	0	0	26	2
1936	7	4	3	0	13	0
1939	2	4	2	0	18	1
1942	2	3	0	0	3	0
1945	0	2	0	0	6	0
1948	1	1	2	0	5	0
1951	0	0	0	0	7	0
1954	2	1	0	0	6	0
1957	3	1	0	0	8	2
1960	0	2	0	1	9	1
1963	0	0	0	0	7	0
1966	1	0	0	0	6	1
1969	1	0	0	0	0	0
1972	0	2	1	0	2	0
1975	1	1	0	0	3	0
1978	1	0	0	0	2	0
1981	2	0	1	0	2	0

ST MARTHA

IV: The Journalist

Dorothy Day was only twenty-two when she made a final commitment to journalism. She had been at it a long time. Before she was eleven, she and her siblings were typing out the little family newspaper. At seventeen at the University of Illinois she joined a campus writers' club and wrote for the town newspaper. Before she was twenty she had overcome her father's disapproval to become a reporter in New York, for the Socialist *Call* and later the *Masses.* Then her vigorous social conscience led her off in another direction for a while. She did enter nurse's training. But her "longing to write" prevailed.[1] At the end of World War I she left nursing, firmly committed to effecting social change through her journalism.

Throughout the rest of her life, Day thought of herself primarily as a journalist, although she also enjoyed producing more lengthy work. In fact, she usually had a book in the back of her mind. When she was nearly eighty, she remarked, "I don't remember the time when I was *not* writing a book."[2] But she was most devoted to journalism. Above all, she felt, writing was to *report.* Advocacy journalism suited her goals far better than the careful crafting of a few novels would have. At a penny a copy, *Catholic Worker* journalism could reach a large audience, especially the poor. And it could be written on the run, without stealing too many hours from Day's other demanding activity, caring for the Catholic Worker family. So successful was her journalism, though, that it found its way into several book-length collections. It also created a readership for her several nonfiction books on her Catholic Worker life.

Day shared the genuine journalist's urge to be read; she always wrote with an audience in mind. She was so committed to getting the Catholic Worker viewpoint in print that if the regular channels of publication were closed to her, she once remarked, she would not hesitate to mimeograph her articles and hand them out on street corners.[3] "Writing was her craft," observed Thomas Cornell, an editor of the *Catholic Worker* in the early Sixties, and she took it very seriously.[4] Father John J. Hugo, Day's friend and confessor for the last forty years of her life, concurred: "She considered herself a writer; she always mentioned that. She considered writing not an avocation, but a vocation."[5] Day herself explained this in a letter she wrote to a benefactor in 1967. She had always viewed writing, she said, "as a way 'to earning a living' which each of us is bound to do as far as he is able before depending on others" (even though we may get "entirely too much credit for a work for which we have a vocation"). She added that she was now writing a pamphlet on the works of mercy to earn funds for the Catholic Worker movement.[6]

Similarly, she had contributed her free-lance writing income to help pay for the very first issue of the *Catholic Worker*. However, Day noted how shamefully "underpaid" writers were. She had earned more, she said, working her way through a year of college at "twenty cents an hour for housework, plus four hours work a day for room and board."[7] In a letter to her biographer, she commented: "My long experience with publishing houses showed me money is not to be made by writing. You just have to do it for the love of it."[8] For Day, the value of writing lay far beyond the income it could provide to aid the poor, or the creative gratifications it offered. Journalism, she believed, was the social activist's prime tool. One could use it "to move the heart, stir the will to action; to arouse pity, compassion, to awaken the conscience."[9] Bemoaning the author's continual low pay, she summarized the real rewards and true value of writing:

> But oh, the joy of seeing one's books (however unworthy of the honor of acceptance by the public) on newsstands, in chain drugstores, supermarkets, bus stations, even airports, handled by media who little know that many books of protest contain dynamite to blow our current unjust, war-ridden, profit-hungry civilization to smithereens.[10]

"I have no faith in our kind of books *selling*," she wrote to William D. Miller in 1970. "If they get on library shelves and influence people—that is enough."[11]

For Dorothy Day, then, writing was a serious vocation, a most worthwhile and significant calling. Naturally shy, she never really enjoyed public speaking, although she made countless speeches on behalf of the Catholic Worker movement. Her talents and interests led her to communicate her ideas primarily through the medium of print journalism. Like many writers who came into their prime during the decade of the Depression, she wanted her work to be socially significant and to inspire social change. Like her friends Elizabeth Gurley Flynn and Mary Heaton Vorse, she started out in Socialist journalism. But after her conversion to Catholicism, Dorothy Day sought to awaken people not only to the plight of the world, but also to their own spiritual condition. Hers became an advocacy journalism informed by a distinctive and profound religious faith. She came to this in part through such youthful experiences as a stint writing Hollywood scripts, which she found frustrating and meaningless; and through the process of writing her pre-conversion novel, *The Eleventh Virgin*, which sold to Hollywood. Thereafter, Day disdained such comparatively mundane, superficial literary endeavors. Resist the temptation of writing trash just to make money, she advised aspiring writers. She sometimes lamented the sad career of a friend in the labor movement, who had gone to Hollywood and made a fortune while "prostituting his great talents as a writer."[12] Rather,

Day admired writers such as Dostoevsky and Tolstoy, who dealt with monumental themes of human life and spirituality, and Dickens, Sinclair, and London, who through their books made greater strides in social reform, she felt, than did many politicians and economists.

Yet at least another, personal reason spurred Day to write. She once explained privately that she wrote *House of Hospitality*, *On Pilgrimage*, *The Long Loneliness*, and *Loaves and Fishes* — journalistic accounts of the Catholic Worker movement and her life within it — "to ease an aching heart and a discouraged mind." Such writing, she said, was "a most effective way of working things out for oneself as well as trying to make others understand."[13] If her book-length collection of 1948 columns entitled *On Pilgrimage* was "preaching and didactic in parts," she suggested at its end, "it is because I am preaching and teaching and encouraging myself on this narrow road we are treading."[14]

Dorothy Day's overall vision of journalism is shared by many advocacy journalists. In their sociological portrait of print and broadcast journalists, *The News People* (1976), John W.C. Johnstone, Edward J. Slawski, and William W. Bowman identified ideology as the "cornerstone" of contemporary advocacy journalism collectives such as Liberation News Service (New York) and the *Great Speckled Bird* (Atlanta).[15] Dorothy Day would have agreed. Early in her *Catholic Worker* career, she candidly avowed that the publication's purpose was "to influence the thought of its readers."[16] She often espoused the social change-oriented, "investigative," "analytic," and "interpretive" type of journalism that these researchers found to be so characteristic among advocacy journalists (many of whom were writing, like Day, for small, magazine-style publications). Like those surveyed in *The News People*, Day too was a participant journalist who emphasized opinion over "neutrality," and "interpretation over speed of transmission." Although she admired the artistry of many authors, she herself never wrote simply for the sake of writing; she always had a message in mind. But unlike the *News People* subjects, she did not emphasize "substance over technique." Nor did her ideological allegiances eclipse her commitment to high standards of journalistic excellence, as was the case among so many of them.[17]

Like George Orwell, whose work she admired, Dorothy Day seems to have recognized that clear, direct, personal prose was the basis for open political dialogue among all classes. She was not alone in recognizing the impact of technique on substance, the importance of devising what Kenneth Burke would call a "rhetorical strategy." Editors of many radical publications in the Thirties, including one Day had written for, the *New Masses*, were acutely aware of the power of language to create "potent symbols about which [the] masses could collect for action."[18] And Day had cut her journalistic teeth at the *Masses*, the first radical publication to concentrate on literary finesse as well as content, spicing it with a dash of sophisticated humor.

The journalism of her apprenticeship years suggests considerable talent. Anticipating her later work, it clearly shows a flair for characterization, an ability to discern the telling detail, and a deep sympathy for the poor, whose stories she could so effectively personalize.[19] These elements meshed in a piece entitled "A Coney Island Picture," which the twenty-year-old Day wrote for the *Liberator* in April 1918. First she set the scene: "Last night it stormed. The ocean spit far up on the beach huge cakes of ice, bits of driftwood glazed over with foamy crystals." The body of a destitute young girl had also been cast ashore. Day offered sparse but well-chosen details, memorably characterizing the victim. She mentioned the eighteen cents found in the dead girl's pocket, "Tied up in the corner of her handkerchief," as well as "the blister on her frozen heel as though she had walked—as we all have walked, to deaden the misery or to get warm." Day noted the "many neat darns" on her stockings, and her "thin cotton crepe underwear,... yellow because it had been washed and washed in the bathroom of a rooming house, and hung over the heater to dry. Poor little chemise."[20]

In "South Street," a piece she wrote for the *Masses* about the same time, the young reporter proved she was a sharp observer. In just a few strokes, she evoked the beauty and squalor of life near the harbor. She began: "South Street, where the truckmen and deckmen sit around on loads of boxes and wait for a boat to come in, where men idle in the September sunlight and dream and yawn and smoke, where the horses clatter along the cobbles dragging huge heavy trucks with a noise resembling a mob of people aroused after long repression, and where the kids sit on the edge of the dock and look with wishful eyes at the water below that swirls with refuse and driftwood." Always attuned to natural beauty, Day described "a wave of soft silence, golden in the September sunlight with its autumny smell." She contrasted this with the "heavy foul odor from God knows what storehouse, and from the river that gulps and gulps at the docks all day long," which sometimes replaced "the mellowness."[21]

In critical essays for the *Masses* and the *Liberator*, she also proved herself an insightful reviewer, able to cut through abstractions to reach a book's central ideas.[22]

Deft characterization, bright description, and authentic-sounding dialogue enriched her muckraking series on dance halls, which she wrote for the New Orleans *Item* in 1924. Presented in the first person, the articles piled up details to reveal such sordidness as easy-flowing "whisky and dope smokes."[23] The series was given page-one prominence, and it led New Orleans organizations such as the Business and Professional Women's Club and the Federation of Clubs to press successfully for some reforms.[24] Day also wrote for the *Item* a series on women at the races and gaming tables, entitled "The Thrills of 1924." She studded the articles with colorful personality sketches.[25] Day was equally adept at interviewing boxers and capturing the excitement of a close match.[26]

Later on, of course, a deep religious dimension would inform her writing. From her early, pre-conversion apprenticeship, Day brought to the *Catholic Worker* firsthand knowledge of the synergistic effect of literary technique on one's message. She indicated her awareness of technique's importance when she wrote in 1948: "An ordinary journalistic device is to paint a picture with contrasts. It is an emotional way of making a point."[27] How well this characterized much of her writing. Doubtless too, Day's appreciation of style for its own sake also helped keep her ever conscious of its meshing with substance. And so she crafted columns and articles for the *Catholic Worker* that used a wide array of the fiction writer's techniques, laced with her pungent comic irony.

While *Catholic Worker* journalism was her major focus, Day also viewed letter writing as an important calling, indeed as an "apostolate." Whenever she sat down to write an article, she said, she did so "with the oppressive sense of having many letters that have come into the *Catholic Worker* mail bag waiting to be answered." She regretted that no one could spare uninterrupted time for letter writing, which she identified as one of the "big jobs" in the *Catholic Worker* office.[28] Away on speaking trips, she always toted a bundle of letters to read and answer on the subway, the bus, the train, or anywhere else she could snatch a few spare moments.[29] Notebooks also accompanied her on her travels. She filled them with jottings to be used in her monthly *Catholic Worker* columns. "I'm a compulsive scribbler," she said, explaining their great number.[30]

Articles for the *Catholic Worker*, letter-answering, diary-keeping: Day considered all to be important aspects of a writing vocation and devoted herself to them. She constantly urged others to do likewise: "We all should (keep a diary)," Day exhorted, "no matter how brief and factual—and be careful, in letter and diary, not to err in charity and write things that may hurt others."[31] Joseph Zarrella, a Catholic Worker veteran, recalled how Day was "always after me to write for the paper." Although he did not consider himself a journalist, he finally obliged with an article entitled "Joe Zarrella Writes."[32] Similarly, Stanley Vishnewski, a lifelong Catholic Worker, recalled Day's continual encouragement of his writing attempts, as well as others'.[33]

Perhaps Day sought to galvanize aspiring (and non-aspiring) writers because the art came so naturally to her. "I am rather like the sorcerer's apprentice when I get at the typewriter," she confessed. "When I am turned on, a flood of words come and hundreds of new pages pour out."[34] Many of those who worked closely with her, such as Nina Polcyn Moore and Florence Weinfurter, Catholic Workers and friends of Day's for over forty years, strongly agree.[35] Because Day "was such a skilled and practiced writer," Thomas Cornell recently remarked, "she could get away with writing one draft, then correcting it in pencil."[36]

Exactly how many articles Day wrote for the *Catholic Worker* cannot be determined, because many of the paper's unsigned pieces were also hers. During the Thirties and Forties, Joseph Zarrella often observed Day at the printer's where, he remembered, "if we were short of copy, she'd pound out copy to fill the space. She was like a machine gun—she could write just like that." He judged that she did "much of the writing" for the *Catholic Worker*, at least in the first decade or so, including most of the articles without bylines.[37] His wife Mary Alice Lautner Zarrella, also a Catholic Worker in the Thirties when she worked closely with Day, agreed. "Dorothy wrote most of the paper," she said. "It kind of fell on her. There were enough writers to fill the paper up, but not enough had the necessary personal discipline—so Dorothy wrote."[38] Indeed, as

late as 1946, when she and her followers were busy rebuilding ranks that had
been diminished by wartime defection, Day commented: "I wish we had more
writers in the Catholic Worker movement. There are so many things of interest
to report, and the workers are so busy, on all fronts, that we don't have the
written reports we should."[39]

In the *Catholic Worker*'s early years, Day contributed investigative, muckraking
reports on such topics as tenant evictions, the seamen's strikes of the Thirties,
the 1936 Vermont marble workers' strike, and the 1937 Republic Steel massacre.
As a young radical reporter she had honed her descriptive skills, and they
sparkled in her 1936 series of articles on Arkansas sharecroppers, which appeared both in the *Catholic Worker*[40] and in *America:*

> It was seventeen above zero when we started out this morning with a carload
> of flour, meal, lard, sugar, coffee, and soup. . . .
>
> It wasn't until late in the afternoon that we reached the worst place of all, just
> outside Parkin, Arkansas. There drawn up along the road was a tent colony,
> which housed 108 people, four infants among them, and God knows how
> many children.
>
> The little girls giggled and laughed with their arms around each other
> while we talked to this evicted crowd of sharecroppers. Only one of them had
> on a sweater, and the heels and toes of all of them were coming out of their
> shoes. Their giggles started them coughing and woke up one of the babies who
> cried fretfully, weakly. . . .
>
> The little tent where we stood on the frozen earth was filled with fourteen
> children and there were thirteen more in the camp. Here too were four
> infants, wrapped in scanty cotton blankets. . . .
>
> While surveys are being made and written the Southern Tenant Farmers'
> Union carries on . . . organizing the sharecroppers. . . . They have had a hard
> struggle in the past and the future looks dark. But combined with faith and
> charity they have hope, and the terror that walks by day and by night in Arkansas
> does not daunt them.[41]

In articles like this, the discerning reader could see she was as concerned with
technique as with substance. This strategy only intensified the impact of her
message, as Day surely knew. She had learned her lessons well at the *Masses*.
And people in high places felt her impact. In the White House, Day's reports
came to the attention of Eleanor Roosevelt, herself a socially concerned author
of a nationally syndicated, daily newspaper column. The First Lady informed
the Governor of Arkansas. (He made a personal investigation, but the report
sent to the press concluded that nothing was amiss, that the unfortunate publicity was probably concocted by a "Catholic woman" who made "fat salaries off the
misery of the people."[42])

Dorothy Day also wrote some outstanding pieces for the *Catholic Worker* on
the labor movement of the Thirties.[43] Pro-worker, the paper quickly developed
inside sources for the coverage of unions, strikes, and other labor issues. Day
herself knew many national labor figures, and interviewed union heads such as
Philip Murray, John L. Lewis, John Brophy, Joseph Curran, and Harry Bridges.[44]

In 1936 Day covered a speech by the Rev. Stephen Kazincy, the "labor priest," in Braddock, Pennsylvania. She captured the essence of the event with evocative sensory details, and sparse but sonorous quotation. Her matter-of-fact, unsentimental tone underscored the gravity of the steel workers' plight:

> The steel workers spoke first and the sun broiled down and the men and their wives stood there motionless, grave, unsmiling, used to hardship, and thinking of the hardships to come if the steel masters locked them out.
>
> And then Father Kazincy was announced. He got up before the microphone, a broad, straight man of about sixty. His hair was snow white, his head held high ... his words came abrupt, forceful, and unhesitating....
>
> 'Remember that you have an immortal soul,' he told them. 'Remember your dignity as men.
>
> 'Do not let the Carnegie Steel Company crush you.'[45]

One of Dorothy Day's most passionate pieces in the Thirties, which combined muckraking with advocacy, described the Republic Steel massacre. Usually the *Catholic Worker* aimed to "announce," not to "denounce." But when police opened fire on striking steel workers and their families at the gate of the Republic Steel Company in South Chicago on Memorial Day, May 30, 1937, Day could not be silent. She spoke out in hope that "the only way to stop such brutality is to arouse a storm of protest against it." In concrete but unsensationalized detail, she gave her readers a vivid picture of the violence that took ten lives and injured more than a hundred others:

> Have you ever heard a man scream as he was beaten over the head by two or three policemen with clubs and cudgels? Have you ever heard the sickening sound of blows and seen people with their arms upraised, trying to protect their faces, stumbling blindly to get away, falling and rising again to be beaten down? Did you ever see a man, shot in the back, being dragged to his feet by policemen who tried to force him to stand, while his poor body crumpled, paralyzed by a bullet in the spine?

Day went on to compare the Chicago violence to contemporary brutality in Italy, Russia, and Nazi Germany. Instead of piously assigning blame for the Republic Steel tragedy to the police, or to company personnel, she acknowledged a more universal guilt. "Have pity on us all, Our Lord of Gethsemane," she wrote, "—on Tom Girdler [of Republic Steel], those police, the souls of the strikers, as well as on all of us who have not worked enough for 'a new heaven and a new earth wherein justice dwelleth.' "[46]

Once Day established the *Catholic Worker*'s tradition of muckraking she began to leave such writing more to others. But she kept the journalist's sense for telling quote and graphic detail that she developed so early in her career. Throughout her life she retained her ability to write solid, informative, compelling muckraking and advocacy journalism, whether describing Cesar Chavez's struggles in the California vineyards, her 1962 travels to Castro's Cuba, or the problems of racial integration in the South.

These skills also enriched the analytical background pieces which she occasionally wrote.[47] In "Krushchev and Alexander Nevsky" (1960), she delved into Russian history, describing the life of a thirteenth-century national hero and saint of the Russian Orthodox Church.[48] In "Theophane Venard and Ho Chi Minh" (1954), she presented a lengthy (about 3,500 words), well-researched piece on the political history of Vietnam, concluding with a warning against American involvement.[49] From time to time she also contributed perceptive spiritual commentaries and critiques of sophisticated theological and literary works.[50]

As the years went on, Day increasingly devoted herself to her column, originally called "Day by Day," shortly changed to "All in a Day," then to "On Pilgrimage" in 1946. Even today her column is often reprinted, and then it forms the heart of the paper. Dwight Macdonald once aptly described it as a combination of Pascal's *Pensées* and Eleanor Roosevelt's "My Day." In her column Day ruminated in a conversationally warm, appealing manner. She touched on subjects as diverse as children, visitors to St. Joseph's House of Hospitality, animals, the saints, the weather, the soup line, prayer, pacifism, putting out the paper—sometimes mentioning them all in the same piece. All of Day's writing tended to be personal, discursive, and a bit repetitive, but "On Pilgrimage," whose column format afforded a great degree of creative freedom, was especially so. Day often added to this personal ambiance by conversing about her role as mother and grandmother. "I may repeat myself," she acknowledged in the foreword to her book *On Pilgrimage*, "but mothers always do that to be heard."[51] Readers of Day's columns were treated to poignant tales about Tamar Teresa's growing up; for instance, how at eight the little girl "was filled with the small chatter so dear to a mother's ears."[52] Day sometimes reported some of Tamar's childish chatter in order to make more lasting points. Her December 1934 editorial is a moving example. "Christmas is coming," Day began, telling how Tamar and her playmate Freddy were drawing pictures of the Nativity. Hearing the children "tell the story to each other," she wrote, "each filling in the gaps," brought it "fresh and clear" to her mind. " 'And the cow breathed on the little baby Jesus and kept it warm,' Teresa says delightedly. 'Cows are very warm animals, I know. . . . I'm sure the baby Jesus didn't mind being in a stable at all. Probably there were chickens, too. And maybe the shepherds brought their littlest lambs to show them to him.' "

Then Day reported her response. She told the children that "Christ came to live with the poor and the homeless and the dispossessed of this world, . . . and he loved them so much that he showed himself to the workers—the poor shepherds—first of all. It wasn't until afterward that he received the Kings of this earth. So let us keep poor—as poor as possible—

" 'In a stable with cows and chickens,' [Tamar] finished joyfully. 'And then it will be easier for me to have God in my heart.' "[53]

After Tamar grew up and married, readers savored the many homey details Day offered of her country visits to her daughter and nine grandchildren, from baking bread and spinning wool to "feeding and consoling babies." In one column based on such a visit, Day told her *Catholic Worker* audience that she did "not know of a happier way to spend an afternoon than sitting in a shallow brook with babies paddling happily around."[54] Her use of the first-person voice gave the column a personal immediacy, as did the many sensory details, and liberal use of dialogue and quotation. Day wrote "most personally," she said, "because I am a woman who can write no other way."[55] Like Day's autobiography, her columns clearly show that she had the sensibilities of the successful novelist — the sensory sensitivity, the scene-setting and storytelling skills, the ear for authentic speech, and a well-developed sense of the comic, which permeated much of her writing.

Even in the most depressing and difficult situations, Day's sense of humor was acute. Her description of the last days of one of the Catholic Worker's most irascible visitors is a fine piece of comic irony. In the Thirties, an eccentric racist named Edward J. Breen, "sputtering with rage," "his dirty white hair tossing, his eyes bulging out of his apoplectic face," had long tried the patience of those at St. Joseph's, where he remained until he died. "As the end drew near," Day recounted, "we all sat around his bedside, taking turns saying the rosary." With comic restraint, she recorded Mr. Breen's final words to her: " 'I have only one possession left in the world — my cane. I want you to have it. Take it — take it and wrap it around the necks of these bastards around here.' Then," Day went on, "he turned on us a beatific smile. In his weak voice he whispered, 'God has been good to me.' And smiling, he died."[56]

"Franciscan spirit grows hereabouts," Day remarked drily in 1935, telling how a Catholic Worker guest who was devoted to a certain cat "was discovered washing her chest with my washrag and drying her with my towel and then anointing her with a warming unguent for a bad cough!" Meanwhile, she added, a Worker had appropriated one of her blankets "to cover the old horse who helps us deliver our Manhattan bundles of papers every month."[57] In 1948, Day lamented that the typical busy mother had no time for books. Neither did she have the "gay companions of her youth," Day added, because "their nerves can't stand it."[58] At the age of eighty-one, her sense of humor was as sharp as ever. "We had hard, baked potatoes for supper, and cabbage overspiced," she recounted to readers in her February 1979 column. "I'm in favor of becoming a vegetarian only if the vegetables are cooked right."[59]

In some ways, Day's approach to writing resembled that of engraver and *Catholic Worker* illustrator Fritz Eichenberg. Like Eichenberg's art, Day's communicated a deep concern for peace and social justice, often with a satirical leavening that served to intensify the message. Like Eichenberg and like artist Käthe Kollwitz, whose work she greatly admired, Day perpetually sought to arouse consciences by detailing the lives of the poor. No doubt Dorothy Day could have been a successful writer of fiction, but her conversion to Catholicism deepened her commitment to harness her literary gifts, not to serve her own imaginative vision, but rather to portray and celebrate that artistry already present in God's creation.[60] Day was not an intellectual theorist; she did not try to set forth her ideas abstractly or systematically. In her column, she directed her appeal more to the ordinary "workers," and let other *Catholic Worker* writers appeal to the scholars. With rich spiritual insights, she described people she had known, pressing problems, and concrete situations. In this, as her friend Father Hugo has observed, she resembled the writers of the great literary masterpieces she admired and reread: those who mirror life as they see it. But while Dostoevsky, Tolstoy, and their like saw it imaginatively, she saw life in the raw, and in the profound problems of our age.[61]

In her personal example and in her journalism, Dorothy Day communicated the essence of personalism. It was never theory of which she wrote, but deeply felt convictions arrived at from firsthand experience. "You can't write about things without doing them," she remarked in an interview in 1971. "You just have to live that same way."[62] Her early, pre-conversion reporting had certainly taught her the value of participant journalism, starting with her "diet squad" articles about the problems of destitution and hunger for the New York *Call*, 1916-1917. Then, she had actually tried to live on five dollars a week.[63] and in 1924 for the New Orleans *Item*, she had taken a job as a taxi dancer in order to write exposés of dance hall venalities.

The integrity of Day's life was extraordinary. As Robert Ellsberg recently observed, "there was absolutely no distinction between what she believed, what she wrote, and the manner in which she lived."[64] Constantly in the midst of the poor, she understood their daily struggles as few others could. Day knew exactly what it meant to scrounge in the clothing bin, hoping for a not-too-threadbare pair of fitting socks; she knew what it meant to subsist on borrowed, utilitarian food; she knew what it meant to beg for extended credit on overdue rent, heat, and light bills—and sometimes not to be able to afford heat in the cruelest winter. In her January 1963 journal, Day described her room at St. Joseph's House of Hospitality:

> And then the place where I am, cold, unheatable because the gas flow is meager, cluttered and dusty, Marie's newspapers and magazines piled high—what compulsion is there for her to collect, collect, collect.... Now she brings in two shopping bags for a night, God knows what all besides, ... and the room gets fuller and fuller so there is scarcely a passageway through. And there is always an odor in the rooms. My room is both dirty and cold and I have not the energy or strength to clean. My bones are still with cold and I am tired with the weight of clothes I put on to keep warm.[65]

Because Day lived like those she served, she could describe poverty and sorrow—and joy—in the most personal, vivid, and moving terms.

She was at her best when characterizing some of the everyday people who came by St. Joseph's. "It is people who incarnate ideas, who make ideas come alive," Day often said.[66] Deftly as a novelist she brushed in the destitute as distinct characters, using the details of their lives to communicate her concerns.

Her rhetorical strategy was to introduce them by their first names—Bill, Anna, Millie—as if to say, "They are one of us." With skillful portraiture, sympathetic yet unsentimental, she characterized ordinary men and women, revealing their spiritual qualities and recognizing their dignity—a dignity she knew they had and deserved. Again and again she wrote memorable obituaries for those "least among us":

> All of you who ride the Pennsylvania or the Lehigh pass by those pig farms set in the swamps, ugly as sin, evil-smelling holes, where thousands of pigs are raised and fattened on garbage from New York hotels. . . . John Ryder worked in this setting, cleaning out pig sties, caring for the hogs. . . . On pay days he would come over to New York and too often spend his holidays on the Bowery. He told us the pay was good and the meals too, but it was another case of needing heroic virtue to live under such surroundings. Too often the men sought surcease and rest and dreams in drink. . . . But it is difficult to clamber out of the trough of the destitute. . . .
>
> John, like the prodigal son, came home to us after feeding off the husks of the swine. And he could not be feasted because he was dying. Instead, he had that real feast, the bread of the strong [the Eucharist], and he died and was laid out in the chapel at Maryfarm, and each night before his burial we said the office of the dead as though he were one of the mightiest of the sons of God. . . .[67]

Especially in such remembrances, Day wrote with impressive (and effective) restraint about her sordid surroundings. She did this, first, because she truly recognized God even in the person of the most pitiful; her view of life on earth was not hopeless. Also, she perceived the psychology of her audience. Together, too many shocking details from the Lower East Side would lose their impact, besides inordinately depressing readers. So Day sought not to sacrifice editorial appeal by brooding at length over the daily tribulations at St. Joseph's. This entry from her diary shows how closely in touch with her audience Day was:

> The other day when writing my article and appeal I threw away my article, telling all of our troubles and thought 'This is not what readers want—to be tortured with tales of broken families, men beating their wives and children, etc.' I will write happily of June and its beauties. . . .

"Of course if you do this you get a double share of complaints from all around you who try to make you see how bad everything is," she added ruefully.[68] And this excerpt from one of her columns shows how she maintained the fragile balance between honest reporting and a sanguinity devoid of self-pity, even in the grim days on the eve of World War II:

> When the burdens pile high and the weight of all the responsibilities we have undertaken bows us down, when there are never enough beds to go around and never enough food on the table, then it is good to sit out in the

cool of the evening with all our neighbors and exchange talk about babies and
watch the adventurous life of the street.

The world is bowed down with grief, and in many ways God tries to bring us
joy, and peace. They may seem at first to be little ways but if our hearts are
right they color all our days and dispel the gray of the sadness of the times.[69]

Yes, Dorothy Day believed one could always find solace in the presence of
babies. She had a special love for the very young. "Babies and small children,"
she wrote, "are pure beauty, love, joy—the truest in this world."[70] Once, not
long before World War II, she wrote that she was cutting her column short in
order to take the children at Maryfarm in Easton, Pennsylvania "up the hill to
hunt for salamanders in the spring. In spite of strikes and brutality, controversy
and war," she went on, "this world is filled with joy and beauty and the children
bring it to us anew and help us to enjoy it through their eyes."[71] In their lives
she always recognized a means to dramatize great spiritual themes. This mode
can be glimpsed even in her pre-*Catholic Worker* writing. An outstanding example is "Having a Baby," her delightful and moving account of giving birth to
her only child. First published in *New Masses*, it was later reprinted in leftist
papers throughout the world.[72] Written just before her conversion, "Having a
Baby" does not allude directly to religion, but it captures the mother-to-be's
sense of anticipation. In "A Baby Is Born," printed in the January 1941 *Catholic
Worker*, Day juxtaposed the birthing experience of a destitute, young unmar-
ried mother with the plight of the wretched poor lining up outside St. Joseph's
for morning coffee, and with despairing wounded soldiers. Her masterpiece of
nonfiction technique thus became much more than the usual tale of the unwed
mother's woe:

Every night before we went to bed we asked the young mother, 'How do you
feel?' and asked each other . . . 'Is there taxi money?' in case it would be too late
to call an ambulance.

And then, one morning at five I heard rapid footsteps in the room above,
the voice of the ambulance interne in the hall, 'I'll be waiting downstairs,' and I
realized that the great moment had arrived. It was still dark out, but it was
indubitably morning. Lights were on in the kitchens of surrounding tenements.
Fish-peddlers, taxi drivers, truckmen, longshoremen, were up and on their
way to work. The business of life was beginning. And I thought, 'How cheerful
to begin to have a baby at this time of the morning!' Not at 2 A.M., for instance,
a dreary time, of low vitality, when people sink beneath their woes and courage flags. Five o'clock is a cheerful hour. Down in our little back yard . . . down
in that cavernous pit with tenements looming five and seven stories up around,
we could hear them dragging out the ash cans, bringing in the coffee cans for
the line. . . .

Out in front the line was forming already and two or three fires in the
gutters brought out in sharp relief the haggard faces of the men, the tragedy of
their rags. The bright flames, the blue-black sky, the grey buildings all about,
everything sharp and clear, and this morning a white ambulance drawn up in
front of the door.

> This is not the story of the tragedy of the mother. We are not going into detail about that. But I could not help thinking that while I was glad the morning was beginning, it was a miserable shame that the departure of the young woman for her ordeal should be witnessed by a long, silent waiting line of men. They surveyed her, a slight figure, bundled on that cruelly cold morning (and pain and fear make the blood run cold), come running down from the dark, silent house to get into the ambulance.
>
> Not one man, not a dear husband, not a protector on whom she could lean for comfort and strength. There was no Joseph on this winter morning. But there were hundreds of men, silent, waiting, and wondering perhaps as they watched the ambulance, whether it was life or death that had called it out.[73]

Intensifying this powerful juxtaposition, Day moved to deeper themes. She compared the sadness of a woman giving birth alone to the suffering of the soldier, "with his guts spilled out on the battlefield, lying for hours impaled upon barbed wire." By the end of the piece, she had noted that despite the painful process of labor, the mother could be cheered by the new small life; all war issued for the soldier, though, were agony and death. Whatever the circumstances of a child's birth, she observed, joy reigned: "And this tiny creature who little realizes his dignity as a member of the Mystical Body of Christ, lies upstairs from me now as I write, swaddled in a blanket and reposing in a laundry basket." As Christ came to her in the persons of the hungry men in the morning coffee line—"for inasmuch as ye have done it unto these the least of my brethren, ye have done it unto me"—so too was Christ present in this newborn child, just as Christ himself was once present as a baby boy. But Day was not tritely cheerful as she gazed at the "rosy and calm and satisfied" infant, with his "look of infinite peace and complacency." Without descending into hopelessness, she reflected upon how little the child knows of what is in the world, of "what horrors beset us on every side."

In her March 1951 column, Day wrote of another baby whose presence inspired her to reflect on deeper spiritual mysteries. In her typically homey, personal style she observed: "Downstairs the baby is crying while Rita gets her breakfast ready, mashed prunes, baby cereal and milk, all mixed together deliciously. Little Rachel is three months old now and eats with avidity." But by the column's end, Day had moved adroitly from the child's feeding to a perceptive portrayal of common human ill-will and pettiness. She explained her purpose in doing so:

> It may seem that I am speaking lightly of these things, but these are sorrowful mysteries indeed, the mystery of sin and suffering and how we are all members one of another, and drag each other down, or pull each other up.[74]

Day's aim in such juxtapositions as these of the "baby pieces"—and her consummate gift as a writer—was to unite the everyday and the ultimate. "I think of death every day of my life," she once confided to her friend Eileen Egan.[75] And so, in the most universal, commonplace events such as birth, she recognized profound import. She could make matters of faith seem so relevant to everyday life, for instance linking "nibbling in the kitchen" to the seven deadly sins.[76] She had that rare ability to cut directly to the heart of the matter. In this regard her writing resembles that of E.B. White, who also delved beyond the surface of the apparently mundane to deep truths, often with a comic stroke. Among writers of fiction, one might compare Dorothy Day to Flannery O'Connor, who also recognized God's presence in the lives of an array of grotesque misfits. Like O'Connor (and Fritz Eichenberg), Day successfully used comic irony, no doubt to lighten the despair that could easily be awakened by accounts of such tragic characters and situations. By so doing, Day intensified the impact of her message. And using common events and people as a springboard, she could communicate a moving message to a much wider audience, than if she had simply written theory or bald propaganda—that is, concentrated solely on content. Unlike the advocacy journalists surveyed in *The News People*, Day's ideological commitments did not overshadow her dedication to quality journalism. Instead, they worked fruitfully together. As an advocate, she realized the importance of crafting a lattice of substance and style suitable to achieve the greatest appeal. To this task she applied her considerable talents. Modern advocacy journalists have rarely produced writing of such caliber.

Readers loved her style. The Catholic Worker Papers contain many favorable letters from the paper's audience. Readers often addressed Day familiarly as "Dorothy," sometimes explaining, as one young seminarian did, that after they read her writing they felt as if they knew her personally.[77] One woman wrote Day that her articles were "among the most beautiful pieces I have ever read."[78] When another subscriber read Day's October 1962 column about her Cuba travels, she wrote to share her reaction: "I was overcome with emotion, and said aloud, though I was alone, 'Thank God for people like Dorothy Day!' And I am a person who practically never uses the word 'God'; in this case, there was just no other way to say what I felt."[79] And Dr. Julian Pleasants, now a professor of microbiology at Notre Dame University, found Day's "vivid journalistic accounts" so inspiring that he helped to start a House of Hospitality in South Bend, Indiana, in the early Forties. "Before we ever met her," he said, "we knew her holiness and love of the poor which she expressed so well in words."[80]

Viewed in sum, Day's "fan mail" indicates that her conversational, unpretentious writing provided a necessary balance to the more sophisticated, theoretical articles elsewhere in the *Catholic Worker*. Beyond this, she was at the center—her journalism, the hub around which everything revolved. The result was a publication whose deep well of articles allowed readers with diverse tastes to drink what they needed.

ADE BETHUNE

S†:VERONICA

V: The Lengthened Shadow

From 1933 until a series of heart attacks weakened her in the late Seventies, Dorothy Day firmly held the reins of editor and publisher (not to mention movement leader). Only once did she take a leave of absence, her year-long "sabbatical" beginning in the fall of 1943, which she spent in religious retreat. And even when she "retired" in her last years because of ill health, she did so slowly, her presence still keenly felt among Catholic Workers. For as Emerson observed of institutions, the *Catholic Worker* was indeed the "lengthened shadow" of her single person.

From the beginning, the paper was Day's special endeavor. She chose the articles, wrote much of the copy, and designed the makeup and headlines at times. A shrewd manager, a forceful editor and publisher committed to high journalistic standards, Day communicated authority. Her followers had a special reverence for her. To Stanley Vishnewski, one of Day's earliest and most beloved recruits, she was "the inspiration and the life of the Catholic Worker," without whom the movement "would never have been."[1] Eileen Egan, a Catholic Worker and close friend of Day's, called her "the luminous center" of the movement.[2] Deane Mowrer, a Catholic Worker columnist and intimate friend, wrote to her in 1961: "you are, I think, the real spiritual center of the Catholic Worker [movement] and will continue to be needed in this role."[3] Through the years, many of Day's other associates have also singled out her commanding presence, her ability to hearten others. "She inspired you for a number of reasons," remarked Joseph Zarrella, who worked closely with Day during the Thirties. "There isn't anything I wouldn't have done for Dorothy Day." He described her as the "driving force" behind the *Catholic Worker*, the source of its "vitality."[4] In the Thirties, so much did young *Catholic Worker* illustrator Ade Bethune admire the "tall lanky lady" in charge who at that time still "smoked like a chimney," that Bethune even considered taking up the habit in order to emulate her to the fullest.[5]

Personal charisma often assumes importance in a voluntary organization eschewing credo and constitution. And Dorothy Day's personality wielded an exceptionally pervasive force. Michael Harrington, a *Catholic Worker* editor in the early Fifties, described her simply as "a presence." When she came into a room, "even a stranger who had never even heard of her would realize that someone significant had just entered."[6] Ammon Hennacy, who helped edit the paper in the early Fifties, observed that without Day's "patience and knowledge" the paper "could not have lasted six months." Day "knew what an issue was and she knew how to write it up so as to be understood by the reader."[7] Early Sixties' editor Thomas Cornell agreed that "Dorothy controlled the paper absolutely. Her spirit was so important," he said. "She was the soul of the *Worker* in a Scholastic sense; she informed the *Worker*."[8] According to *Catholic Worker* illustrator Fritz Eichenberg, even in her last months when she was mostly bedridden, Day retained a magnetism which "spellbound" others.[9]

Dorothy Day was a complex personality who sometimes puzzled her closest friends. After knowing her for thirty-five years, Vishnewski remarked, "It is still hard for me to be able to classify Dorothy Day. To me she still remains an enigma dressed up in women's clothing. There are times when I feel that I know her and that I am able to explain her actions, but then she reveals another side of her character and leaves me baffled."[10] Such bewilderment is a common reaction to the paradox of Day's successful use of authority: She was, as one Catholic Worker described her, the "Head Anarch"—clearly at the helm, but not at all one for rules and regulations. How was she able to command such a high level of respect and obedience among her followers?

To come to terms with Dorothy Day as editor and publisher, one must examine how she used her authority. This in turn raises several issues, among them her relationship with her co-founder Peter Maurin; and her personal view of women's roles in social activism. To begin with, Day's authority was most reinforced by the power of her own pristine example. Again and again, Catholic Workers cite the inspirational effects of the witness of Dorothy Day's life. According to Monica Cornell (wife of Thomas Cornell), a Catholic Worker since the early Sixties who was very close to Day, "she remained amazingly pure in her motives," never compromising her principles.[11] As Robert Ellsberg has observed, "All her influence and her authority came from her integrity and her faithfulness." Day lived what she believed, so completely and so well that it "gave her an almost irresistible authority."[12] Judith Gregory, a *Catholic Worker* editor who knew Day well in the late Fifties and throughout the Sixties, made a similar evaluation. Authority at the Catholic Worker does not stem from status but from "willingness to act," Gregory observed. And Day was "always willing to speak what she had on her mind, and to move—to go out and do something" to further her causes, including the outright civil disobedience for which she was jailed several times.[13]

The example she set cast a tall shadow. David J. O'Brien, a Catholic historian, tells an illustrative anecdote: From 1974 to 1976, the American Catholic bishops held their bicentennial program with regional hearings. These were panels of ten to twenty bishops who would receive testimonies from various Catholic leaders. Dorothy Day was scheduled to speak at the Newark hearing. She was quite edgy, according to O'Brien, as she tended to be before any kind of public appearance. When the day dawned, she was especially intimidated by the prospect of addressing such a large panel of bishops—about twenty, when she had expected only three or four. O'Brien was impressed "by how terrified these bishops were that Dorothy was going to appear before them. They were at least as nervous as she was." Day began to fiddle anxiously with the microphone—but it didn't work, no matter how she adjusted it. Every time she tested it to no avail, more and more bishops would jump up to help her. Observing the ironically comic scene, O'Brien was reminded of the Gospel idea of authority arising from service to the community. "It was very true there," he said. "If there was authority and indeed if there was power in that room, it sat in her chair, not up there with the bishops—and they knew it."[14]

But what of Peter Maurin? Day herself consistently argued for a greater recognition of his role as co-founder of the Catholic Worker movement, in public and in private. She was often irritated by the great attention showered on her in later life, such as the wide recognition she received on the occasion of her seventy-fifth birthday (including such media coverage as an entire issue of *America* (November 11, 1972) and Notre Dame University's Laetare Medal as an outstanding American Catholic). To her biographer she wrote, probably in the early Seventies: "As for me, my gripe has always been that I wanted you to write and elaborate on Peter. . . ."[15]

But it is true that the nature and importance of Maurin's role in the movement were debated among Catholic Workers during his lifetime, and much disagreement about it still remains. Maurin has been described by those who knew him best as a brilliant saint—and as a nonstop talker who sought only to engineer his propaganda into the conversation at hand. Certainly Dorothy Day was not blind to his faults. She even confessed that although she was "sure that he was a saint and a great teacher," sometimes she wasn't quite sure that she liked Peter Maurin: "He was twenty years older than I, he spoke with an accent so thick it was hard to penetrate to the thought beneath, he had a one-track mind, he did not like music, he did not read Dickens or Dostoevsky, and he did not bathe."[16] Although Day's lovingly humorous touch softens this appraisal, it has a sharp edge. When Day discussed the failure of the Catholic Worker farming commune at Easton, Pennsylvania, in the February 1944 *Catholic Worker*, she first partially blamed the women. Then she added the clincher: "Perhaps, having so nobly taken the blame on my own sex, we can put some of it on Peter too. He was always willing, for the sake of making his point, to sacrifice order and success."[17]

But Peter Maurin made a major contribution by inspiring Day with his ideas for the Catholic Worker movement. To Day, the ex-Socialist, American Catholic convert, Maurin seemed to supply elements whose lack she sorely felt in her own life. He was a French "cradle Catholic," whose roots went back 1,500 years, a link to the older, more established European Church. He was soundly educated in the classical Catholic tradition. He lived a blameless life of voluntary poverty, modeled on that of Christ Himself. And Maurin was absolutely sure of

himself, repeating his well-developed theory over and over until Day appreciated its intricacies. Maurin was a visionary, a man of abstract principles, and an
eccentric; Day was much more down-to-earth, action-oriented, and typically
American. She was, as Dwight Macdonald called her, a "doer." Maurin probably gave Day a psychological security. He provided a sense of legitimacy and
purpose to her life, inspiring her with a program that appealed to her longing
to serve the masses as a Catholic.[18]

Her affection and respect for Maurin were genuine. He continually called
her to faithfulness, his presence reminding her to rise above the petty irritations
of daily life at the Catholic Worker House to fulfill a much larger purpose. But
once Day understood the ideas of her teacher, she supplemented them in her
own way, making those alterations she deemed fit. She initiated Houses of
Hospitality, which were urban relief centers—despite Maurin's emphasis on
more permanent, rural attempts at alternative lifestyles, the farming communes.
And she did not devote the newspaper exclusively to his Easy Essays, but
included varied copy of much wider appeal. She suppressed other tendencies
in Maurin's thought that she deemed inimical to the success of the movement.
For example, like many other European Catholic social activists, Maurin exhib-
ited some mild anti-clericalism. Day made sure that none of this ever saw print.
"I do indeed keep out some of his stuff which attacks the bishops," she told one
correspondent. "I just don't think it's politic. There are quite a number of
priests who think Peter just quaint when he verbally attacks the clergy, but who
would hold up their hands in horror if we printed the stuff."[19] And it was not
Maurin but Day who truly recognized the importance of clerical support for
their endeavors. Wisely, she saw to it that headlines in the *Catholic Worker* were
carefully crafted to indicate endorsement by Church officials, whenever possible:
"Catholic Workers and Readers Blessed by Pope," "Diocesan Distribution of
C.W. Planned by Bishop," "Priests and Laymen Cooperate," and so on.[20] She
also seems to have understood the legitimacy conferred by support from traditional Catholic lay organizations, as this 1933 headline suggests: "K. of C.
[Knights of Columbus] Distribute *Catholic Worker* at Manresa Retreat."[21]

Once it was clear that Day would be operating the *Catholic Worker*, Maurin
seems to have been content in the role of venerable philosopher, often traveling
by bus around the country to lecture on Catholic Worker ideology. He would
appear at St. Joseph's House of Hospitality in New York for a few days, then set
out again on another round. Once he inspired Day with his ideas, he became
more of a symbolic than an actual helpmate for her. And in later life he was
sometimes a burden. For several years before he died in 1949, he suffered from
what was probably hardening of the arteries or a stroke, and had to be cared for
like a child, by Day and others in the Catholic Worker family.[22]

The evidence indicates that she actually believed his day-to-day role in the
Catholic Worker movement was pivotal—or perhaps unconsciously tried to
convince herself of it. She may have done this for reasons stemming from her
own sense of the limitations of her gender—a result, most likely, of her upbring-

ing and the time in which she lived. For Dorothy Day was a single parent, a career woman, and a Catholic convert, trying to start an unprecedented, radical Catholic publication. Such credentials were hardly likely to impress a sexually conservative Church, especially during the Thirties, a time of increasingly reactionary public opinion on women's roles.

Indeed, that decade saw perhaps the century's most repressive anti-women legislation. The Great Depression had fostered a wave of reaction against any change in women's traditional roles of homemaker and mother. Social historians have noted the striking increase of hostility against working women in the Thirties. Often accused of depriving family men of needed jobs, these women actually were most represented in such typically non-male occupations as clerical work. Nevertheless, legislatures enacted laws restricting the employment of married women; and labor, government, and the mass media all joined in a campaign urging females as a patriotic duty to refrain from taking jobs. The equal-pay rules written into the National Recovery Administration industry codes in 1933 were scarcely enforced. By the end of the decade, prospects for improving women's economic and social status appeared bleak indeed.[23]

Trying to start a radical movement and publication in this milieu was clearly no easy task for a woman, no matter how eager Americans in the Thirties were for new solutions to social problems. Society gave little support to women attempting such leadership roles. And Day's own father had chastised her for wanting to work as a journalist.

Another factor was operating against Dorothy Day in the Thirties, especially: the tension she felt between her old life as a radical social activist and her new one as a Catholic traditionalist devoted to social justice. She did not automatically sever all her old friendships when she converted. Some pre-conversion friends enjoyed her company and she theirs through the years. Even in the early Fifties, such old friends as Allen Tate, Caroline Gordon, and Peggy Cowley with whom Day had celebrated her youth in Greenwich Village, often stopped by St. Joseph's in New York. And occasionally she saw Mike Gold and other old leftist comrades, although many dropped her after she made her religion a public matter. In mixed company, with secular radicals and Catholics, Day sometimes found it difficult to relax. According to Ammon Hennacy, Day could joke "in a cordial environment . . . but she did not go much for small talk when in a group of Catholic priests and radicals." She was "free and happy" when visiting Communist friends, as long as there were no Catholics around; with Catholics only and "with no outside radicals she was also free."[24] She was undoubtedly more sensitive about her radical I.W.W., Socialist, and Communist origins in the Thirties, when she was still a fairly fresh Catholic convert. No doubt to distance herself from her radical origins and achieve a greater credibility among Catholics, Day was more stridently anti-Communist, both in person and in print, during the *Catholic Worker*'s early years.[25]

And so, especially at first, Day probably felt some ambivalence about her proper role as a convert leading the Catholic Worker movement and its publication—and whether, as a woman, she could be effective. "She didn't grab the role of matriarch," Thomas Cornell recently remarked. "In a way, it was her self-immolation."[26] When Day left in 1943 for a year-long sabbatical, many wondered if she would return, as she herself did. In her "farewell" column of September 1943, she explained that Arthur Sheehan would be editor and publisher during her year-long absence, concluding, "And as for what will follow in October, 1944, that is in the Hands of God."[27] For at times she certainly approached her taxing role with mixed feelings. One Thirties entry in her notebook, published in *House of Hospitality*, reads: "Low in mind all day, full of tears."[28]

According to Florence Weinfurter, a friend of Day's for more than forty years, Day "felt herself to be outside the pale of ordinary womanhood." Nina Polcyn Moore believed that "a side of Dorothy yearned to be an ordinary woman." Moore recalled how Day "glorified motherhood. She reveled in the everyday tasks of diapering and tending children," often conversing about them in loving detail in her column.[29] Day never regretted the direction her life took after she met Maurin, but being human she must have remembered wistfully some aspects of her pre-conversion life—in particular, the happy periods with Forster Batterham. For she was still the woman who had once in a review identified a book's most appealing quality as the story it told "of a man and a woman who can love each other, in spite of everything, to the end."[30] In her autobiography she acknowledged "A woman does not feel whole without a man. It was years before I awakened without that longing for a face pressed against my breast, an arm about my shoulder. The sense of loss was there," she wrote. "For a woman who had known the joys of marriage, yes, it was hard." Day was comforted by the loving community she found in the Catholic Worker movement. But there were burdens; among them, that certain loneliness. Edmund J. Egan, a Catholic Worker, has observed that because she was the leader, Day "was in the Worker and not of it; she was of it but not in it. She was in a very different situation from anyone else."[31] She could never have a spouse-like confidante; for a person in her position, that would be "playing favorites."[32]

Not surprisingly, a certain ambivalence about her role sometimes crept into Dorothy Day's expression, both spoken and written. She was self-effacing in conversation; like Saint Teresa of Avila, whom she so admired, she would say, "I'm only a woman."[33] Similarly, she often undercut herself in her writing. For instance, in both the foreword and conclusion to her book *On Pilgrimage* (1948) she diffidently identified herself as a woman. That she would emphasize the fact of her gender is expected, for she also made it clear that she was directing the book primarily toward women. But her tone was incongruously self-effacing.[34] And in her spring 1964 appeal, Day wrote: "You must excuse me if I seem to be writing an Easter sermon, out of place for a woman to do."[35]

She seems to have believed that women could not—should not—escape the roles dictated by the fact of their gender, even if they were involved in radical social movements. "Women can't get away from the fact they're different, physically and mentally and emotionally, from men, thank God," she said.[36] She had

Figure 6. Dorothy Day, about 1938. (Courtesy Dorothy Day-Catholic Worker Collection, Marquette University)

acknowledged as much in her autobiographical, pre-conversion novel, *The Eleventh Virgin*. Unlike other early twentieth-century radicals, Day perceived American culture's peculiarly female dilemma of reconciling family life with serious social activism. In *The Long Loneliness* she commented, "I am quite ready to concede now that men are the single-minded, the pure of heart, in these movements. Women by their very nature are more materialistic, thinking of the home, the children, and of all things needful to them."[37] Such thinking echoes that of C.S. Lewis, whose books she read and admired. The British author also singled out women's "intense family patriotism" and their proper role of deferring to their husbands.[38] Of course this was a common notion in America in the Thirties and Forties.

In a handful of articles during those decades, the *Catholic Worker* indicated its thinking that the role of women was not particularly progressive. The *Worker* sometimes gave space to articles that asserted women's place was in the home, not in the factories. For example, after reporting that a priest had opposed wives working in the mills, the *Catholic Worker's* comment was: "And what about paying a living family wage to men so that the wives can stay home and raise the children?"[39] And an article in the July-August 1942 issue proclaimed that "The greatest gifts any girl can pray for are: a loving husband, [and] many healthy children," for her "real vocation" was to become a wife and mother.[40] In 1944, Day openly blamed the women of the Easton, Pennsylvania farming commune in part for its failure. Because they did not tend the kitchen, she explained, "more time was spent in complaining about food . . . that should have been used to better purpose in building up the community."[41]

In several of her 1948 columns (collected in *On Pilgrimage*), Day expressed views on women's roles that were decidedly traditional, albeit typical of the times. "Women," she asserted, "are most happy in doing that for which they are made, when they are cooking and serving others. They are the nourishers, starting with the babies at the breast and from then on their work is to nourish and strengthen and console." Since "Woman's job is to love," Day wrote, "let her do . . . for *others*, always." She added that a woman could "achieve the highest spirituality and union with God through her [dedication to] house and children."[42]

But women's was a bittersweet role. "God knows women have enough of the ugly and the lowly to do in the work of this world," Day also wrote. "In their sufferings they see clearly the result of the Fall. They are closer both to heaven and to hell than men are in a very literal, material, earthy sense."[43] And she admitted that women's lot was "a raw deal over and over again. They have to work, and then they have to go home and shop and cook the meals and take care of the children. They have about twice the burden of men, yet greater fragility."[44] Even living on the land, in Christian communality, she felt that men "have an easier time of it." They could be refreshed by invigorating outdoor work, "chopping wood, dragging in fodder, working with the animals," while "women are held pretty much to the house."[45] And Day observed that whether living in city or country, "women's bodies, heavy with children, dragged down by children, are a weight like a cross to be carried about." Constantly "preoccupied with cares," women found their path to be "a road once set out upon, from which there is no turning back.

"Every woman," Day continued, "knows that feeling of not being able to escape, of the inevitability of her hour drawing ever nearer." She firmly believed that such a "path of pain" was "woman's lot." But it was also "her glory and her salvation. She must accept."[46]

Yet at least by the Fifties, according to Thomas Cornell, Dorothy Day was acutely attuned to any "discrimination on the basis of gender" at St. Joseph's. She was always "well aware" of the male-female ratio among Catholic Workers at St. Joseph's, and "she was afraid of men taking over."[47]

But Dorothy Day had no sympathy for the women's movement which burgeoned in the early Sixties. It was "too lacking in love" for her.[48] She herself had always found revolution to seem most "possible" when it was "homelike," as she had long ago stated in one of her book reviews for the *Masses*.[49] She did not find the women's liberation movement to be at all that. Worse, it seemed to be largely an upper-class effort. "When I hear about women who are thinking in terms of salaries, it's all on the part of the rich," she remarked. "The poor haven't time for this luxury. They'll participate in strikes. You'll find the poor working for the poor."[50] To Day, a woman who had fought and overcome crass sexism early in her life, the women's movement probably seemed superfluous. Sixty-six when *The Feminine Mystique* stirred the women's liberation movement in 1963, Day had already accomplished many of the things authors such as Betty Friedan and Simone de Beauvoir were now advocating as women's right. Day voiced her belief that "if a woman sees something that has to be done, she doesn't need a movement in order to do it."[51] Day probably felt she faced much more challenging and important tasks than those associated with the new activist feminists' struggle. Furthermore, she seems not to have been aware of some of the accomplishments in cooperation and community that were growing out of the women's liberation movement.[52]

No doubt, too, Day's traditional view of sexuality did not build any bridges between her and some feminists. In fact, she seemed to think the focus of the women's movement was sexual promiscuity—something she emphatically rejected.[53] She once admitted that as "a product of the Catholic middle class, Irish-American," she knew the "tinge of Jansenism." While Day always honored sex (sans artificial birth control) as an "integral" part of a "holy marriage," she disdained any other varieties. At seventeen, when she encountered Havelock Ellis's *Sexual Pathology* at the University of Illinois, she found it "an ugly shock" best reserved for "doctor and priest."[54] In the Twenties, Day had admired Emma Goldman's revolutionary spirit—but not the activist's frank espousal of "free love." "I was revolted by such promiscuity," Day wrote.[55] Some fifty years later, Day was greatly distressed when two "brilliant women" came to her to proclaim themselves lesbians. In a letter to her friend Sister Peter Claver, Day lamented that the pair paid "no attention" to Scripture or the writings of St.

Paul on this subject. "It is all 'women's lib,' " she continued. "And I am just not 'with it' anymore, and you can imagine the kind of desolation I feel."[56] Day's personal revulsion at homosexuality did not prevent her from approaching homosexuals with genuine Christian love, although undoubtedly she found this most difficult. As early as 1952, long before their civil rights became a major issue in America, the *Catholic Worker* asserted that "Society has been very unfair" to homosexuals.[57]

Day held fast to her view of the women's liberation movement. When reporters inquired whether she had any sympathy with feminists in politics, she deftly changed the subject, quoting William James:

> I am done with great things and big things, great institutions and big success, and I am for those tiny invisible molecular moral forces that work from individual to individual, creeping through the crannies of the world like so many rootlets, or like the capillary oozing of water, yet which, if you give them time, will rend the hardest monuments of man's pride.[58]

As a Catholic traditionalist, Day accepted the Church's most conservative view of women's roles. "I wouldn't want to go to confession to a woman," she said. "I wouldn't want to get up and preach a homily" (although she often informally did).[59] The barring of women from the priesthood did not trouble her; there were, Day maintained, more important things for women to do. One, most assuredly, was motherhood. "So many mothers run away from their children," Day had lamented in 1948, "or put them in nurseries or go out to work because they can't stand . . . the suffering that [parental] love entails."[60]

When the women's liberation movement was blossoming in the summer of 1970, Day addressed a conference at a college in Westchester, New York. First Betty Friedan and other feminists spoke in near-militant terms, denouncing American society. Then Dorothy Day walked gracefully to the podium. Nearly seventy-three, she remained statuesque, her snow-white hair wound crownlike in neat braids as she had worn it most of her life. An account in *Commonweal* described her as "perhaps the oldest person in the room, the most personally courageous, in action and practice, already the most liberated." The article continued:

> She said nothing about women's liberation, never mentioned the words, never stated her views on the subject of economic equality, careers, chores, society's institutions. Instead, she reminisced about her life, her daughter, the families she'd known, the poor, the work she'd done, in jail, in the streets, in her Houses [of Hospitality].[61]

The audience reacted with spirited applause.

An additional perspective on Day is offered by historian Susan Ware. She views Day as belonging to an early twentieth-century generation of radical women social activists who were "unwilling or unable to generalize from their own experiences to a full-scale critique of women's roles in society." Perhaps because they experienced the financial and social disaster of the Thirties, Day, Elizabeth Gurley Flynn and Ella Reeve ("Mother") Bloor of the Communist Party, and others, devoted their energies not to a feminist revolution, but to a primarily economic one. When the entire system seemed in a shambles, the individual, personal dimension mattered less. Rather than choose traditional feminism, which they may have viewed as "selfish, personal, and totally divorced from economic issues," this generation of radical women activists committed themselves to movements (especially Communism) which they saw as broader and more socially significant.[62] If this was Dorothy Day's viewpoint, it did not seem to change in the Sixties. And if her thinking about women remained traditional, her paper did not emphasize this. The *Catholic Worker* of the Sixties and later did not explicitly focus on the issues raised by the women's movement. There were no articles like those of the Thirties and Forties which had advised women that their proper place was at the hearth. Perhaps this was due in part to Day's diplomacy; but also, she felt that issues such as Vietnam and civil rights transcended all others.

An ingenuity, perhaps unconscious, characterized all Day's expressions of feminine deference. She neatly avoided entanglement in the often vitriolic debates and discussions at the Catholic Worker House by pleading that it was a man's job to argue and to talk, and a woman's to serve and to administer. But however she regarded sex roles, male Catholic Workers seemed to feel that she understood and appreciated them. She dealt deftly with their bombast. The average man who confronted her was pleasantly silenced by Day's blithe rejoinder: "I have no time for arguing and besides I think like a woman."[63] Stanley Vishnewski described the consternation of a young professor who lectured at St. Joseph's in the early days of the *Catholic Worker*, when the women in the audience knitted nonstop through his presentation. When he complained to Day about this apparent lack of courtesy, she smiled and replied that "women actually could think best when they had something to do with their hands and that they were able to work and talk at the same time." Day herself had been known to sit at Friday evening discussions with a knitting project in her lap. (But perhaps her real meaning was indicated on another occasion, when she observed Maurin deeply engaged in discussion with a visiting intellectual. Day commented that "men would rather talk than work," and that they "seemed incapable of carrying on an intellectual conversation and working at the same time."[64])

"I am sure we 'got away' with a lot because I was a woman and a convert," Day confided to Dwight Macdonald.[65] To Thomas Cornell she made the same remark many times, adding that "people don't pay that much attention to women, or excuse their excesses more freely."[66] Cornell believes Day's self-deprecation of herself as a woman, especially as she grew older, was "a gambit" she used in response to the tiresome, repetitive questions that each new generation needs to ask. By the time Day was sixty, she had lived for some twenty-five years alongside a succession of youthful Catholic Worker recruits, and doubtless she felt a bit world-weary and wise. "She found ways of making life a little easier for herself as she aged," Cornell said, "by shifting the onus onto Peter [Maurin], or saying, 'Well, what can you expect? I'm only a woman,' and then going off and doing ten times more than any man could accomplish."[67]

Still, for Dorothy Day, who was raised to believe that their very nature limited women to certain roles, Peter Maurin's presence undoubtedly provided a measure of confidence and security. She confessed that "the Catholic Worker movement would not have had the cooperation it has had from so many brilliant young men had it not been for Peter's influence. Far be it from men to follow a woman."[68] Her viewpoint may explain why, indeed, so many *Catholic Worker* editors have been men—especially in the paper's early years when it sought to build a following. Then, with the exception of two journalists—Dorothy Weston, who began a long association with the *Catholic Worker* beginning with the second issue, and Eileen Corridan, whose name, starting with the February 1934 issue, also appeared on the masthead as an assistant editor—Day even tended to discourage women from writing for the paper. At least one Catholic Worker from the Thirties, Mary Alice Zarrella, remembered that then, "writing was a closed shop." Although she had journalistic talent (she later edited the Catholic magazines *Marriage* and *Child and Family*) and got along well with Day, Zarrella was not at all encouraged to write for the paper.[69] Several Catholic Workers from the Thirties have recalled Day's tendency during that decade to discourage women from working at all at the New York House. Conscientiously, Day was worried that their safety would be endangered in the near-Bowery location during those tumultuous years.[70] Yet she seems to have been little concerned with her own safety as a woman living and working in the slums. She would do what she would not think of asking others to.

Usually chatty about her helpers, Day wrote little about her first two volunteer editors, Eileen Corridan and Dorothy Weston. Corridan, a former "newspaperwoman" (according to Day's biographer),[71] was described by Day as "a fierce worker like her cousin (the priest who was portrayed in the film 'Waterfront')," who left the *Catholic Worker* after the June 1934 issue to start "a magazine of her own."[72] Although Weston, a Manhattanville College journalism graduate, served three years as assistant editor (until June, 1936), Day also offered little characterization of her, but for these physical details: Weston, Day wrote, was "a dainty young Irish girl with black hair and bright blue eyes." Unfortunately, she had the bad habit of "sleeping until noon" (because she liked to work late at night). "It was embarrassing," Day went on, "to have a beautiful young creature asleep on a couch made up in the room in back of the office, her arms flung up on either side of her head, her black hair silhouetted against the pillow." A screen could not eliminate the sense of "her presence," and "the fellows who came in to help us had to go through the room to get to the kitchen for water or a midmorning cup of coffee."[73] Day seemed to be saying that women, especially attractive ones, could be a distraction in the workplace.

Day's practical desire to build a credible movement and newspaper also seems to have motivated her, perhaps unconsciously, to encourage more male participation, at least in the beginning years. She could point to a male co-founder and male editors and achieve a greater credibility and subsequent acceptance in the sexually conservative Catholic Church than if she were operating alone. Furthermore, Maurin's presence as a birthright Catholic minimized her sense, as a convert, of risk-taking in unfamiliar waters. The resonant echo of Maurin's oft-repeated "Man proposes, woman disposes" provided Day with a convenient rationale for taking action without offending those who believed in the "natural" supremacy of masculine ability. Although she bristled at the ring of that phrase, she overcame the message's inherent sexism. Indeed she proposed and carried out some of her own innovations for the Catholic Worker movement, carefully eliminating any proposals of her co-founder that violated her own understanding of it. All the while, she was using the age-old feminine device of achieving her goals, at least in part, through a man.

The question may linger: why did she devote her life to the Catholic Worker movement? Everything in her life points to her genuine, profound sympathy for the poor, and her commitment to realize the most radical principles of the Gospels. Despite some ambivalence over what was to be her proper role as the female head of the Catholic Worker movement, Dorothy Day persevered in her leadership. She drew her strength from a spiritual faith that deepened as the years went on. As she explained: "I would not dare write or speak or try to follow the vocation God has given me to work for the poor and for peace, if I did not have this constant reassurance of the Mass, the confidence the Mass gives."[74]

Leader of the paper, leader of the movement—Dorothy Day often acknowledged her pivotal role, albeit in modest terms. Frequently she described herself in both capacities as "the mother of a very large family."[75] As such, she confessed to "some authoritarian aspect" in her attitude. She continued:

> The one realm in which I do have the last say, is the *Catholic Worker* itself. I do choose what is to be published and what is to be left out. The mistakes we make, I am responsible for, and many an editorial slip I have made, many a mistake.[76]

The evidence for the pervasiveness of Day's role, the strength of her personality, is substantial and convincing. James Forest, a *Catholic Worker* editor in the early Sixties who helped form the Catholic Peace Fellowship in 1964 and now directs the International Fellowship of Reconciliation from Holland, recently wrote, "Dorothy ... wasn't for what might be called 'democratic process.' There wasn't a democratic bone in her body."[77] Forest has also commented on Day's "tendency to make a decision, and that was that." He recalled that once when Day thought many of the men staying at Peter Maurin Farm were alcoholics, she banned drinking in all individual rooms. She had decided "we should voluntarily choose to share their anguish with them," Forest said. "Invitations are one thing, but orders are quite another.

"She's not all sugar," Forest continued. "See, she's tough, she's stubborn, she doesn't listen well all the time, she holds grudges, and like other Catholic radicals, she has a problem about sometimes being too judgmental." Nevertheless, he judged her "a genius and a saint."[78] Forest has also called Day "nobody's sweet little mother." She was "more like a tough old matriarch, one who's not so fond of her children that she's afraid to give them a harsh word or two just to keep them in line."[79]

Thomas Cornell described Day as "fierce," "judgmental," and "hell on wheels" — anything but a "sweet little grandmother." Those who knew her only in the last few years of her life, he said, "didn't realize how cantankerous she could be earlier on, in her prime." In the Fifties and early Sixties, Cornell found Day "very tough" and "very protective" as far as the movement was concerned. She herself acknowledged her tendency to be "judgmental." But Cornell never found these to be negative qualities. "I don't think she was excessive," he said. For the good of the movement, Day exercised a forceful leadership which was "as painful for her as it was for those who bore the brunt of it."[80]

Stanley Vishnewski remembered Day was "rather sarcastic at times," with "a cutting edge to her tongue." Especially in the early years, he recalled, she "had a habit of cutting people down to size if they were ornery or proved to be too disagreeable. This was a fault she freely acknowledged and that she prayed to overcome." Vishnewski felt Day's seeming severity — most pronounced in the Thirties — stemmed from her being "nobody's fool. She had to be a strong and valiant woman" to maintain the paper's "even keel."[81] Another participant has described the atmosphere around St. Joseph's House of Hospitality during the greening time of the Thirties as one of wildly swinging moods and "plenty of friendly and not-so-friendly discussions" whose intensity was often lightened with "puns and levity."[82] In such a highly charged atmosphere, Day's forceful stability often must have been welcome.

Thomas Cornell agreed that Day "sometimes found it difficult to suffer fools gladly, and she was surrounded by them." At times St. Joseph's seemed to number "more neurotics and psychotics than a mental hospital" among its visitors, he said, "and they could drive you mad." In the Thirties, Day was still capable of being "quite abrupt" with such people, retaining a certain pre-conversion brashness in her language. Catholic Workers often tell an anecdote about Day's response to the breathless visitor who asked her, "Do you have visions?" Day's response, the story goes, was an expletive followed by, "Just visions of unpaid bills." But Day mellowed a bit with the years as her spirituality strengthened.[83]

Edmund J. Egan, a Catholic Worker, summarized Day's role in a revealing statement:

> Unless Dorothy had had the place she had and has in the Worker, there wouldn't have been so much bitching about her and so much complaining about her. . . . Dorothy is not a person without moods. But there was great affection for Dorothy. She was the leader, she was the founder, and she was someone whom everyone took very seriously and I think most of us loved very much.[84]

Dorothy Day was the capable manager of a movement and a newspaper whose very natures were at odds with formal organization. No committees ever oper-

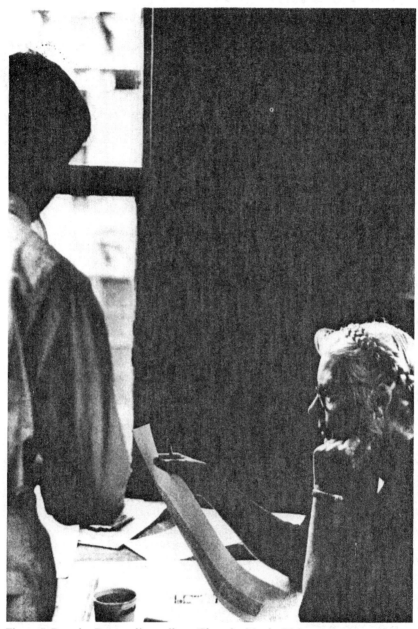

Figure 7. Dorothy Day reading galleys. (Photo by Mottke Weissman)

ated within the structure of either. Certainly an editorial meeting was a rare, if existent, convention. Anyone who came to the *Catholic Worker* office was liable to be pressed into service by Day for whatever tasks were at hand that day. A visitor might be dispatched to babysit for a poor family or to assist victims of eviction or to distribute leaflets at a rally. When a Fordham University teacher once appeared with an armful of donated clothes, Day promptly talked him into giving blood for a destitute man at a nearby hospital.[85] One of Dorothy Day's most "endearing" qualities, according to Thomas Cornell, was the way she "forwarded people," especially women who might otherwise be overlooked. In a godmotherly way, "Dorothy made sure that people got assignments in keeping with their talents," then praised them publicly (often in the *Catholic Worker*), "even if the results weren't up to the standard expected."[86] But she was equally adept at squelching the many "oddballs" who sought to enlist her support for all types of impractical projects. Her technique, as Stanley Vishnewski described it, was to listen "patiently and tentatively" to whatever scheme the person was trying to sell her. Then Day would inform the person "to go ahead with the idea, since it was his brain child, and no one else could do it more effectively."[87]

Day's exercise of editorial control grew naturally from the respect commanded by her integrity. But it was also buttressed by her financial control. She signed the checks, or carefully designated someone else to have an authorized signature. "Everyone knew they were living on funds that came to the Worker because of Dorothy's appeal letters and public speaking," and the force of her personality, remarked Thomas Cornell. This tended to quash any palace revolts.[88]

Besides responsibility for money, she distributed a few other jobs such as management of the paper and running the House of Hospitality. Remaining jobs were simply absorbed one way or another. In the words of James Forest, Day functioned as a sort of "reluctant but necessary abbot" whose "constant hope was that those who had particular responsibilities would manage to handle them responsibly, without infuriating everybody else." He recalled how "decisions, often out of alignment with each other, seemed to occur by spontaneous combustion," at times resulting "in some nasty burns."[89] Though the crises were over petty matters, they could spark into conflagrations. Day recalled an occasion when she put on the masthead the name of a man who helped with the business affairs of the paper. Then, "an editorial worker announced that if this one's name was on he didn't want his own on, and in the ensuing dispute, which somehow involved everyone, *all* the names came off." Another time so many were listed as editors that Ammon Hennacy demanded the removal of his own name.[90] Usually Day tried to let the participants settle their own arguments, but occasionally she would make the necessary and final decision, as leader of the movement or as editor and publisher.[91]

Day allowed her writers and editors creative freedom, but within what she perceived as Catholic Worker principles. She usually screened everything that went into the paper, with few exceptions—when she took a leave in 1943-44, and when late material was occasionally used at once, assuming her approval. Commenting on all this, she wrote, "Perhaps on two or three occasions I disapproved of the emphasis given by the placing of material as well as by the articles themselves. But no *great* harm was done."[92] Yet Day did not hesitate to eliminate anything that she thought deviated from Catholic Worker philosophy. In 1961 a woman sent in a letter advocating certain constrictions of freedom of expression. She was told that her message could not be printed in the paper because it contradicted the Catholic Worker viewpoint. "We are very much opposed to any limitation of the right of free expression, either in print or verbal," the *Catholic Worker* replied. The basic principle of democracy is that people can govern themselves; and if so, "then they are able to choose for themselves — and to choose they must have a chance to hear all sides — no matter how unpopular or wrong they may be."[93] Dorothy Day was too astute to fail to see the irony in this reply. What comes across is her willingness to endure a minor charge of inconsistency (the writer *was* being denied "free expression") in favor of an overall consistent fidelity to the Catholic Worker viewpoint.

More often than not, however, consensus among Workers ensured little conflict over what was printed. No one would approach the *Catholic Worker* as a contributor unless he or she "were in agreement with Dorothy's principles," Florence Weinfurter observed.[94] "There was no confrontation, no casting into outer darkness of people who disagreed with some of the planks of the [Catholic Worker] program," Joseph Zarrella recalled. "We never disassociated them." Dissidents discovered they could still devote themselves to those aspects of the program they found palatable. Thus, the Catholic Worker movement was like "a big umbrella, with some people interested more in specific areas than in others."[95] However, Zarrella doubted "whether we would have published an article against pacifism." During World War II, the paper was united on the pacifist question. James O'Gara, Tom Sullivan, and John Cogley, Catholic Workers who could not agree completely with Dorothy Day on this matter, published their viewpoint in the *Chicago Catholic Worker*. Perceiving her stand, they did not approach her with the aim of printing their view in *her* newspaper. Such self-censorship was common among the writers and editors of the (New York) *Catholic Worker*. Usually they just went elsewhere if they could not agree with Day. She herself acknowledged this:

> How much coming and going there is around the *Catholic Worker*! I remember one of the very early editors left because I, as managing editor, refused to throw out another editor. Peter [Maurin] said, 'No need to eliminate anyone, they eliminate themselves.'[96]

However, if Day sensed an editor was inclined to steer the editorial policy away from the direction in which she had set it, that person's tenure would be quite brief. "I wouldn't have lasted thirty seconds," Thomas Cornell remarked, "if what I wanted to do with the paper was contrary to Dorothy's decisions or if I did it behind her back." Day "felt it was her spiritual duty" to "root out anything building that was contrary to her understanding of the Worker [movement]," he said, even if that meant "kicking people out." When Day exercised her authority as leader, it was final. Cornell recalled the efforts of Dianne Gannon Feeley (later a Socialist Workers' Party committee candidate in California) to enact content and design changes in the paper in the early Sixties, without consulting Day. "She clashed with Dorothy," Cornell said, "and Dorothy threw her out. And there was no calling of an editorial meeting to appeal her decision." According to Cornell, about the same time — 1961 — Day showed another Catholic Worker the door for having used the facilities to publish a magazine she judged obscene. Supposedly intended as a parody of pornography, the publication advertised, among other things, "Poems by Catholic Worker poets." This Day would not allow. Catholic Workers still refer to this incident as "The Great Stomp."[97]

Almost from the beginning, calls poured in from churches and organizations across the country, asking Day to lecture. As she increased her traveling and speaking engagements, she delegated some of her editorial responsibilities. Always, Day recruited her editors informally, but as carefully as she selected her check-signing proxy. Once she made up her mind, she was likely to draft the person with little fanfare. Cornell recalled how he, a Catholic Worker with a bent for writing but no publishing experience save for editing his high-school literary magazine, suddenly became editor of the paper in September 1962. In a hurry to travel to Cuba, Day ordered Cornell to come to New York a week early. "Basically, she said, 'Take up thy sleeping bag and follow me,'" Cornell recalled. "Dorothy put a bunch of manuscripts and galley proofs in my hands and said, 'Here, edit the paper.' I was petrified." She did instruct him in the basics. She told Cornell, "Use short paragraphs because they're easier to read; break up those paragraphs with subheads; use a lot of graphics; and don't butt headlines."[98]

On the road, ever the conscientious editor and publisher, Day always checked on the paper according to the degree of trust she had in the person editing it. She participated through frequent memos and other correspondence. Joseph Zarrella recalled that in the Thirties when Day was gone, she often sent letters suggesting articles, reviewing them, and in general "keeping control of the paper."[99] Nina Polcyn Moore remembered that Day was "constantly in touch with things published in the paper."[100] Of course, away traveling, she could take part fully in "no more than three issues" during Cornell's entire editorship in the early Sixties. But he was more than aware of her editorial preferences. Whenever he had any questions, he dutifully shipped her manuscripts, and she invariably replied, usually agreeing with his decisions. Occasionally, when she could not be reached, he had to decide intricate matters of the paper's public posture by himself— for example, whether to run a controversial appeal. Then, Cornell often consulted with Martin J. Corbin, second in command at the paper. It was for such reflective caution that Day had chosen Cornell as editor, after all. She had a high degree of trust in him; he knew what she wanted.

Still, Day and her trusted editor occasionally clashed. She criticized Cornell a few times for not using enough subheads to break up the type. And he remembered how "she bawled me out for the October '62 issue" (which contained the three clerical contributions). Day stressed that the *Catholic Worker* must remain a layperson's paper. And she also berated him for not commemorating, in the May 1964 issue, the fifteenth anniversary of Peter Maurin's death. "She got pretty mad about that," Cornell recalled. "We used to fight like cat and dog . . . but it was very much, too, like mother and son," he said. Sometimes difficult, their relationship was "always very loving. We knew each other well enough so that we could afford to shout at each other." He went on:

> She knew that if she bawled me out one day, I would take it to heart and so
> she'd always make it up to me on the next. She'd take me out to Chinatown or
> to one of those little joints on Mulberry Street or Mott Street for a plate of
> spaghetti or what have you . . . or take me to [her sister] Della's and cook a little
> something, and chat . . . she loved to chat and I loved it more than anything-
> her reminiscences.[101]

And it was not enough that Day's editors agree with her on the substance of potential pieces for the *Catholic Worker*; she wanted them to pay attention as well to style. "She probably hit some kind of editorial chutzpah," commented Edmund J. Egan, "when she took out a paragraph of something Mike Harrington had written and inserted a paragraph which she thought was better, which she had written."[102]

Her attitude towards her own writing seems to have changed over the years. Robert Ellsberg, who served as editor from 1976 to 1978, says Day "regarded her own work with extraordinary detachment." Although she was "rarely satisfied with her own writing," he said, once she completed an article she went on to other tasks. She often handed him her copy "with a look of resignation, saying, 'Here it is. Do what you want with it.'" Ellsberg states further that Day gave her editors at this time "broad license," although "most of them tended to extreme caution in tampering with Dorothy's prose."[103] Such detachment may have been a development late in Day's life, when she was beginning to relinquish some of her authority, but it is not the way Cornell tells it about a decade earlier.

Then, Day was sometimes irritated by Cornell's editing of her untidy, much-penciled-over manuscripts. She apparently felt that this seemed to undercut her professional autonomy. "Mostly I just took care of housekeeping details," Cornell said, but sometimes she noticed his editing, and then "complained furiously." Day gave him "the dirtiest copy I'd ever seen . . . scratches all over it, syntactical lapses," doubtless because she had had to write it on the run. When she rewrote it, tightening passages by curbing her natural tendency to digress, Cornell said, "it came out beautifully." When he rewrote it, she could be "very girlish, almost adolescently picky, especially about splicing a sentence of hers. If you changed something out of grammatical or syntactical necessity and she noticed it, she'd fuss and fume, saying you'd changed the meaning when you had not. If she didn't notice it," Cornell went on, "you were all right."

Although she was unsurpassed at writing the annual Catholic Worker appeals (to be printed in the paper and mailed separately to many supporters), Dorothy

Day did not relish the task. One year in a fit of pique, she told Cornell: "*You write the appeal!*" "She had said this before," Cornell recalled, "but this time I took her up on it." Realizing he could hardly equal Day's masterful appeals, he culled from the files various samples from the past. Selecting a paragraph here, a paragraph there, and writing a few connecting sentences, he fashioned an amalgam from several of Day's finest efforts. When it was sent out, Cornell said, it drew "something like $50,000, a little bit better than the normal amount." But Dorothy Day was "furious." She told Cornell, "You sat there at your desk laughing all the time you wrote that, mimicking my style, saying, 'here, the pious old thing would write something like this, wouldn't she?'"

"No," Cornell replied, "no, Dorothy, those were your own words. It's just two or three sentences I wrote, to sew them together." But Day apparently thought Cornell was being cheeky. "She did criticize me for a flippant attitude," Cornell acknowledged, "which was often not without foundation. Oh, but she was mad as a wet hen over that," he went on. "I don't know what made her more angry, the fact that it was successful or that she didn't think she had written it." Cornell found such sensitivity "endearing, because you could see she hadn't reached perfection, hadn't reached absolute detachment. And that was comforting, because she was saintly enough."[104]

Certainly Dorothy Day sometimes lacked objectivity about her own work. Thomas Sullivan, a Catholic Worker starting in the Thirties, who worked at both the Chicago and New York Houses, and helped edit the paper in the late Forties and early Fifties, shares this anecdote. When her autobiography *The Long Loneliness* appeared in 1952, Day wanted it reviewed by Michael Harrington in the *Catholic Worker*. "I don't think it's the thing to do, you know," Sullivan advised her, "—have the book reviewed by a writer for the paper." But Day's wishes prevailed. And the review Harrington wrote was "a beautiful, beautiful valentine to Dorothy." Sullivan recalled that when he read it, he said, "Geez, you aren't using that, Mike! If you look back at that a month from now you'll wonder, 'What the hell possessed me! It's not a review—it's a love letter to Dorothy Day!' We don't want to print a love letter." Sullivan advised Harrington instead to write a resume of the book's contents. Harrington complied, and when it went to press, Day complained to Sullivan. Once more he pointed out that the original review had been so glowing that it was "an out-and-out love letter." Then he asked, "You wouldn't want to have that printed in the paper, would you?" "Why not?" Day replied. "Why not have that?" "There was no discussion," Sullivan recalled. Characteristically, she had been "very frank and outspoken," letting "her feelings come right through."

While Day sometimes seemed acutely sensitive to criticism of her own work, expressing her hurt feelings plainly, she could also bear censure graciously. Sullivan recalled how Day was "rankled" when the Rev. Hans A. Reinhold gave her autobiography a mixed review in *Commonweal*. The priest found *The Long Loneliness* "a bit weary, disenchanted, repetitious, rather too meditative."[105] Such remarks, Sullivan observed, were bound to "sting" one as "sensitive" as Day. But when Father Reinhold came to St. Joseph's a few days later to make peace, she never indicated her displeasure. Day "just sat down there and talked with him very pleasantly."[106]

In Thomas Cornell's experience, Day only lightly edited others' copy, probably because she had assigned articles with care. Day's friend and confessor, Father Hugo, made a similar observation: "I don't think she edited things much," he said. "If someone shared her *ideas* on social justice, she published their articles." Nevertheless, it was Day who ran the paper and put her "special stamp" on it.[107] And as Joseph Zarrella pointed out, Day did little editing because "somehow it was *understood* what went into the paper. There was a common understanding among us of what we stood for, what needed to be said."[108]

As editor of the *Catholic Worker*, Day's hours were surely much longer, year in and year out, than those of the typical advocacy journalist. From the start of the paper in 1933, her working day began at a dawn Mass and often ended at midnight.[109] "Like many exceptional people, she didn't realize it [her exceptionality]," observed Mary Alice Zarrella. "She expected that everyone else was too — and that everyone else would write, too."[110] Co-workers remember that she constantly urged others — at first, usually men — to write for the paper, even the non-writers. Day always supported high standards of journalism when she dealt with readers who wished to write for the paper. The Catholic Worker Papers contain many letters from Day to readers, seeking to inspire them to elaborate in a full-length article the small pieces of information they had just sent in. One of her typical replies read:

> Thanks again for the clippings. Can't you come down and talk over the textile business with us, and if you haven't time to do that write us, in more detail about the attitude of the mill owners. You need not sign the letter if you don't wish to.[111]

Conscious that the personal and the concrete would command a broader appeal, Day coached one would-be contributor: "Personal experiences are always so much more valuable than vague generalizations."[112] This, of course, had always been her own journalistic strategy.

But Day did not confine herself solely to editorial matters. Not only did she enjoy designing the paper — looking at the various cuts, determining which would be used — but she also cut up the galleys and even folded the printed issues.[113] Joseph Zarrella remembers Day "happily doing the headlines and makeup."[114] Despite having assigned others to do this, she felt she should make the trip to the printers' to personally oversee the makeup of the paper.[115] Such attention to detail was just one example of Day's commitment as editor to producing the best possible *Catholic Worker*.

As publisher, Dorothy Day's role centered on her relationship with the Catholic Church. At first she had resisted the idea of converting to Catholicism, for she glimpsed little in the way of social consciousness among Catholics. Later, her perceptions of Catholicism, perhaps intensified because she was a convert, meant charity, caring for the poor, and pacifism. All these things were at odds with the reality of a church which owned huge amounts of property, had enormous financial investments in the capitalist system, and associated itself with privilege and power. Day admitted that sometimes she grew "impatient at the luxury of the Church, the building programs, the cost of the diocesan school system, and the conservatism of the hierarchy."[116] But she would also frequently remark that, "warts and all, I love the Church."[117] Despite the bourgeois Catholicism she saw all around her, she believed it to be the church of the poor. She focused on those aspects of Catholicism that were true to her sense of Christianity's original character: helping the poor, the weak, and other rejects of society. And when she found social apathy in the Church, she forged ahead as an activist.

Dorothy Day had the convert's zeal for her chosen religion, regularly attending Mass and rising daily before dawn to pray in solitude. In *Divine Disobedience*, Francine du Plessix Gray wrote revealingly of Day's demeanor at a Mass celebrated by Father Daniel Berrigan at St. Joseph's House of Hospitality:

> He said the litany calmly, softly, with a deadpan air that verged on boredom. His entourage exchanged amused looks, for a Berrigan liturgy, these days, would more likely consist of long readings from Pablo Neruda, Auden, T.S. Eliot... but today he had conceded, with delicacy, to Dorothy Day's traditional tastes. And she followed the service reverently, wearing on her head a black lace mantilla similar to the one she had worn to receive Communion a few years earlier, from the hands of the Pope.[118]

In theological matters and in liturgy, Day was an ardent Catholic conservative. She acknowledged as much in her March 1966 column: "I am afraid I am a traditionalist, in that I do not like to see Mass offered with a large coffee cup for a chalice."[119]

Although she was a widely acknowledged inspiration for the Catholic Left of the mid-Sixties and early Seventies, whose style was protest, even disobedience, this was never Dorothy Day's style in Church matters. Though the *Catholic Worker*'s strict adherence to pacifism put it outside mainstream American Catholicism, Day would never be found in an underground church. Rather, she would be kneeling in the back pew in the humble, liturgically conservative churches she loved so much on the Lower East Side. While others greeted the Berrigan priests as "Dan" and "Phil," she called them "Father Dan" and "Father Phil," because to her they would always be "priests and prophets."[120]

Many of the Catholic radicals whose views she helped to create disagreed with her unquestioning obedience to the Church hierarchy and her refusal to challenge Church tradition in areas such as abortion, birth control, and liturgy. According to James Forest, many were most disturbed by Day's "complete acceptance of Catholic dogma and Church structure."[121] Furthermore, Day believed in obedience to those in religious authority. She subjected herself to the direction of priests and bishops, although it is true that when she was a new convert and her confessor objected to her social interests and to her writing "on the ground that it is too late to do anything except prepare for death, " Day quickly left him and found another, rather than disobey.[122] For Day permitted no criticism of priests or bishops in her presence, immediately coming to their defense. She suppressed Peter Maurin's mild anti-clericalism from the *Catholic Worker*. She told Stanley Vishnewski that Catholics should emulate St. Francis of Assisi's attitude of respect and reverence toward clergy.[123] Without priests, she asked, "what would we do? They are so vital a part of our lives, standing by us as they do at birth, marriage, sickness, and death—at all the great and critical moments of our existence—but also daily bringing us the bread of life, our Lord Himself, to nourish us."[124] Thus Day readily submitted to ecclesiastical review in 1934 at the suggestion of Msgr. Arthur J. Scanlan, Office of Censor of Books, who had received a barrage of letters denouncing the *Catholic Worker's* support of the Child Labor Amendment. In a diplomatic letter, Day suggested that the Rev. Joseph McSorley, her spiritual adviser, become her editorial adviser. She pointed out that the Child Labor Amendment had been and was supported by Msgr. John A. Ryan and other Church officials. She wrote:

> It is, after all, a matter of opinion, and it has nothing to do with faith or dogma, so we did not think we were treading on dangerous ground in upholding this piece of legislation. . . . And after all, isn't there room for a difference of opinion on this matter?[125]

After the Fair Labor Standards Act was passed in June 1938, the child labor situation improved so that the subject was no longer discussed in the *Catholic Worker*; simultaneously, the issue of Chancery review of the paper was apparently dropped.[126]

Throughout her tenure as *Catholic Worker* editor, Day sometimes remarked that "If the Cardinal [Francis Cardinal Spellman of the New York diocese] asked me to stop publishing, I would."[127] She elaborated: "First of all, I cannot conceive of Cardinal Spellman's making such a request of me, considering the respect he has always shown for freedom of conscience and freedom of speech." But if such an "improbable" event were to occur, she declared, "my respect for Cardinal Spellman and my faith that God will right all mistakes, mine as well as his, would lead me to obey."[128] When an alarmed *Catholic Worker* editor asked Day if such a spirit of obedience might eventually cause the paper to abandon its pacifist advocacy, she replied: "Not at all. But... then we [would] only use quotations from the Bible, the words of Jesus, the sayings of the saints, the encyclicals of the Popes—nothing of our own." These are, in fact, the *Catholic Worker's* primary sources. But when the editor remained appalled at the acquiescence Day had in reserve for such a potential abuse of authority, she explained, "I'm Catholic, not Quaker. If you want to edit the *Quaker Worker*, you're at the wrong place."[129] As long as she followed her conscience by putting her best efforts into the *Catholic Worker*, success as the world measures it meant little to her. If the New York diocese had ever directed Dorothy Day to stop publishing, she would have graciously accepted the mandate. Probably it would not have been long, however, before she ventured to another diocese. Once there she would not have sought officially endorsed status for the *Catholic Worker*, for she always wished to keep it a lay publication. But there is no doubt that she would have maintained an attitude of respectful obedience toward the hierarchy.

Day's answer to the question of what to do if the Chancery ordered her to stop publishing illuminates her relationship with Catholic Church authorities over the years. At first she was viewed with intense suspicion, as "a borderline heretic who rightly belonged in the prison cells she so often inhabited."[130] As Day herself often put it, "the bottle always smells of the liquor it once held." There were quite a few attacks on Day by publications such as the *Brooklyn Tablet*, the *Wanderer*, and the *American Mercury*, which in 1935 described Day as "a former Greenwich Village habituée and recent convert ot the Church," an unmistakable sign of the downfall of the Catholic Church in the United States."[131] One cannot imagine that the New York hierarchy was delighted to have Day in its archdiocese, at least during the *Catholic Worker*'s early years. Then, Thomas Sullivan recalled, Day was "really a persona non grata in the Church. She had a few priest friends around, but very few. Mostly nobody wanted to deal with Dorothy Day."[132]

But as the years showed Day to be a loyal Catholic traditionalist, obedient to and reverent toward the Church hierarchy, she was more and more accepted. By 1972, she had been named the "Outstanding American Catholic" of the year by Notre Dame University.

Dorothy Day was one of the American Catholic Church's most devoted consciences. She never chided the Church for what it taught, only for its failures to live up to its teaching, to communicate the heart of the Gospels. She completely respected and obeyed the Church when it spoke with its full religious authority. Furthermore, she saw to it that nothing in the *Catholic Worker* was ever fabricated; sources were revealed upon request, and ultimately they originated from unimpeachable authorities such as the papal encyclicals, the Bible, the words of Jesus, and the sayings of the saints. Thus no bishop or priest could ever accurately charge Day and the *Catholic Worker* with undermining Church doctrine.

This was the unbreakable thread—fidelity to the teachings of the Gospels. It unified Dorothy Day, radical editor and publisher of the *Catholic Worker*, and conservative Church authorities. Theirs was a complex relationship, intensified during times of war when her pacifism and sponsorship of the first conscientious objectors were glaring departures from the mainstream of recent Catholic thinking. Through the years that relationship grew, in large part through her diplomacy.

One of the principal issues between Day and the New York Chancery was her use of the word "Catholic" in the paper's name. When Msgr. Edward R. Gaffney, Day's post-World War II contact at the Chancery, questioned her on this point, she responded in a long, careful letter that illustrated her sagacity. She began by assuring the Monsignor that because Catholic Workers did not wish to "take advantage" of the "generosity of this archdiocese," nor "to count on the official protection which the name 'Catholic' brings us," they would opt to change the *Catholic Worker*'s name rather than cease publication. "You very rightly advised me," Day went on, "to talk matters over with the staff here and to let you know the results of our conference."

Then she reported on the consensus among her flock: "No one of course wishes to change the name. All feel that the *Catholic Worker* has been in existence for eighteen years . . . under that name, and that this is no time to change it so late in the day." She was sure, she said, that no one would think that the Catholic War Veterans, who also use the adjective Catholic, represent the archdiocese's viewpoint any more than they think the *Catholic Worker* does. But to clarify matters, she offered to print a box under the paper's masthead each month disavowing any official connection with the Catholic Church.

Having made one practical suggestion, Day now interjected this reassurance: "We are all ready to receive respectfully and give practical heed and application to all scientific, scholarly criticism and correction of mistakes; to all disciplinary directions as to . . . wrong doing, and to all theological or . . . spiritual errors." Then she clearly stated her position: "But we cannot simply cease the publication of a review which has been built up, with its worldwide circulation of 63,000. This," she told the Monsignor, "would be a grave scandal to our readers and would put into the hands of our enemies . . . a formidable weapon."

Quickly, she assumed responsibility for any mistakes the paper had made. "I personally am at fault," she wrote, "in not being more careful as editor and censor. It is my job as publisher and editor and it has always, I know, been expected of me at the Chancery Office." She confessed that she had "not given sufficient time to the matter of the paper, being occupied with so many other cares. . . ."

But she also argued persuasively for her ideals. She pointed out that the *Catholic Worker*'s "opposition to the Capitalist order" was "no new thing," and went on to cite a recent warning by "the Vatican paper" [*L'Osservatore Romano*] not to consider capitalism and Communism the only two political alternatives. The Catholic Worker movement, she said, was "trying to make the kind of society which does not make for war, a society where each is not seeking his own, a functional society in which there will again be a philosophy of work."

By now, Day added, no one could consider Catholic Workers to be "anything but pacifist in our techniques of changing the social order." She found it difficult to understand why their criticism of capitalism and labor unions had "aroused such protest."

She ended on a moving conciliatory note, pledging "to be less dogmatic, more persuasive, less irritating, more winning."[133] And so *Catholic Worker* the name remained.

It is true that in her life as a Catholic Worker, Day was banned by several bishops from speaking to religious groups in their dioceses; the paper was banned from some churches; and Day was sometimes sharply criticized by the clergy. But the Catholic Church never actually stopped her work. Even such arch-conservative leaders of the New York diocese as Patrick Cardinal Hayes, James Cardinal McIntyre, and Francis Cardinal Spellman—all of whom had dealings with Dorothy Day—would not presume to silence her, primarily for two reasons: There was the doctrinal purity of the Catholic Worker philosophy, with its irrefutable sources, the same as the Church's. And the hierarchy could not fault Day's emphasis on the works of mercy, or her active resistance to the works of war, positions rooted in the Gospel command to love one another. Certainly Day's mollifying mien smoothed her dealings with the Chancery, too. "I think you approach a bishop as a human being and a member of the human family," she said in an interview. She likened Cardinal McIntyre to her "old father, who was a racist from Tennessee." Mr. Day, she wrote, would say: " 'Of course nothing is so cute as a little nigger baby. Baby mules and baby niggers are the cutest things on God's earth.' " But "we have to love our father just the same," Day declared. "Who are we to go ahead in righteous indignation and condemn?"[134]

Day's responses to clerical criticism showed finesse and restraint. To an arch-bishop in 1942, she wrote: "We are going to concentrate on peace and the land in all the coming issues of our paper to try to keep these ideals alive." She assured him that "If our Bishop asks us to cease, we will, of course, obey immediately," but then gently reminded him that after all, Church authorities "permitted us to continue in the Spanish Civil War, when we were again opposed to the use of force in spite of widespread controversy here over our refusal to uphold war as holy."[135]

When a priest chastised the *Catholic Worker* in the Thirties for "publishing abuses thereby stirring up unrest," Day thanked him for his "gentle rebuke." She informed him that the staff was well aware of this danger, and that they had strived "to make our criticisms constructive rather than merely carping, by pointing out wherever possible the many good and helpful things being done by the Church and churchmen in the reconstruction of the social order." Tactfully, she continued with another apology, then expressed her delight at a different part of his letter which had extolled voluntary poverty. Finally, Day mentioned Peter Maurin's advocacy of voluntary poverty as the "only genuine Catholic antidote for social evils."[136] Day's restrained, considered tone, her use of the editorial "we" and her mention of her co-founder's name, dispelled any doubt that a lone woman was subverting the Catholic Church.

The Catholic Worker Papers contain many other letters from Day to the Chancery that illustrate her prudent diplomacy. Perhaps because she herself exercised authority, she could well understand the difficulties of others who wielded it. Also, as one priest put it, "The veiled mystery of womanhood which celibate clerics approach with awe gives such great women [as Dorothy Day] their due influence and elicits in them the more noble, gentlemanly and fatherly instincts." Thus, rather than damn Day as a Communist sympathizer, he rationalized that she was "so thoroughly a woman, a mother and a sister that she sees only persons, wretched lives and human failures; when she meets radicals, in spite of their wild language, she sees in them only wounded, flaming hearts."[137] It cannot be denied that Day sometimes played the role of deferential woman in her dealings with Catholic Church authorities; she knew bishops and others were more likely to forgive the mistakes she made, on the grounds that she was, after all, not only a convert but a woman. And she accepted that.

Perceptively, Day had early recognized that because a movement like the Catholic Worker was bound to make mistakes, it should remain fully a lay endeavor. Day knew that lay people could afford to make errors that clergy and bishops could not. But her mistakes were so few, as a matter of fact, that there wasn't much to worry about. "We have been given, from the first, the freedom which is to be expected we laymen should take in handling temporal affairs, which after all is our province," she wrote.[138] She summarized her dealings with the New York Chancery: "We've enjoyed the utmost liberty in this diocese. They leave us alone, and let us edit the paper the way we want to. Oh, we used to hear from them on a few things, but not anymore." She admitted that "when Cardinal McIntyre took over as chancellor, he was somewhat perplexed by us." She could still remember him inspecting a double-page *Catholic Worker* spread about the evils of conscription, and muttering, "They didn't tell me about this in the seminary." But the Cardinal "bore up pretty well."[139] Indeed, Cardinal McIntyre (then a bishop) once offered to sponsor a $15,000 bank loan for the Catholic Worker movement to ease its housing problems.[140] On another occasion she remarked that Cardinal Spellman "has given us absolute freedom and shown us courtesy and kindness."[141] [Richard] Cardinal Cushing sent the *Catholic Worker* $500 every time its editors went to jail for civil disobedience and referred to Day as a "saint" in the German edition of her autobiography, *The Long Loneliness*.[142]

But Dorothy Day did not wait for priests, bishops, or cardinals to officially approve her ideas; she went ahead and took immediate action. As the years went by, her radical origins became less an issue. Always a Catholic first and an activist second, she was an old-style radical who adhered to the established forms while she tried to change them. Day sought, as Peter Maurin had adapted the old I.W.W. slogan, "to build a new society within the shell of the old." As a loyal, obedient Catholic convert, a woman who could claim a male co-founder, her way was made smoother. By the time of the Second Vatican Council in 1962, Day was respected not only among Catholic clergy, but among all levels of society and worldwide. Former *America* editor Donald R. Campion remembered that "Suddenly you found yourself talking with a bishop or theologian from Africa and Australia and discovered that the first stop he had made in the States on his way home from the seminary days in Rome, just before World War II, was to the Worker house."[143] And when Dorothy Day died in November 1980, the acclaim from the Church was truly impressive.

As editor and publisher, as leader of the Catholic Worker movement, Day was extraordinarily pressed to travel, to lecture, to advise, to console. Hundreds who read her columns wrote to her seeking spiritual advice, or requesting her prayers. Sometimes people telephoned long-distance seeking her counsel. Marge

Hughes, a Catholic Worker, wrote to an absent Dorothy Day about the reader who called one morning, "enduring terrible physical pain" and begging for Day's personal prayers.[144] And hundreds more, both humble and famous, journeyed to the Lower East Side to see Day in person. Each year even more came, as, in the words of Thomas Cornell, Day's position was more firmly rooted as "the mother of us all."

Characteristically modest to the end of her life, Day always insisted that others be given more credit for the Catholic Worker movement. To her biographer she wrote, "I am deathly sick of all the interviewings and publicity I got around my seventy-fifth birthday and exhausted from all the visitors, telephone calls, and requests for talks, etc."[145] She was especially irritated by the label of "saint" that was constantly pinned on her in her later years, not wanting the Catholic Worker movement or its paper to be so easily dismissed. That appellation invokes an image of the superhuman linked to the supernatural. Day saw herself as down to earth, even matter-of-fact — a woman relying on her conscience, as her wartime stand on pacifism aptly demonstrated.

ST·MARTIN DE·PORRES·

ADE BETHUNE

VI: Ominous Times, Valiant Decisions

Many in the Union Square crowd on May Day, 1933, were nonplussed by a Catholic paper advocating social justice. Although it was not well known at the time, substantial papal precedent undergirded the *Catholic Worker*'s activism. More than forty years earlier, in May 1891, Pope Leo XIII had presented a detailed social justice program in *Rerum novarum*, an encyclical on the condition of labor. Social justice, the Pope asserted, must mediate between the two conflicting systems of the day: one, economic laissez-faire liberalism, which scorned moral and political intervention in industry; the other, socialism, which exaggerated the role of the state in industrial life. Though non-socialist, Pope Leo's program was radical. Historian Aaron Abell summarizes it as stressing that religion "enjoined employers to carry out all equitable agreements freely made and employers to respect the human and Christian dignity of their workpeople, and to pay them just and adequate wages." The Pope further directed all who enjoyed a material surplus to share with those in need.[1]

Pope Pius XI enlarged these themes in his encyclical on reconstructing the social order, issued in May 1931 on the fortieth anniversary of *Rerum novarum*. In *Quadragesimo anno*, Pope Pius declared that justice required that workers be compensated with wages of "ample sufficiency." He recommended that co-partnerships be made where possible, to enable workers to share in some way in the ownership, management, or profits of industry. Should economic depression prevent employers from paying adequate wages, employers and employees, aided by public authority, should act together to remedy the situation. Pope Pius also advocated trade unions to promote justice and the common good.[2]

Thus the stage was set for a sympathetic relationship between the Catholic Church and the working people, who had composed the great majority of the American Catholic Church ever since the period of heavy immigration, about 1830-1850.[3] But as time went on, American Catholicism's minority self-consciousness as an immigrant church, its organizational immaturity, extremely rapid growth, and the prevailing climate of anti-Catholic hostility by nativist groups, all combined to retard the development of a truly unified, coherent American Catholic Church that could effectively grapple with the problems of modern industrialism.[4] Unfortunately, the period of greatest Catholic growth—after

1830 — coincided with a tremendous burst of Protestant evangelicalism. According to historian Philip Gleason, many revivalists connected Protestantism and the national destiny, in millenial terms. These evangelicals judged the existence of Catholicism to be "utterly incompatible with the millenial promise." They viewed the growing strength of the Catholic Church in the United States (from 35,000 in 1790 to 300,000 in 1830 to 1.6 million in 1850 to 3.1 million in 1860) as "the work of the Evil One," and battled it strenuously.[5] In order "to surmount its minority complex and 'Americanize' itself," historian Richard Hofstadter has written, some American Catholics either devoted themselves to denouncing aspects of American life as "materialistic" or "secularistic," or overidentified with other aspects that struck them as more acceptable.[6] Yet a native-born Catholic liberal tradition did arise in the United States, as exemplified by Orestes A. Brownson, James Cardinal Gibbons, Archbishop John Ireland, and Msgr. John A. Ryan. But on the whole its voice was not yet heard. When the *Catholic Worker* appeared in 1933, the Church was still fairly preoccupied with providing for the immediate spiritual and social needs of its thousands of immigrants, so that it hardly addressed the problems of modern society expounded in the papal encyclicals.[7] At best, its dissemination of the ideas of "social Catholicism" had been weak.

And as Francine du Plessix Gray has observed, the nature of American Catholicism had also fostered its distinctive position on war and the state. Medieval Catholics had recognized the power of the state as God-given. There followed a long tradition of viewing commands of the state as unchallengeable, even sacred. Thus as late as 1966, when Francis Cardinal Spellman was asked to comment on the United States' Vietnam policy during a trip to Saigon, he asserted: "My country, may it always be right. Right or wrong, my country" (a paraphrase of the words of Stephen Decatur, a nineteenth-century naval hero). While Protestant pacifists came from churches steeped in a tradition of dissent against secular power, dating from the Reformation, Catholics were much more likely to espouse a blind patriotism.[8] This was especially true of Catholics eager to be assimiliated into mainstream America in the first half of this century.

When Dorothy Day hawked the first issue of her paper in Union Square on May Day, 1933, the title's union of "Catholic" and "Worker" — a union of religious and social action — seemed preposterous, even sinister to many Americans, for only Communists were addressing the laboring masses in any concerted way. When Richard Deverall and a friend sold the paper in downtown Newark in 1935, they were approached by an angry Irish policeman who thundered, "Mabbee it's Catholic... but it says *Worker* and that means you two must be darty Communists."[9] And when Clement D. Brown was an undergraduate at St. John's University in Brooklyn, which he described as "an extremely conservative school dominated by Vincentian priests," he and some friends began to distribute the *Catholic Worker* to fellow students. Brown recalled that several of the priests objected, calling the paper Communist. When the dean ordered them to stop, they continued to pass out the *Catholic Worker* on the subway —

until a traveling Vincentian spotted them. He informed the dean, but the students were rescued from his wrath by a "kindly" priest who offered to serve as adviser, but then took no active role. Brown and his friends continued to distribute the *Catholic Worker* outside the immediate University area.[10]

At first, many Catholics viewed the paper as undermining their newly achieved respectability in American society. An early letter to the editors addressed this concern:

> Catholicism pertains to religion, and has no bearing on industrial and economic life.... It is very distasteful to find you making remarks which certainly must embitter the attacked people against the Catholic Church.... the Church is at its greatest when adhering to thoughts only on religion.[11]

And when the *Catholic Worker* accelerated its coverage of pacifism as the Thirties wore on, Catholic reaction was often similar. Many criticized the paper for

Figure 8. Soupline at St. Joseph's House. (Courtesy Dorothy Day-Catholic Worker Collection, Marquette University)

championing pacifism during the Spanish Civil War and World War II. Some even considered the *Catholic Worker* to be advocating treason.

The story of how the *Catholic Worker* survived the Thirties and the Forties emphasizes Dorothy Day's courageous role as leader. From the beginning, she kept the paper engaged with modern, major social problems. Peter Maurin often repeated his dictum that "Strikes don't strike me," but Day felt strongly otherwise. She instinctively recognized that as the Great Depression dragged on, people desperately craved a new message of social change. "You have to remember the times," Joseph Zarrella has pointed out. "The right to organize, unions, strikes, unemployment, breadlines—these were the big issues in the early days of the *Catholic Worker*."[12] Catholics were beginning to discover the papal encyclicals. They were in a new mood of reform, indicated, for example, by their overwhelming support of Franklin D. Roosevelt and the New Deal.[13]

Dorothy Day forged ahead over Peter Maurin's objections, shrewdly addressing in her paper the immediate, ubiquitous problems of labor, thus creating a mass appeal. In its first few years, much of the *Catholic Worker*'s news, features, and editorials dealt with labor issues such as strikes, unions, wages, unemployment, and the exploitation of black workers. The *Catholic Worker* supported labor for "the fundamental truth that men should be treated not as chattels, but as human beings, as 'temples of the Holy Ghost.' "[14] It backed up its viewpoint with frequent, judicious quotations from the social justice teachings of the papal encyclicals. Such content, in the reform-minded years of the Great Depression, won for the paper an impressive following. From 2,500 copies in its premier May 1933 issue, circulation jumped to 110,000 by May 1935.

While Maurin rejected any sort of government intervention in the economy and completely opposed the New Deal, Day took a more moderate course. To her, "the whole program of unemployment insurance, Social Security, was a confession of the failure of our whole social order" and of basic "Christian principles." It showed "that man, in fact, did not look after his brother. That he had to go to the State." Day recognized a vexing dilemma here. Again and again, the Federal Government has to protect people from injustice, as "in the South." Yet "ideally," such matters "should not be the business of the State. The State," she declared, "should never take over functions that could be performed by a smaller body. The State should only enter when there are grave abuses."[15]

So, as she stressed the importance of personal responsibility toward the poor and the moral superiority of the small group as reformer, Dorothy Day asserted that "the State is bound for the sake of the common good, to take care of the unemployed and the unemployable by relief and lodging houses and work projects."[16] She concluded that an emergency the magnitude of the Great Depression demanded immediate, government-sponsored relief. At the same time she continued to acknowledge the evils of big government, noting the tension of "autonomy as against immediate need."[17] Day thus expressed, especially throughout the *Catholic Worker*'s first few years, an editorial viewpoint on the New Deal that was more winning than her co-founder's absolutist position.

Figure 9. Serving soup. (Bob Fitch photo, courtesy Dorothy Day-Catholic Worker Collection, Marquette University)

During its first year, the *Catholic Worker* contained only occasional articles that directly addressed pacifism. In 1933, when the Depression's brutal realities were far more salient, few could glimpse the clouds gathering abroad. Not until the fifth issue did a short pacifist item appear, an announcement that Catholic Workers would be delegates at a peace conference of the United States Congress Against War.[18] Thereafter, throughout its first three years the paper offered regular if limited coverage of pacifism. Not until its third birthday did the *Catholic Worker* unequivocally assert its pacifist nature:

> The *Catholic Worker* is sincerely a *pacifist* paper.... We oppose... imperialist war. We oppose, moreover, preparedness for war, a preparedness which is going on now on an unprecedented scale and which will undoubtedly lead to war.... We must be brave enough and courageous enough to set the example.... A pacifist who is willing to endure the scorn of the unthinking mob, the ignominy of jail, the pain of stripes and the threat of death, cannot be lightly dismissed as a coward afraid of physical pain. A pacifist even now must be prepared for the opposition of the mob who thinks violence is bravery. The pacifist in the next war must be ready for martyrdom. We call upon youth to prepare![19]

Now there could be no doubt where the *Catholic Worker* stood. And throughout its existence, it has never violated its pledge of absolute pacifism.

The first test of the *Catholic Worker*'s commitment came during the Spanish Civil War, 1936-1939. Early in the war, it was evident that American majority sentiment rested with the Loyalist central government. In July 1936, the Loyalists savagely attacked Catholics, and a Catholic general named Francisco Franco stepped forward to defend the faith. As civil war ensued, thousands were murdered, churches were burned, and bishops, priests, and nuns were routed from their beds to be tortured and murdered. It was an awkward time for United States Catholics, whose sympathy with their coreligionists in Spain now placed them once more in a minority position in American society. The position for American Catholics seemed clear: Franco and his rebels were on the side of God. To oppose him was to oppose Catholicism, to support Communist anarchy. "Almost to a man," observed historian David J. O'Brien, "the hierarchy and the American Catholic press supported the Franco side, insisting that the loyalist government was Communist-dominated, did not represent the will of the Spanish people, and was bent upon destruction of the Church in Spain."[20]

The Spanish Civil War was certainly an arduous trial for any Catholic publications leaning towards pacifism. When the liberal *Commonweal*, led by managing editor George Shuster, abandoned its pro-Franco stand for neutrality, it lost one-quarter of its circulation. By mid-June of 1937, irate readers and clergy forced Shuster to leave, and *Commonweal*'s founder and editor changed the policy to conform to the prevailing American Catholic viewpoint.

But Shuster's old friend Dorothy Day stood firm. Always, she and her paper opposed the war. The *Catholic Worker* was the sole Catholic publication to remain consistently neutral and pacifist throughout the conflict.[21] Early in the war, Day published an editorial that unmistakably clarified the viewpoint of the *Catholic Worker:*

> Poor blood-drenched Spain is the most talked about subject today.... Who is right and who is wrong? We are inclined to believe that the issue is not so clear cut as to enable either side to condemn the other justifiably....
>   Our main concern is that the 'members of Christ tear one another.'
>   ... Spain doesn't need favorable publicity for the rebels. She doesn't need condemnation of the loyalists. What she needs is the prayers of the rest of the Mystical Body. Pleas to God that Members will stop hating each other....
>   The *Catholic Worker* makes this appeal to its readers: Forget your anger. Let your indignation die. Remember only that the Body is rent asunder, and the only solution is Love.[22]

To the many American Catholics who supported Franco, who thought that at least the fascists were defending the Church against Communist oppression, Day pointed out the persecution of the Church in Germany by Nazi fascists.[23] In the December 1936 *Catholic Worker*, a one-inch, five-column banner headline proclaimed: "Spanish Catholic Flays Both Sides." Below, a long letter written by a Catholic Spaniard to Emmanuel Mounier, the French philosopher and editor of *L'Esprit*, vigorously argued the neutral position.[24]

Meanwhile, individual Catholic Workers were taking direct action to protest the Spanish conflict, as they would during wars to come. They picketed both Communist and United Front (a leftwing coalition) meetings, where they distributed the *Catholic Worker* and Catholic pamphlets to the participants. In June 1938, Catholic Workers Joseph Zarrella, Stanley Vishnewski, and Bill Callahan picketed Radio City Music Hall to protest the showing of the film "Blockade," which was an emotional appeal to remove the embargo on arms to Spain, with a script by Clifford Odets.

Reaction to the *Catholic Worker*'s stand was bitter among both Communists and right-wing Catholics, who sent in their cancellations. Joseph Zarrella recalled that "We were torn apart from both sides. We were anathema because of our pacifist, neutral position." Catholic schools cancelled their bundle orders.[25] A typical letter to the *Catholic Worker*'s editor read:

> I think that you are still a dirty Communist parading as a loyal Catholic.... I think, finally, that you are a two-faced hypocrite, a wolf in sheep's clothing, serving your Red monster, Joseph Stalin, who guides you from his capitol at Moscow.... Scallions to you, Dorothy Day, and to all your fellow travelers— Jewish or Gentile.... I hope I meet you in the dark some night, when you are accompanied by some of your 'Red' butcher friends as I have a burning desire to achieve martyrdom for the Faith.[26]

Because of its stand on the Spanish Civil War and on pacifism in general, the paper's circulation plummeted from a high of 190,000 in early 1938 to a low of 50,500 during World War II. Shorn of bundle orders, the *Catholic Worker* was excommunicated by the Catholic Press Association. (In later years, when "grassroots murmur" had elected Dorothy Day the first lady of American Catholicism, the *Catholic Worker* was invited back into the C.P.A., but it declined.[27])

Disgruntled clergy also fired off furious missives. The bishop in Worcester, Massachusetts—like many of his peers around the country—began to discourage priests from visiting any Catholic Worker Houses of Hospitality. The Providence, Rhode Island, bishop exhorted a group against starting such a residence there.[28]

The press also attacked the *Catholic Worker*. Patrick Scanlan, editor of the *Brooklyn Tablet*, the diocesan newspaper, was appalled by *Catholic Worker* pacifism. An article in *Social Justice*, the weekly of the demagogical radio priest of Royal Oak, Michigan, the Rev. Charles E. Coughlin, was especially vitriolic. The article announced: "There is no middle ground between Catholicity and Communism." Despite all the *Catholic Worker*'s "references to the saints, the Popes and the Encyclicals," its "attitude on the Spanish question" made Coughlinites "wonder if the thing were downright communism, camouflaged with Catholic paint."[29]

Even Day's old friend Mike Gold turned bitter against her and the *Catholic Worker* over the Spanish Civil War, as he later would over her unyielding pacifism in World War II. But Day remained resolute in her stand, even as she "got it from both sides."[30] In a 1938 editorial, she acknowledged the tension of the pacifist position:

> We all know there is a frightful persecution of religion in Spain.... In the light of this fact it is inconceivably difficult to write as we do. It is folly—it seems madness—to say as we do—'we are opposed to the use of force as a means of settling personal, national, or international disputes.' As a newspaper trying to affect public opinion, we take this stand. We feel that if the press and the public throughout the world do not speak in terms of the counsels of perfection, who else will?
>
> ... As long as men trust to the use of force—only a superior, a more savage and brutal force will overcome the enemy.

But neither did Day condemn those who had seized arms and were now engaged in war, for she added:

> Who of us individuals, if he were in Spain today, could tell what he would do? . . . From the human natural standpoint men are doing good to defend their faith, their country. But from the standpoint of the Supernatural—there is the 'better way'—the way of the Saints—the way of love.
>
> . . .If we do not, as the press, emphasize the law of love, we betray our trust, our vocation. We must stand opposed to the use of force.[31]

Day even sent a cablegram to both the insurgents and the loyalists, urging them to observe on Good Friday 1938 the Truce of God, a medieval tradition requiring Christians engaged in combat to lay down their arms on certain Holy Days and seasons. (On Holy Saturday the *New York Times* reported in a dispatch from Spain that not a single shot had been fired on Good Friday.)

In March 1939 the Spanish Civil War ended. Many Catholics rejoiced as

Madrid surrendered unconditionally to Franco's troops. But the *Catholic Worker*, preoccupied with the new war that was imminent, was steadily increasing its coverage of the pacifism issue, despite Peter Maurin's counsel to the contrary. According to William D. Miller, Maurin "never reached the point of making his pacifism a pronouncement," although he had urged neutrality during the Spanish Civil War. Miller suggests that boldly speaking out for pacifism might have offended Maurin's personalist sense.[32] According to Maurin's biographer Arthur Sheehan, the Frenchman's pacifism resembled that of the early Christians, who "refused to become judges because they might have had to sentence men to death."[33] However, later research indicates that while Maurin personally embraced pacifism, he also realized how fully the American public had come to accept the concept of war as an instrument of national policy. Marc H. Ellis, author of a recent study on Maurin's thought, says that because Maurin realized "the difficulties Dorothy Day was having in her vocal opposition" to World War II, he "counseled her that for a time silence would be better than continuing vocal opposition to war."[34] "Perhaps," Maurin told her, "it is time to be silent; they are not willing to listen."[35]

But Dorothy Day was committed to the most extreme form of pacifism, utterly rejecting war. According to Father Hugo, she abhorred war as "the matrix of all other evils that disfigure our society." But she was not just a "political pacifist," he said. She embraced peace through "fidelity to the Beatitude, 'Blessed are the peacemakers, for they shall be called children of God.' "[36] Day's views and approach prevailed. As World War II neared, the *Catholic Worker*, joined by *Commonweal*, signalled the first American Catholic rejection of the traditional just war theory, that is, the right to war under certain circumstances, with unrestricted methods of warfare.[37]

At first, through 1939, the *Catholic Worker* opposed conscription through arguments based primarily on history. But as the war threatened, Father Hugo sent Day a letter that suggested she make clear the deeper philosophical wellsprings of her pacifism. "No doubt [pacifism] is all clear to you; but then you have not tried to work it out doctrinally," he wrote. "If you knew no theology, it would probably be simpler to make a solution. Yet the decision must be based on doctrine. Pacifism must proceed from truth, or it cannot exist at all." He added that her attacks on conscription were "the most extreme form of pacifism."[38] Day recognized that for many American Catholics, a priest spoke with utmost authority; and so the writers who articulated the *Catholic Worker*'s pacifist theory were often learned clergy. One was Father Hugo, who began in 1941 to contribute many substantive pieces on pacifism and the primacy of the individual conscience. He wrote two major series of articles, which were later published as pamphlets. His "Weapons of the Spirit" series stressed the theological and moral basis for *spiritual* combat. Father Hugo identified the evil nature of Nazism, which he claimed required not conventional warfare, but Christ's warfare— spiritual action such as prayer, penance, fasting, and self-sacrifice.[39]

In his second series, Father Hugo developed a "Gospel of Peace," arguing that contrary to current belief, the Gospels directly address the problems of peace. He defined peace not as a state of material wealth or security, but as a spiritual state achieved when the individual follows the teachings and example of Christ. True peace must be based first on this internal peace of each person. He further argued that war was immoral because it violated the fundamental law of Christianity: to love one's neighbor as oneself.[40]

When the Rev. Barry O'Toole of the Philosophy Department at Catholic University began to contribute articles outlining the theological basis of Catholic nonconscription, 1939-1941, *Time* announced that "U.S. Protestant pacifists might have to move over on the bandwagon to make room for some Catholics."[41] Father O'Toole argued that the destructiveness of contemporary weapons meant that no Christian could morally participate in modern war. Twentieth-century technological sophistication, he declared, had made moot the age-old Christian concept of a "just war." He also concluded that all conscription was a form of slavery that violated the true meaning of vocation, that of a voluntary choice of state in life.[42]

The Hugo and O'Toole pieces, along with the "Christ and the Patriot" series by Msgr. Paul Hanly Furfey, the distinguished sociologist, formed a comprehensive theory of pacifism. By the end of World War II, the *Catholic Worker's* pacifist rationale was fairly sophisticated.

Of course, the paper had been pacifist all along. Throughout the early Thirties, for example, it condemned war preparations, advancing this argument in the April 1934 issue:

> Never before in peacetime and seldom in wartime, have we spent the hundreds of millions for war now being appropriated. . . .
> Nothing is a substitute for conscience. Conscience would probably put an end to war if it were given its rights. But when wars arise or even rumors of wars, the first thing that is killed is conscience. And there is the supreme crime and tragedy of war, not the killing of the enemy but the killing of conscience.[43]

In 1935 the *Catholic Worker* condemned poison gas an an immoral weapon. In April 1936, the paper predicted a war in Europe and urged Catholics to examine their consciences while they could still be objective.[44] The *Catholic Worker* also advocated a boycott of the Hearst newspapers, because of the press lord's "absurd red-baiting and militaristic propaganda."[45]

And as early as 1935 the *Catholic Worker* had discussed the concept of conscientious objection, maintaining that modern war was intrinsically immoral because it included brutal attacks on civilians. The *Catholic Worker* declared that "Catholics should and must refuse to take part in any modern war."[46]

The paper also sounded an early warning against American anti-Semitism, publishing a sharp condemnation in its sixth issue.[47] Likewise, the paper was quick to condemn Hitler's persecution of Jews. The *Catholic Worker* eclipsed most—perhaps all—American publications, both religious and secular, in the speed and concern with which it disclosed the Jewish persecution. By the end of

1933, all German laws restricting or excluding Jews from public life, education, government, the arts, and the professions were firmly in place.[48] In May 1934, the *Catholic Worker* warned that the Church in Germany was "heroically fighting a battle against the quiet insidious persecution of Hitler's brownshirts." It mentioned that Michael von Faulhaber, the outspoken German cardinal, was "frequently in danger of arrest and personal harm" because he had publicly attacked "Hitler's persecution of the Jews, the hampering of the Catholic youth organizations, and the direct spurning of the terms of the concordat."[49] In the same issue, an article outlined Catholic teaching which condemned two recent books, *The Cult of the Twentieth Century* by Alfred Rosenberg, Minister of Education in the German Reich; and Ernest Bergmann's *German National Church*. "God is the universal sovereign," the *Catholic Worker* wrote. "All men are brothers in Adam and in Jesus Christ." It quoted St. Paul's reminder: "There is neither gentile nor Jew . . . but Christ is All and in all."[50]

In a letter about a year later Day wrote, "As Catholics we too feel called upon to protest against the Nazi persecution of Catholics and Jews, by demonstration and distribution of literature. We feel that we would be neglecting our duty as Catholics if we did not do this."[51] Less than a year later, in April 1936, the *Catholic Worker* declared its stand in the most explicit terms:

> A writer in the *Jewish Examiner* warns us that we must be always on guard against the anti-Jewish feeling cropping up at most any time. We intend to follow his warning and spike every rumor and whisper that reaches our ears. It is not enough to appreciate the fact that the small-time organizations, engaged in this despicable business of spreading hate, are composed of mentally diseased morons. We must inform the healthy minded bystanders of true Christian teachings on this subject.[52]

As Jews moved into the most horrifying period of their history, the *Catholic Worker* continued to speak out. Sometimes Nazi persecution was mentioned in articles focusing on other themes; sometimes it was highlighted in separate pieces. Although the *Catholic Worker* aimed to "announce," not "denounce," it took on the increasingly perverse, anti-Semitic Rev. Charles E. Coughlin. As the decade of the Thirties wore on, his *Social Justice* singled out the Jew as the culprit simultaneously responsible for domestic capitalist depression and international Communism. On July 19, 1939, *Social Justice* descended into new depths of inhumanity when it began to publish the fabricated "Protocols of the Elders of Zion," a series of twenty-four lectures supposedly by Jewish leaders on how to conquer the world. On the front page of its December 1938 issue, the *Catholic Worker* condemned the "Protocols," systematically exposing each one.[53] In an open letter to Father Coughlin in its May 1939 issue, the *Catholic Worker* declared: "If a real wave of anti-Semitism sweeps the United States, if in the future Jews are persecuted as they are in Europe, you, Father Coughlin, must be ready to assume a goodly part of that responsibility."[54]

Peter Maurin always had a special love for the Jewish people, and as they were increasingly persecuted both abroad and in America, 1936-1939, the *Catholic Worker* printed more of Maurin's (and others') articles in protest. The front page of the July-August 1939 issue displayed a bold headline: "Let's Keep the Jews, for Christ's Sake." Underneath was a collection of seven Easy Essays reminding readers that Jews were also members of God's family.[55] In the January 1940 *Catholic Worker*, Maurin wrote in part:

Hitler needs to read
the old Testament
and the New Testament
if he wants
to lead men
into the Promised
    Land
where people
do no longer try
to cut each other's
throats
and where the lion
comes to lie down
with the lamb.[56]

In Germany during November 9-13, 1938, through successive nights of terror that collectively came to be called *Kristallnacht* ("Night of Broken Glass"), Jews were beaten and killed, their stores looted and burned. The following month, besides exposing the fakery of the *Social Justice* "Protocols," the *Catholic Worker* printed a front-page piece by Archbishop Joseph Francis Rummel of New Orleans that acknowledged Nazi racial violence and appealed for prayers for the persecuted.[57] The *Catholic Worker* also printed another bishop's article that similarly denounced the Jewish pogrom, expressing "revulsion, disgust, and grief."[58] Surely the madness of Nazism was now undeniable. But by 1939, anti-Semitism in the United States was reaching its zenith; that year there were a reported one hundred and twenty-one anti-Semitic organizations active.[59] And millions of American Catholics listened faithfully to Father Coughlin's radio tirades against Jews.

Besides setting the *Catholic Worker* squarely against anti-Semitism, often using many clerics as writers to achieve greater credibility, Dorothy Day took other action. In December 1938 she sent a statement to several newspapers and to the *New Republic*. It read:

Inept and untimely was the radio broadcast of Father Coughlin in which he admonished the Jews on Communism, and equally inept and untimely was its pugnacious defense by Mr. Patrick Scanlan, editor of the Brooklyn *Tablet*. It is to be hoped the Jews of America will consider both cases not in the light of anti−Semitism but rather as two cases of extraordinarily bad manners.[60]

And in May 1939, Day helped to organize the Committee of Catholics to Fight Anti-Semitism. The committee's first executive secretary was Prof. Emmanuel

Chapman of the philosophy department at Fordham University. He was joined by Edward Marciniak, a Catholic Worker; Marie Antoinette Roulet, a worker in the labor movement; the Jesuit Martin Carribine; and Prof. Herbert Rattner of the University of Chicago. Soon there was a distinguished list of sponsors and a paper, the *Voice*, was sold on the streets of New York — sometimes in direct confrontation with *Social Justice* salespeople.[61]

Just as it defended Jews, the *Catholic Worker* denounced the internment of Japanese-Americans. "I saw a bit of Germany on the West Coast," Dorothy Day wrote in one report. She described the federal government's relocation policy, stating that if she did not protest it, she would be guilty of failing in the works of mercy.[62]

Catholic Worker spin-off organizations that worked for peace included PAX (later called the Association of Catholic Conscientious Objectors), formed in October 1936. Modelled on the English PAX organization, it sought to organize Catholic pacifists into a "mighty league of CO's." PAX members claimed that the conditions of modern warfare made a "just war" impossible, and they wished to form a permanent group that would assist Catholic conscientious objectors and spread Catholic pacifist ideas. In 1941, the National Service Board for Religious Objectors offered one of its work camps to the Catholic Worker movement. This was quite a precedent, because until World War II, pacifists belonged to Quaker, Mennonite, Church of the Brethren, and other primarily Protestant denominations — certainly not the Catholic Church. By September 1943, the Catholic objectors were publishing their own quarterly, the *Catholic C.O.*, which grew into a scholarly journal covering the pacifism issue. According to one of its founders, Arthur Sheehan, the group believed that a separate paper was needed, because of the sheer "amount of peace material and the need to give space to other matters in the *Catholic Worker*."[63] The *Catholic C.O.*, with contributions from Dorothy Day, Peter Maurin, Ammon Hennacy, Gordon Zahn, and other Catholic Workers, continued until 1948 when it merged with the *Catholic Worker*.

Meanwhile, Dorothy Day herself remained resolutely pacifist. She opposed even registering as a conscientious objector, considering this to be a form of cooperation with war-making. In December 1942, Day was the first signer and prime organizer of a manifesto that appeared in the *Catholic Worker*. Forty-seven other women added their signatures to hers, pledging that they would refuse to register for any proposed draft of women. In another article the following month, Day announced that not only would she not register, but that she would not submit any statement whatsoever to the draft board. Thus she would not cooperate in any form with conscription, because she believed "modern war to be murder, incompatible with the religion of love."[64] This was a far more radical position than that taken by the conscientious objectors she was advising. Nevertheless Day respected the consciences of those who took the comparatively moderate approach of registering their dissent within the law, and supported them.[65] So Day allowed PAX, through a regular monthly column in the *Catholic*

Worker, to call for signatures to support a Catholic's right to conscientious objection. She also allowed PAX to print a box in the paper urging men not to register for the draft. While the government seemed not to notice this, Church authorities did. Soon Day was called to the New York Chancery and told, "Dorothy, you must stand corrected." "I was not quite sure what that meant," she later wrote. But she agreed not to print such explicit admonitions to resist the draft, because she "realized that one should not tell another what to do in such circumstances." She added: "We had to follow our own consciences, which later took us to jail; but our work in getting out the paper was an attempt to arouse the consciences of others, not to advise action for which they were not prepared."[66]

As always, Day was diplomatic, toning down an extreme stand but never jettisoning it. She never compromised the larger question of pacifism, even as American isolationism crumbled and Roosevelt prepared the country for war. In October 1939, a month after Hitler invaded Poland, and Britain and France declared war on Germany, Day addressed an editorial to workers. She told them she knew that appeals were being made to their "selfishness," as they were "told that prosperity will accompany a war boom, that if the United States shall sell to warring nations or other nations to be transferred to warring countries, the long-awaited lift from unemployment and depression is at hand." But Catholic Workers, she said, wished to "address another appeal: an appeal to your idealism, to your desire for justice, to your Charity." She continued:

> No matter how the legislative tide turns, no matter what laws are passed abridging the neutrality of the United States, you hold it in your power to keep our country aloof from the European war. This is our appeal, then, that you use your power as workers to refuse to manufacture or transport articles of war that are intended for foreign nations, warring or neutral. That you serve notice on your employers, in organized fashion, that you will have no part of such blood money, and that you will strike if necessary to maintain your position.
> . . . It is yours to say whether the United States shall dip its hands in the blood of European workers. You can say NO![67]

When Congress in 1940 began to consider the possibility of a military draft, the *Catholic Worker* intensified its condemnation of conscription. Day asserted that "To fight war we must fight conscription. To this fight THE CATHOLIC WORKER PLEDGES ITSELF AS LONG AS WE ARE PERMITTED TO EXIST."[68] In July, she traveled with Joseph Zarrella and Msgr. Barry O'Toole, author of the *Catholic Worker*'s "The Morality of Conscription" series, to Washington, D.C. There they voiced their disapproval to the Senate Military Affairs Committee conducting hearings on the proposed Burke-Wadsworth Compulsory Military Training Law.[69]

As war loomed, the soul-searching among Catholic Workers heightend. "We all knew that it was but a matter of months," recalled Stanley Vishnewski, "before we would have to declare our stand as conscientious objectors. We had to decide whether or not we were to abandon our intellects and our consciences

Figure 10. Catholic Workers, Thirties; second row, starting third from left: Day, Maurin, Tamar, Ade Bethune. (Courtesy Dorothy Day-Catholic Worker Collection, Marquette University)

in the hands of Mother State or were we to look in our hearts and decide for ourselves."[70] As United States entry into World War II seemed ever more certain, criticism of Day and her *Catholic Worker* grew more strident. "It seems to be," she wrote to a priest friend in May 1940, "that opposition to our work and to our ideas is pretty consistent." She added that since the Paulist church in San Francisco had thrown out the *Catholic Worker* as well as her books from its library, "there are still plenty of good, healthy obstacles to be overcome."[71] In another letter just before the war's outbreak, she admitted to "differences of opinion" among Catholic Workers. "Although that has caused grief," she went on, "I do not think it has jeopardized the strength of the Catholic Worker movement. Articulate or inarticulate, no matter how clumsy we are in expressing ourselves, there is a great sense of unity among us."[72]

Then on December 7, 1941, in a terrifying show of force, the Japanese attacked Pearl Harbor. On December 22, the Most Reverend Edward Mooney sent a letter on behalf of the Catholic bishops to President Franklin Roosevelt, promising the support of all Catholics in this newly declared war. Dorothy Day immediately recognized that the pacifist position would become more troublesome, as this letter, which she sent to all the Houses and farms and published in the January 1942 *Catholic Worker*, indicated:

Dear Fellow Workers in Christ:

Lord God, merciful God, our Father, shall we keep silent, or shall we speak? And if we speak, what shall we say?

. . . We are still pacifists. Our manifesto is the Sermon on the Mount, which means that we will try to be peacemakers. Speaking for many of our conscientious objectors, we will not participate in armed warfare or in making munitions, or by buying government bonds to prosecute the war, or in urging others to these efforts.

. . . We understand, of course, that there is and that there will be great differences of opinion even among our own groups as to how much collaboration we can have with the government in times like these. . . . there will be many continuing to work with us from choice, who do not agree with us as to our position on war, conscientious objection, etc. But we beg that there will be mutual charity and forbearance among us all.

This letter . . . is to state our position in this most difficult time.

Because of our refusal to assist in the prosecution of war and our insistence that our collaboration be one for peace, we may find ourselves in difficulties. But we trust in the generosity and understanding of our government and our friends, to permit us to continue, to use our paper to 'preach Christ crucified.'[73]

Members of other peace organizations applauded her position. When Clarence E. Pickett, the Executive Secretary of the American Friends Service Committee, read the *Catholic Worker*'s Pearl Harbor editorial, he told Day that he "thanked God and took courage." He would "fully expect" the *Catholic Worker*'s viewpoint to be shared by any Quaker, Mennonite, or Church of the Brethren paper. He knew that pacifism "quite as naturally springs from the deeper spiritual roots of a devout Catholic." But because the institutional Catholic Church had not "historically maintained a consistent pacifist testimony," Dorothy Day's word contained "a special weight."[74]

There continued to be much discussion among Catholic Workers about their proper role. Some felt that they should be silent about the war, only concentrating on the works of mercy and keeping the movement alive so that they could help reconstruct the world afterwards.[75] Joseph Zarrella, who worked with the American Friends Service Committee during the war, recalled that it was a most painful time to be a pacifist. "Everybody wanted to go off and fight for justice."[76]

But Dorothy Day and her *Catholic Worker* never budged from a comprehensive pacifism. In a letter written early in 1942, she outlined her editorial plans to Church authorities. She explained that she intended to concentrate on peace in future issues. She assured the hierarchy that if asked to cease, she would "of course, obey immediately." But then she mentioned ever so gently that Church authorities had allowed "us" to continue publishing the pacifist point of view during the Spanish Civil War.[77]

Thus, a year after the Japanese attack, while Americans were spiritedly singing "Remember Pearl Harbor," the *Catholic Worker* headlined an article, "Forget Pearl Harbor." It suggested that Americans "humbly apologize and beg forgiveness for our past mistreatment of the Japanese people."[78]

The World War II years were thorny for the *Catholic Worker*. From time to time, FBI men visited its Mott Street headquarters, to check on those who had declared themselves conscientious objectors.[79] The agents were also amassing a substantial file on Dorothy Day and her "subversive" pacifist activities. Nearly six hundred pages, spanning a period of about thirty years, were recently declassified from the FBI's Dorothy Day-Catholic Worker file. Because the Bureau made its major investigation before the height of its surveillance powers during the Cold War, the Catholic Worker file is comparatively modest in design and detail. There is no indication, for instance, that the FBI watched the mail that came to the Houses of Hospitality. The size of the FBI's documentation on groups such as the Socialist Workers Party and the Black Panthers is, as Robert Ellsberg has pointed out, much more impressive.[80] Nevertheless, the FBI's Catholic Worker file illuminates some of the problems peculiar to a pacifist publication during times of national crisis.

The Catholic Worker movement first attracted serious FBI attention in 1940, when the Bureau was tipped that a radical group was using "The Dorothy Day Art Studio" in New York City as a front. Three months of "careful investigation" did not confirm the existence of such an Art Studio, but it did uncover information about a certain Dorothy Day. She was described as having been "at one time a well-known Communist but at present a Catholic convert residing in voluntary poverty and operating a shelter for the destitute on the Lower East Side." The FBI further identified her as publisher of the *Catholic Worker*, "widely read by Catholics."

Then the Bureau unearthed a much more suggestive reference on Day already on record, an index card bearing her name with the label, "Communist." Ellsberg described it as one of the file's "more extraordinary items." It described her as "a Russian who came to this country, visited Chicago in the spring of 1939 and attempted to interest people in Communistic activities; is doing same work in Harlem section of New York City; is editor and publisher of the *Catholic Worker*... in which the July-August, 1940 issue opposes the Compulsory Military Training Bill." Actually, as Ellsberg observes, this is a combined and confused version of the activities of Day and her friend the Baroness Catherine de Hueck Doherty, who was running a shelter called Friendship House in Harlem at the time.

Then, on December 10, 1942, the FBI's file began to fatten. A "reliable informant" phoned his supervisory agent. His remarks were recorded and a transcript made. On the basis of his conversation, the Catholic Worker movement was investigated on charges of sedition for the next two years, an effort that ultimately required the services of agents in twenty different American cities. The informant had avidly read the December 1942 issue of the *Catholic Worker*, which contained Day's front-page call to women to refuse to cooperate with the draft. "Say, listen," the informant began. "I think this Dorothy Day has gone off the reservation again. ... here is what she's doing now," he went on. "She is going out and persuading women to refuse to register in case the government registers them! Now on the initial list there are quite a few on it, also a couple of girls who are daughters of millionaires...." He was also upset about Day's pieces on the wartime mistreatment of Americans of Japanese descent. "Any Jap that seems to be up against it in this country," he said, "they try to give him help! It's cockeyed.

"I don't like it," he continued, discussing other instances of disguised sedition in the December 1942 issue. "From my religious standpoint, I'm getting pretty sick of it...." And there was not a single article in the "whole darn thing," he added, "that doesn't tingle—well, I'll put it this way: It's almost complete pacifism." He had one more charge to level: the *Catholic Worker* was "stirring up a Negro question about race equality and God knows, you know how bad that is!"

The informant's supervisor, an agent named Conroy, brought this information straight to Director J. Edgar Hoover, who ordered a new investigation to determine "whether the publication of this paper constitutes a violation of the sedition statutes." Meanwhile, the original informant, acting only on the basis of his penny copies of the *Catholic Worker* and his patriotism, provided the Bureau with two galvanizing background memos. One opened with this ominous warning: "I realize I am messing around with dynamite in discussing this publication.... Please note the article 'Forget Pearl Harbor.' This article itself is just one nice mess of disguised sedition. As a matter of fact, I think the whole group should be put in jail until the end of the war.

"Last but not least," the memo concluded, "there are two columns titled 'farming commune'; notice the sickle at the side of the article.... The writer of this happens to be a Catholic but I place my country first and I believe that here is a nest of people that are using the Church as a window dressing to carry on something that is quite sinister.... Personally I don't like it a bit."

The other memo was entitled "Something to Think About," and gave this summary: "Dorothy Day was at one time an 'out in the open red.' Next she supposedly refudiated it [*sic*]. Then we found her running her Catholic flophouse and commune in New York. In a short time she started playing around with the leaders of the National Maritime Union. Whenever there was an affair to draw in the intellectual Reds, she was around. Several weeks ago her paper had an article giving praise, in a way, to the Jap people.

"The December issue is certainly fine reading," the memo continued. "It has plenty of questionable items that are of a hocifistic nature [*sic*]. Now the Day woman has collected together forty-eight women who declare they will defy the law (names attached)."

This shocking information mobilized the FBI's Internal Security Division, and agents were sent around the country, to Philadelphia, Cleveland, Detroit, Buffalo—apparently, wherever there was a House of Hospitality. It proved difficult indeed to pin down the elusive nature of the Catholic Worker movement's brand of subversion. The FBI decided Day and her colleagues were quite clever in camouflaging their sedition. Wendell Berge, Assistant Attorney General, was of the opinion that the *Catholic Worker* was "a 'front' publication of the Communist Party." His proof? A passage in the paper that stated, "so that we may have, if need be, a 'Christ Inn' in every parish come the revolution or whatever the future may hold." He was certain that this sentence had sinister implications. J. Edgar Hoover wanted to know what this "Council of Perfection" alluded to in several *Catholic Worker* pieces was all about. He had a hunch that it was some kind of anti-draft group based in New York City. He himself thought the Catholic Workers were operating some sort of underground "haven" for conscientious objectors. As a result, the investigation turned to Maryfarm in Easton, Pennsylvania. Several agents slipped into the rural community for a tour and "spent hours conversing with some of the twenty-three occupants there." Devising some excuse, they also poked at length into the library, but discovered only "literature of a religious nature" there. The agents concluded that the Catholic Worker farm was a "mysterious place" that sheltered "dirty people" who "take the attitude that the world owes them a living." Maryfarm, they stated, was "a hanging out place for people who will not work." Furthermore, "It was the opinion of the agents that the occupants of Maryfarm are of low mentality and moral standards."

Meanwhile, Dorothy Day almost made Hoover's supreme line-up—his "Custodial Detention List" which included the most feared radical elements of all: those who should be arrested and interned in time of war, to preserve national security. On April 3, 1941—eight months before the United States entered World War II—Hoover filed a memorandum with the Special Defense Unit of the Justice Department, recommending that Day be added to this list, "in the event of a national emergency." For the next six months, FBI agents checked into her background, using such sources as the Board of Health, Immigration Service at Ellis Island, and for some reason, the New York telephone directory, all with "negative" results. The New York Chancery office was cooperative in answering the Bureau's questions. It stated that the Catholic Worker had never "requested nor been granted permission by the Church to use the name 'Catholic Worker' " —and that this had caused "no end of trouble" in the way of "frequent complaints by members of the diocese." But the Chancery also mentioned Catholic Workers' "sincerity." At the end of this investigation, agents could only report that Day's "work and relief ideas [are] radical compared to those generally accepted today, but Church officials believe her to be an honest and sincere Catholic, having entirely given up Communism."

On February 3, 1942, the Justice Department issued its conclusion as to Dorothy Day's "dangerousness." She was "tentatively" placed in "Group C"—the list reserved for those "individuals believed to be the least dangerous and who need not be restricted in absence of additional information, but should be subjected to general surveillance." And pending confirmation of her supposed Russian birth, Day was also classified as a "naturalized citizen."

Finally, in June 1944, following four years of investigation, the Justice Department sent Hoover a memo stating that there was inadequate documentation to support the prosecution of Day and the Catholic Worker movement for sedition. Her file was apparently closed — until the next time Catholic Workers appeared "to engage in activities of a questionable nature."[81] The movement's next significant tangle with the FBI would not be too long in coming.

But Hoover's FBI was not the only group that questioned the patriotism of Day and her associates. Reaction from other publications to *Catholic Worker* pacifism was often bitter. For instance, the *Denver-Register* remarked:

> The *Catholic Worker* has promoted some strange things. Its latest is a Committee to Feed the Axis, on the idea that the enemy will be turned into a friend if we send him food. Does not Christian love of our enemies sometimes insist that we forcibly bring these foes back to their senses when they go berserk, just as a father must punish an erring son? It is Christian duty today for Americans to protest Christianity against attempted extinction. To argue that complete pacifism is called for is to break with all Christian tradition.[82]

The article concluded with a recommendation of Archbishop Francis Spellman's "excellent book," *The Road to Victory*, which summarized "the correct attitude of the Church in New York towards the war."

The *Catholic Worker's* unpopular pacifist stand accelerated the decline in circulation that had started during the Spanish Civil War. "The pacifism you preach is false, unpatriotic, and dangerous," one disaffected reader wrote. She would not make another contribution to the movement until Dorothy Day assured her that "not one cent" of her contribution would be spent for "pacifist propaganda." A notation on the margin of the letter gave the guarantee: "Yes, we'll buy beans for soup."[83] The Rev. Charles Owen Rice disassociated his Catholic Radical Alliance from the Catholic Worker movement over the peace issue, a decision he was to regret in later years.[84] By 1945, the bundle copies had reached a low of 27,500. Still, the single subscriber copies rose during the war to a new total of 23,000. Apparently while organized groups — churches, parish organizations, schools — opposed the *Catholic Worker's* pacifism, many individual subscribers did not.

During World War II, the Catholic Worker movement lost many members, some to the armed services, some to the C.O. camps. Soon Houses of Hospitality closed their doors for lack of personnel; by 1944, only nine of the thirty-two remained open, and only seven farms operated.[85] And certainly support for Day's brand of pacifism was not unanimous; hence, there were additional defectors. Indeed, in the words of one observer, "The only thing like a split" among Catholic Workers "came as a result of the *Catholic Worker's* pacifist stand during World War II. Many of the most militant and energetic" Catholic Workers "simply were not pacifists — or found they were not after Pearl Harbor."[86] A letter from one of the Houses of Hospitality to Dorothy Day summarized the feelings of many in the movement:

> Damn war! Damn Pacifism and stands!... How I wish you weren't a heretic!
> And sometimes I wish that I were one too. But to agree with you means cutting
> off from a much larger world and that pain is one you must know well, so that
> my anguish of separation is meager in comparison.
>
> Please pray for me.... It will be a new world to face—new attitudes, new
> viewpoints. I wouldn't be half so grim about it could I bring the Catholic
> Worker [movement] with me—but I can't.[87]

Abigail·McCarthy, who volunteered at the Minneapolis House to replace drafted male volunteers, remembered that she felt "the [Catholic] Worker [movement] was the answer to Christ's call to serve the poor," but she could not reconcile herself to "Dorothy Day's unyielding pacifism."[88] (But later, as a columnist for *Commonweal* and other magazines, McCarthy transmitted many other Catholic Worker ideas.)

Like Houses of Hospitality in Pittsburgh and elsewhere, the Seattle House stopped distributing or reading the *Catholic Worker*. According to its correspondent to the New York House, the Rev. H.A. Reinhold, the paper "was filled almost entirely with 'pacifism' and tended to arouse the 'pacifists' to new outbursts that were far from pacifist." So, like other nonpacifist Houses, the Seattle House read and distributed the non-absolutist *Chicago Catholic Worker* instead.[89] The situation was even worse in the Los Angeles House, where some Catholic Workers burned bundles of the *Catholic Worker* as soon as the paper arrived from New York.[90]

Internecine dissent so rent the Catholic Worker Houses that in June 1940 Day sent them all an ultimatum. "We know," she began, "that there are those who are members of Catholic Workers groups throughout the country who do not stand with us on this issue." She admitted that "We have not been able to change their views through what we have written in the paper, or by letters, or by personal conversation." The dissidents still wished "to be associated with us, to perform the corporal works of mercy."[91] She was not of the opinion that those who performed the works of mercy must be absolute pacifists, but in other cases where Catholic Workers were actually suppressing the paper, she felt that disassociation was necessary.

Day repeated these points two months later at a Catholic Worker retreat at Maryfarm. She had sent out a call to all the Houses of Hospitality: seventy-five Workers came, perhaps wondering if it would be their last official gathering.[92] At the retreat's conclusion, the issues of pacifism and conscientious objection were frankly discussed. Day told her delegates that the Catholic Worker movement was pacifist, from its genesis and always. According to Stanley Vishnewski, "she made it clear that anyone who did not wish to be associated with the movement in its pacifist stand should leave the work." Day further declared that Houses actively opposing the stand taken by the *Catholic Worker* "to the extent of suppressing the paper," ought to "disassociate themselves" from the movement. Those who disagreed with the pacifist stand but still wished "to remain part of the movement not in active opposition" were "at liberty to do so." She added, "We are only too happy to continue in this way."[93]

And that is exactly what happened. The band of Chicago Catholic Workers including Thomas Sullivan, John Cogley, and James O'Gara, continued for a time to perform the works of mercy and publish the *Chicago Catholic Worker*, in which they could express their more qualified view on pacifism. As the war approached, Cogley and several others were becoming interventionists, arguing that the conditions necessary for a just war were present in the conflict with Hitler.[94] Later, Cogley admitted that he had "long found it hard" to take the *Catholic Worker* "very seriously" on the question of pacifism because what it had to say usually struck him as "simplistic, evasive, and even sentimental. But I am ready," he said, "to admit these very weaknesses may have been the *Worker*'s great strength. Its position has been so extreme that it succeeded in making it impossible for nonpacifists like me to accept violence unthinkingly."[95]

But Cogley and the Chicago group never sought to insert their opinions into the New York *Catholic Worker*; so while there was much dissent within the movement, that paper's pacifist stand was never compromised. According to Joseph Zarrella, "During World War II, the paper was *united* on the pacifism question. No one on the paper ever disagreed with Dorothy on that."[96] The self-censorship that Florence Weinfurter had first observed in the Thirties continued to guarantee a staff united behind Day's principles. The movement's emphasis on personal responsibility and direct action contributed to this self-expurgation. If people disagreed strongly with any aspect of the movement or the paper, they were encouraged, Quaker-fashion, to secede politely and start their own ventures. Eventually, after intense soul-searching, Cogley broke with the movement over the pacifist issue and joined the army. In June 1941, the *Chicago Catholic Worker* was discontinued. But Dorothy Day remained on friendly terms with the dissidents. Before going to war, Sullivan and Cogley visited her in New York. Day greeted them as close members of her family, though she tried to dissuade them one more time.[97]

And yet there were occasional bright moments for her during the war. By 1943, the number of individual subscribers was again increasing. James F. Powers' account of his prison experiences for noncompliance with the draft law ("Night in the County Jail") brightened the May 1943 issue. And that fall a party of several young men in uniform came to Mott Street to talk to Day about her work and outlook. All night long, they talked of war and peace and humanity and the state. Later Day would recall two of the young men, brothers Joseph and John Kennedy.[98]

In September of 1943, Day announced that she was taking a year-long absence from the movement and the paper. She was undoubtedly saddened by the decline in membership and bundle orders. And to complete her troubles, Peter Maurin's health was beginning to fail. Still, she remained ardently pacifist. In her last column before Arthur Sheehan took over as editor and publisher, she made that clear:

> One thing, of course, I wish to stress, and that is that there is no change in
> my convictions in regard to War and Peace and the means to attain it. I have
> been and still am a Christian pacifist, opposing class war, race war, civil war
> and international war. . . . if conscription comes for women, I still will not
> register, and if breaking of the law means still further retirement, of course, I
> shall consider myself privileged to go to jail.[99]

During the next year, Day spent time in a convent and also with her daughter.
While on retreat she had time to remember all the young people who had
helped start the Catholic Worker movement. So many were gone now, on Navy
ships, in Army tanks, in weapons factories, in conscientious objector camps. In
the December 1943 *Catholic Worker*, she mentioned O'Gara and Sullivan, now in
the armed forces on the Gilbert Islands. She had taken a leave, she wrote, "to
have time to gather and hold in my prayers all these members of our family, all
these dear to us."[100]

By October 1944, Day's name was back on the mast as editor and publisher.
When the war ended in 1945, she did not rejoice. The *Catholic Worker's* account
of the German surrender tersely noted: "On April 25, the feast of St. Mark,
advanced units of the armies of the U.S. and of the U.S.S.R. met and shook
hands in Germany. Capitalism met and fraternized with Communism over the
dead body of Nazism in the homeland of the latter." Almost prophetically, the
article continued: "Already people in this country are talking of the 'inevitable'
war which is sure to come between the two remaining great powers of the
earth."[101]

Many Americans rejoiced when the war was ended — and two Japanese cities
spectacularly destroyed — by a formidable new weapon. Newspaper headlines
everywhere throbbed with excitement over the untold promise represented by
the opening of the nuclear age. But Dorothy Day recognized immediately what
the awesome new weapon portended. Even before the beginning of the nuclear
era, she had predicted the folly of the arms race. In 1938, if not earlier, she had
stated that "as long as men trust to the use of force — only a superior, a more
savage and brutal force will overcome the enemy."[102] And so, about Hiroshima
and Nagasaki Day wrote:

> Mr. Truman was jubilant. . . . True man. What a strange name, come to think
> of it. . . . Truman is a true man of his time in that he was jubilant. He was not a
> son of God, brother of Christ, brother of the Japanese, jubilating as he did. . . .
> *Jubilate Deo.* We have killed 318,000 Japanese.
> . . . they are vaporized, our Japanese brothers, scattered, men, women and
> babies, to the four winds, over the seven seas. Perhaps we will breathe their
> dust into our nostrils, feel them in the fog of New York on our faces, feel them
> in the rain on the hills of Easton.[103]

In a telegram sent to President Truman, Day and her followers expressed
their horror over his "jubilation over the havoc inflicted upon Japan. We beg
you in the name of Christ crucified," the telegram implored, "to do all in your
power to cause this abomination of desolation, this new discovery to be buried

forever. Far better to be destroyed ourselves than to destroy others with such fiendish and inhuman ingenuity."[104]

But the *Catholic Worker's* conscience was clear. Led by Dorothy Day, it had maintained a consistently pacifist stand despite a major loss of circulation, the closing of most of its Houses of Hospitality, the bitter opposition from both foes and old friends. Yes, the price the *Catholic Worker* paid for its pacifism was sometimes staggering. In the July-August 1947 issue, Dorothy Day noted that only ten Houses of Hospitality remained. "They are neither as they were before in the depths of depression and with the energy of emergency and crisis upon them and the new-found joy of a fellowship in the lay apostolate;" she wrote, "nor are they centers of Catholic Action as Peter Maurin envisaged them. We are in a transition state and we need to do a great deal of writing and talking to work out programs of action and a modus vivendi."[105]

But though the *Catholic Worker* was bruised, it was not broken. Now it turned to rebuilding the world, offering its moral succor to returning soldiers. "Many former GIs," began an article in the March 1947 issue, "are today hesitant sheep wandering with both ears cocked for the clear, confident voice of their Shepherd. They are wondering about the justice of their various activities in the past war . . . because the promised era of peace and justice grows daily more improbable."[106] And within four years, many of these same soldiers were at war in Korea. How the *Catholic Worker*, led by Dorothy Day, survived the first major conflict of the nuclear age—and those conflicts that followed—is the story of the next chapter.

ADE BETHUNE

VII: Civil Disobedience and Divine Obedience

The ghastly carnage of Hiroshima and Nagasaki underscored the destructive capability of the new atomic weapons, intensifying public fears about the prospect of nuclear annihilation. In September 1945, eighty-three percent of Americans polled acknowledged the "real danger" of "most city people on earth being killed by atomic bombs" in the event of another world conflict.[1] Now, in the years immediately following World War II, many Americans who had never opposed conventional warfare began to advocate and make respectable a "nuclear pacifism."

Meanwhile, from a World War II low of 50,500, the *Catholic Worker's* circulation rose by 1949 to 60,000. Although it is impossible to make a conclusive connection between public opinion and the paper's circulation, the *Catholic Worker* probably enjoyed increasing popularity because of Americans' general mood of limited pacifism based on self-interest. But the paper continued to denounce the immorality of the very concept of war. Rather than focus the *Catholic Worker's* energies on such causes as nuclear arms control and the improvement of international government, Dorothy Day—still an absolute pacifist—allotted much column space to the condemnation of conscription.[2]

In 1946 and 1947, the Catholic Worker movement teamed with other pacifist groups, including the War Resisters League, the Fellowship of Reconciliation, and the Committee on Nonviolent Revolution, to oppose President Harry Truman's proposed peacetime draft and Universal Military Training. When the draft was passed in 1948, the *Catholic Worker* continued to advocate noncooperation and publicized accounts of draft resisters' struggles. In April 1948 the paper reprinted the full, lengthy text of Father Hugo's "The Immorality of Conscription"; 75,000 pamphlet copies were also printed and distributed.[3]

But limited pacifism soon lost its appeal for many Americans. During the period from September 1949 to June 1950, several startling events unfolded. First, Communists occupied all of Mainland China; then the Soviets exploded their first atomic bomb. Communist North Korea attacked the Republic of South Korea; and Alger Hiss, a high-ranking diplomat who had accompanied President Roosevelt to the Yalta Conference, was linked to Communism and convicted of perjury. Meanwhile, newspaper reports indicated that Russia's nuclear bomb capability was aided by technical information from a spy ring headed by Klaus Fuchs, a German-born scientist, when the latter was arrested in England. Public anxiety over the atomic bomb soon coalesced with a general perception of a Soviet menace that was literally worldwide. The result was a national terror of anything even vaguely Communist. Soon Senator Joseph McCarthy was leading a crusade against the Communist subversion he and many other Americans believed to be smoldering in nearly every area of American life. Mandatory loyalty oaths and investigations into "Un-American Activities" became symbols of the period.

As usual during wartime, the more moderate pacifist groups disbanded or changed their emphasis; the radical groups met much public hostility. Nevertheless, the *Catholic Worker* fared better during the Korean War than it had during World War II. Despite the Chancery's uneasiness, the paper retained the name "Catholic"—a kind of "protective coloration" which provided a measure of respectability.[4] Also, Dorothy Day's ever-increasing public speaking tours— and her rising stature as a loyal, traditional Catholic who happened to be a radical social activist—helped draw support. By 1950, the paper's circulation at 63,000 had clearly recovered from its World War II slump; then it experienced a moderate decline, dropping to 60,000 in 1952 and to 58,000 in 1953. But by 1959 it was back at 63,000; and by 1960, at 65,000. (Again, caution dictates against making an exact correlation between these fluctuations and the decade's events. But the demise of McCarthyism in the late Fifties certainly meant a climate more favorable to the expression of alternative viewpoints such as the *Catholic Worker*'s. And by then the United States was not directly involved in any war, which also may have increased the pacifist publication's acceptance.)

Another factor in the *Catholic Worker*'s comparative stability during the Korean War may have been the paper's moderation in criticizing the war. Of course its stance was pacifist. In the first issue following the invasion by the North Koreans, Dorothy Day reiterated her position against all war. "It is heartbreaking once again to see casualty lists in the *New York Times*," she wrote. "We believe that not only atomic weapons must be outlawed, but all war, and that the social order must be restored in Christ. . . ."[5] In the same issue, associate editor Robert Ludlow declared there was "an immediate need of individual resistance to war and all that it implies." He argued that war was basically immoral—murder— and that the pacifism Christ expounded in his Sermon on the Mount should be the basis of international morality. But Ludlow did not condemn individual soldiers, only "those who knowingly participate" in war.[6]

And Dorothy Day focused not on the specific wrongdoing of the United States, but on the centrality of love in resolving the conflict. "We are on the side of the poor," she asserted. She identified "the poor" as "our soldiers in Korea fighting in zero weather, thousands of them suffering and tortured and dying. . . ." The poor were also "the Koreans themselves, north and south, who have been bombed out, burnt out in the rain of fire from heaven." Then she pointed out that all on both sides were "our brothers, made to the image and likeness of

God, temples of the Holy Ghost."[7] Articles condemning the immorality of conscription continued to be staple *Catholic Worker* features, but there was also a warning to objectors not to oppose war "with pride, with condemnation of others, with bitterness," lest they make their viewpoint also "questionable."[8] And during the entire Korean War period, the *Catholic Worker* mentioned only one occurrence of direct, protesting action — in December 1950, when Ammon Hennacy picketed the Phoenix Post Office to oppose President Truman's declaration of a state of emergency.[9]

On other issues of the day, the *Catholic Worker* said little. In the January 1951 issue, Robert Ludlow commented: "We have our secret police, our thought control agencies, our over-powering bureaucracy."[10] But the paper did not really address the McCarthy phenomenon until the height of the hysteria in 1953. Then, in the March issue, Ludlow lamented that "guilt by association is fast becoming the accepted method of judging." He found it "frightening indeed" that this pervaded "all levels of society." Worse, "our patriotic Catholics and our wretched publications do not see this."[11]

Dorothy Day was silent, perhaps now following Peter Maurin's principle that Catholic Workers should be "announcers" and not "denouncers."[12] Faced with another hot war in less than a decade, and an oppressive cold war, the general mood of pacifists in the early Fifties was bleak indeed, and the *Catholic Worker* editors were no exception. At the time, Dorothy Day confessed: "It grows ever harder to talk of love in the face of a scorning world."[13] "Sometimes," wrote Robert Ludlow about a year later, "our fellow pacifists who are not Catholics wonder why we continue in the Church, wonder because most Catholics are not pacifists and very few priests are and the official policy seems to be to encourage hatred of Communists and to prepare the laity for war with Russia. Yes," he went on, "we are weary of all this and carry on with a sort of automatic faith in our position and a conviction that one has to go on. . . ."[14]

A letter Day wrote in June 1952 also showed a tone of discouragement. She was afraid that "most American Catholics" had hardly reached the awareness that "modern war presents a moral problem," even though they faced "perhaps the most gigantic manifestation of imperialism and practical atheism that the world has ever seen." She deplored a widespread tendency among Catholics to assume that "*whatever* is necessary for offensive war is legitimate." She felt that American Catholics' "tendency to conformity and patriotism" was imperilling their "religious values." While she didn't expect everyone to be a conscientious objector, she found it "a tragic comment on our society that most don't even consider war a problem." Day confessed her fear that the Church would "surrender the vision of Christ for acceptance, for conformity, for assimilation." If there were a clear choice to be made between Americanism and Christ, as in nineteenth-century France and twentieth-century Spain, she added, "the Catholic knows his way." She acknowledged that in the United States, the choice was not yet clear; "but *someone* must criticize the tendencies that go to secularize our culture and bring that choice closer and closer."[15]

Accordingly, the *Catholic Worker* denounced specific, glaring evils, for which it was often widely excoriated. It assailed the anti-Communist Smith and McCarran Acts, which Dorothy Day considered totalitarianism of the far right. The Smith Act criminalized the teaching or advocacy of the violent overthrow of the United States government, or membership in any organization which held such views. The McCarran Internal Security Act forbade radical aliens from entering the United States, allowed the deportation of foreign Communists, and established a dictatorial control board. Of it, the *Catholic Worker* wrote:

> We now have an official police State. We now have federal agents melo-dramatically banging on doors at 2 o'clock in the morning . . . and dragging non-citizens from their families. People charged with no crime other then that they have not the permission of the State to live. . . . The pseudo-democracy of our times merely substitutes for the absolutism of a fictitious entity conceived as being more than the people who compose it. And now it is called the State.[16]

The *Catholic Worker* also spoke up for Julius and Ethel Rosenberg, who had been accused of atomic spying after the arrest of Klaus Fuchs in England in February 1950. The Rosenbergs were found guilty and sentenced to be executed in June 1953. As the day drew nearer, the *Catholic Worker* increased its outcries against their fate. "On both sides," Robert Ludlow wrote, "it is prejudice and not a concern for the facts in themselves that determines the attitude taken. It is not a just age we live in," he declared, citing the public's fear of holding "unpopular opinions," and teachers' reluctance to "teach the truth, as they see it."[17] The Rosenbergs protested their innocence right to the end. Although Pope Pius XII made a plea for clemency, they were put to death on the evening of June 19, 1953 — while Dorothy Day was at the farm. Later in the *Catholic Worker* she recounted her thoughts that summer evening, when "the air was fragrant with the smell of honeysuckle. Out under the hedge at Peter Maurin Farm," she wrote, "the black cat played with a grass snake, and the newly cut grass was fragrant in the evening air." In her most personal style, Day told of bathing her grandson just before the Rosenbergs were electrocuted: "My heart was heavy, as I soaped Nickie's dirty little legs, knowing that Ethel Rosenberg must have been thinking with all the yearning of her heart, of her own soon-to-be-orphaned children." If the Rosenbergs were indeed spies for Russia, then "they were doing what we also do in other countries." Day observed that in their way they had been "serving a philosophy, a religion." And how distorted religion can become, she went on, "when Christian prelates sprinkle holy water on scrap metal, to be used for obliteration bombing, and name bombers for the Holy Innocents, for Our Lady of Mercy; [and] bless a man about to press a button which releases death on fifty thousand human beings, including little babies, children, the sick, the aged, the innocent as well as the guilty." She concluded: "Let us have no part with the vindictive State and let us pray for Ethel and Julius Rosenberg. May their souls, as well as the souls of the faithful departed, rest in peace."[18]

Conservatives had long taken issue with the *Catholic Worker*'s willingness to defend Communists as "our brothers," to join with them in mutual opposition to certain aspects of capitalism. Now, fueled by the national anti-Communist psychosis, they reacted stridently to the paper's condemnation of the Smith and McCarran Acts, and its support of the Rosenbergs. Senator Joseph McCarthy himself took notice of the *Catholic Worker*. His shrill alarms put some pressure on the movement. McCarthyites hinted darkly of the paper's Communist ties and nicknamed Dorothy Day "Moscow Mary," as some reactionaries still call her.[19]

Among the many publications that censured the *Catholic Worker* during the Red scare years was the *National Police Gazette*. In 1954, it charged that Day's paper was "one of the most extraordinary publications in the United States" and labelled it an "instrument of the Communist conspiracy." Castigating Day for her piece on the Rosenbergs, the article identified her "specialty" as "prescribing pro-Communist pills with a religious sugar coating, as strange a concoction as one can find in the world today. In all [its] years," the article concluded, "the outpourings of this publication which exploits the name Catholic have been more odd than influential."[20]

Reviewing Day's *The Long Loneliness* in the *New Republic*, Francis E. McMahon called Catholic Worker pacifism "another excess. Extreme pacifism," he wrote, "has no sanction from theology, philosophy, or common sense. . . . War remains a legitimate ultimate resort against the unjust aggressor."[21] Like many readers who wrote to Dorothy Day's paper, a priest asserted that Catholic Workers were not Catholic at all. He challenged them to "come out in the open, declare yourselves Bolshevik Communists, and fight the Church like men." Furthermore, Catholic Workers were "ungrateful parasites" who "bite the hand of the country that feeds [them]." As for the *Catholic Worker*, it "boasts of and encourages the way of life of loafers, draft dodgers, traitors to their country and sensational publicity-hungry psychotics."[22]

Before long, Day's post-World War II contact at the Chancery, Msgr. Edward R. Gaffney, was questioning her about the paper's use of the word "Catholic" in its title. Undoubtedly thinking of the McCarthy witch hunts, Day responded in a long, diplomatic letter that human truth "has to grow organically, one mind meeting another mind in the struggle for agreement only to go on to more struggle for more truth." Such organic growth was "seldom an orderly, neat affair."[23]

Nevertheless, according to Michael Harrington, who joined the staff in 1951, the danger of anti-Catholic Worker violence was "omnipresent" during the McCarthy era. In June 1951, the first anniversary of the beginning of the Korean War, he and a fellow picketer represented the Catholic Worker movement in a New York anti-war march. By the end of the demonstration, Harrington's companion had been punched squarely in the jaw and knocked over by an irate anti-Communist who was sure that Catholic Workers were camouflaged Reds. Soon after, Harrington was assigned to be picket captain because he was Irish. He recalled that when the police would demand to know the identity of the group's leader, he would "step forward" and state his name. Usually there was "a stunned silence," followed by "some remark like, 'Michael, my boy, what are you doing with *these* people?' " One time Harrington and company were picketing the British and Irish Railways office in Rockefeller Center. After the "regular conversation," a baffled sergeant inquired, " 'But Michael, how can you march against the Irish Railways?' 'That,' " Harrington informed him, " 'is the North of Irish Railways.' " Harrington observed that "the law gave us most friendly protection the rest of the day."[24]

The *Catholic Worker* office needed such comic relief in the early Fifties. A very conservative FBI director regularly dispatched his agents to check up on the paper and its staff. Thomas Sullivan, who served as an associate editor from the October, 1947 through the April, 1955 issues, described the tension of those days, including one when St. Joseph's was "contacted by the FBI agents on three different occasions. Their presence still makes me sweat," he acknowledged, "no matter how many times we have met them."[25] Only six months later, he remarked: "I don't know how it is with you, but we have had a steady run of FBI agents paying us visits."[26] However, Thomas Cornell, who first came to St. Joseph's House of Hospitality in 1953, was unaware of "any kind of paranoia about being watched" during the rest of the Fifties. "I don't remember anyone ever expressing concern about surveillance," he said, "or [about] being blacklisted in the future because of what we were doing now." Monica Cornell pointed out that "always, taking care of the people who came to the house" was a distraction from such anxieties.[27]

Dorothy Day seems not to have been much ruffled by the presence of federal investigators. "Some FBI man by the name of Daly came down to query me about one of our friends who is a conscientious objector," she announced in her January 1954 column. "He asked the usual questions as to how long I had known him, how he stated his position as c.o. or pacifist, whether or not he believed in defending himself. Evidently, one of my answers offended him," she went on, "because he pulled back his jacket and displayed the holster of a gun under his armpit, which he patted bravely as he said, 'I believe in defending myself.' I could not but think," she recounted, " 'How brave a man, defending himself with his gun against us unarmed women and children hereabouts.' "[28]

Her remarks nearly launched another FBI investigation of the Catholic Worker movement. Special Agent Daly denied that he had ever displayed his firearm, even though, as the FBI's file reported, he had been piqued by Miss Day, who "repeatedly endeavored to engage him in a discussion of pacifism." The Bureau also noted in its file Dorothy Day's opposition to the Smith and McCarran Acts, and her spoken criticism of the House Un-American Activities Committee. The FBI concluded that Day's activities "strongly suggest that she is either consciously or unconsciously being used by Communist groups. From our experience with her it is obvious that she maintains a very hostile and belligerent attitude toward the Bureau and makes every effort to castigate the Bureau whenever she feels inclined to do so."[29] This profile, prepared by Director J. Edgar Hoover himself, was especially derogatory. It characterized Day as "a very erratic and irresponsible person." Ellsberg has noted the ironic appending of this profile to a letter in which Hoover notes that the "FBI is strictly a fact-finding agency and does not draw conclusions or make evaluations as to the character and integrity of any organization, publication or individual."[30] Hoover then placed Day on a special "no contact list," meaning "no further attempt be made to interview subject regarding her comments in the *Catholic Worker*, since any additional contacts may well be distorted by her and result in further unfavorable comments regarding the Bureau."[31]

The next letter in the file declared that Day was not only mentally unstable, but "something of a fascist." Apparently the FBI did not view this as a contradiction of its earlier characterization of her as "consciously or unconsciously being used by Communist groups."

Such judgments represented a reversal of the relationship which had existed between the Catholic Worker movement and the FBI since the late Forties. Then, after nearly a decade of investigation, the Bureau had concluded that the movement was not a Red plot to infiltrate the Catholic Church and gave it a grudging respect. The Bureau's file during this period contains comparatively non-judgmental appraisals of Dorothy Day and her associates, describing their work as "pacifist and anti-Communist." Now the FBI was not so sure.

Neither were the FBI's correspondents. For several years, a few dozen citizens had written to the FBI to ascertain how Communistic the Catholic Workers were. According to Ellsberg, such letters "increased considerably" during the Cold War Fifties. One letter writer expressed concern over the proximity of one Catholic Worker community to an isolated coastline, "ideally suited for smuggling persons or material into the country." A schoolgirl wanted J. Edgar Hoover's help for a term paper on "Dorothy Day and the Communist Party."[32]

Dorothy Day seems to have taken FBI probing in stride. She never appeared uncomfortable in the presence of agents. When they visited St. Joseph's House of Hospitality, she was sure to express her views on pacifism in no uncertain terms. And Catholic Workers continued to protest redbaiting by their visible presence at functions of the Communist Party. A Catholic Worker always spoke at the Mayday Communist rallies in Union Square, at least into the early Sixties. "That way, if they smeared anybody for associating with Communists, they'd have to smear us too," recalled Thomas Cornell. "And to smear the Catholic Worker [movement] even by then was difficult," he said, partly because of the word "Catholic" in its name. He sensed that by the mid-Fifties, Catholic Workers' "integrity" was recognized, "at least in some quarters."[33] However, frequent visits by investigators may indeed have had a chilling effect on the *Catholic Worker*; at least, compared to its outspokenness during World War II, the paper seemed a bit subdued during the dark days of McCarthyism and the Korean War. But muted resistance to the war was probably not a *direct* result from intimidation by McCarthyism. And like most pacifists of the time, Catholic Workers were despondent at the buildup of arms and Americans' general disinclination towards the cause of peace.

Yet during those bleak days, the paper itself was outstanding. If the world was doomed, Day seemed to be saying in her personalist way, at least the *Catholic Worker* could strive for quality. And the first post-World War II decade — 1946 to 1956 — saw probably the highest, most consistent quality in the paper's history. Thomas Cornell recalled the environment he perceived in 1953 when he first visited Day and the *Catholic Worker* office: "It was a wonderfully rich atmosphere, the best place to be . . . exciting, stimulating. It was like being parachuted into third-century Athens."[34]

Dorothy Day's column — changed from "Day by Day" to "On Pilgrimage" in the February 1946 issue — continued to be the paper's mainstay. But there were also moving pieces about Europe's postwar poor by Doris Ann Doran; Irene Mary Naughton's thoughtful articles on strikes and economic issues; John Cogley's occasional articles and reviews; and Gordon Zahn's accounts of his experiences with mentally retareded children at the Rosewood Training School in Owings Mills, Maryland.

By December 1951, Michael Harrington was an associate editor whose contributions appeared regularly. Thomas Sullivan recalled that when Harrington had first appeared at the door of St. Joseph's, then in his early twenties and clad in "a camel-hair coat," he had seemed to be just "another hand to help mail out the papers." Then, the already quite erudite Harrington tried writing his first piece for the *Catholic Worker*. Sullivan read it, but he "couldn't figure out what the hell this guy (was) saying!" So Sullivan passed the abstruse article to Dorothy Day, who commented, " 'What in the heavens does he mean? I can't make heads or tails. Give that back to him.' " Sullivan then decided to try out Harrington as a reviewer, and handed him a book. In the space of forty-five minutes, the newcomer had not only finished the book, but produced an able review. From then on, he was a contributor.[35]

Later, Michael Harrington would remember that "All I knew of the Catholic Worker when I walked into its House of Hospitality on Chrystie Street just off New York's Skid Row... was that it was as far Left as you could go within the Church. In those first innocent days when I had just begun to discover the complex world into which I had blundered," he continued, "Dorothy startled me over coffee one morning when I mentioned one of my favorite poets, Hart Crane.

" 'Oh that Hart,' she said. 'I used to have breakfast with him all the time when I was pregnant with Tamar.' "[36]

Harrington stayed two years. The Catholic Worker spirit affected him so profoundly that it almost led him to the penitentiary as a conscientious objector during the Korean War. A volunteer for the Army Medical Reserve, he endured several crises with military authorities who tried to get him to rifle practice. "What maintained and stiffened my will," he later wrote, "was that almost primitive Christian sense of mission that pervaded the Worker [movement]."[37] Eventually Harrington recorded his experiences with Dorothy Day and her associates in *The Other America*. The book became a topic of conversation in the intellectual circles of the Northeast corridor, came to the attention of President John F. Kennedy, and inspired the beginning of his anti-poverty program.

SERMON TO THE BIRDS 1964

Sullivan, a friend of John Cogley's who had been with the Chicago Catholic Worker group before World War II, was a regular contributing editor during the postwar decade. His "Mott Street" and "Chrystie Street" columns presented humorous insights and observations as he chronicled the events of the New York Catholic Worker family. Sullivan was joined by Robert Ludlow, whose learned analyses of anarchism, pacifism, and mental illness (often based on his experiences at the Rosewood Training School) added substantial depth to the postwar *Catholic Worker*. Occasionally, Ludlow's sophisticated diatribes were rather obscure, prompting Day to write in her column on one occasion that she personally stood behind "everything Bob Ludlow writes, though his way of expressing himself is at times peculiar, to say the least." With characteristic humor she admitted, "I don't think the majority of our readers know what he is talking about when he says, 'The compulsion to revolt is explained as a manifestation of the libido.' "[38]

Quaker artist Fritz Eichenberg became a regular contributor of magnificent wood engravings in 1950. In the gloomy years of the early Fifties, the Catholic Worker movement was invigorated, too, by a colorful, old-time pacifist and anarchist. Descended from Quakers, Ammon Hennacy had sold the radical Socialist paper, *Appeal to Reason*; studied journalism under Willard Bleyer at the University of Wisconsin; joined the I.W.W.; and written, like Day, for the Socialist *Call*. Their common friends included Hugo and Livia Gellert, Claude McKay, Mike Gold, and Maurice Becker. Not until 1937 did Day and Hennacy meet, in Milwaukee, where Hennacy was busy living his self-proclaimed "One-Man Revolution." A World War I draft resister who had spent nearly two years in Atlanta federal prison for conspiracy (July 1917 to March 1919), Hennacy was especially attracted to Catholic Worker pacifism and tax resistance.[39]

In August 1952, Hennacy began to devote his multi-faceted energies to the Catholic Worker movement. His personal "Life at Hard Labor" series about his experiences as a migrant day laborer in the Southwest had brightened the pages of the *Catholic Worker* during much of the Forties; now Hennacy continued to write of his picketing and traveling about the countryside to spread the Catholic Worker message. "Every month his article came in," Dorothy Day recalled, "and every month, I am sure, each of us members of the staff was shamed by ... his true life of poverty and hard work, and his utterly consistent pacifism."[40] Often, Hennacy's comments were quite blunt:

> Truman and other politicians tell us the lie that we are defending freedom throughout the world against Communist imperialism. The fact is that we tried to defend a corrupt government in South Korea and the property of the New Korea Company whose exploitation caused the Korean peasant to have the lowest standard of living among seventy countries.... Likewise in Indo-China and the Dutch East Indies we have upheld the imperialism of the French and the Dutch. The only freedom our leaders are interested in is the freedom to exploit.[41]

Eternally in and out of jail, fearless, witty, and capable of enormous feats of physical endurance such as unrelieved days of fasting to protest each anniversary of the Hiroshima bombing, Hennacy was an idiosyncratic associate editor. The Catholic Worker Papers contain many of his letters to figures of such stature as Khrushchev, Kennedy, Castro, Tito, and Nehru. Hennacy dashed off quite a few letters to world leaders, inviting them to visit the Lower East Side, proselytizing for peace, and proudly enclosing copies of the latest *Catholic Worker*. Just before the 1960 Presidential election, he sent this note to Senator John F. Kennedy:

> In the heat of this campaign you have other things to do than to think about anarchists and pacifists, even if they are at the same time Catholics, as we are here at the Catholic Worker [movement]. We do not vote and we do not shoot and we are the most radical group you will find in this country. Yet we go to Mass and communion daily. . . . In the next issue I have in my column the reasons why we would not vote for you or for Nixon. Nevertheless, personally, I feel kindly toward you, and would always hope that you veered to the left rather than to the right.[42]

Compared to the turbulent Sixties, the Fifties were generally subdued, non-activist years. But Dorothy Day and Ammon Hennacy inspired Catholic pacifists, and others, to revive a time-honored kind of American activism in a creative fashion. During the years 1955-1961, they and other Catholic Workers were often jailed for various acts of civil disobedience to protest the prevailing cold war mentality of war preparations.

Their first act of protest occurred on June 15, 1955, when there was a full-scale dress rehearsal of the Civil Defense organizations in the United States, Canada, and Mexico. "Operation Alert" began at noon and continued until two p.m. the following day. In Washington, President Dwight Eisenhower and key Executive Department employees rushed to secret bomb shelters; across the nation, state and city Civil Defense authorities and the public were asked to cooperate by rehearsing their reactions to a nuclear attack, including participating in a ten-minute mock air raid drill. The degree of compliance with this request varied around the nation, but in New York City, it was comparatively high. The *New York Times* urged cooperation. "We hope and pray that day of horror will never come," it wrote. "But your duty and your self-interest require that you make ready for the worst by taking part in this drill."[43]

In New York, ten Catholic Workers and eighteen others from the War Resisters League and the Fellowship of Reconciliation, including A.J. Muste, sat quietly on their benches in City Hall Park when the sirens sounded the mock alert at five minutes after two. As was their custom, they had publicly announced their intended actions, notifying the Mayor of New York, the New York police, Associated Press, and United Press. With customary brashness, Ammon Hennacy had also notified the FBI that Catholic Workers intended to advise noncooperation with the drill. He added a personal note for the benefit of J. Edgar Hoover: "We are, as you know, subversives, though no more than always."[44] Soon, auxiliary police wearing elaborate uniforms studded "with much brass, stars, and ribbons of past battles," marched over and ordered the group to take shelter. When they refused they were arrested and detained for nine hours until they could each raise the fifteen hundred dollars for bail.[45]

In the next issue of the *Catholic Worker*, Ammon Hennacy explained their actions. "In the name of Jesus, Who is God, Who is Love, we will not obey this order to pretend to evacuate, to hide. In view of the certain knowledge the administration of this country has that there is no defense in atomic warfare," he wrote, "we know this drill is to be a military act in a cold war to instill fear, to prepare the collective mind for war." Catholic Workers, he said, "refuse to cooperate."[46] In a front-page story in the same issue, Dorothy Day explained that the demonstration was also intended to be "an act of public penance for having been the first people in the world to drop the atom bomb, [and] to make the hydrogen bomb." Perhaps anticipating Chancery criticism, she added: "We are engaging only ourselves in this action, not the Church. We are acting as individual Catholics."[47] Catholic Workers linked noncooperation with the air-raid drills to other forms of nonviolent resistance, including voluntary poverty, through which one could avoid the military-supporting income tax.[48]

On December 22, 1955, Judge Hyman Bushel found the group guilty of violating the New York State Defense Emergency Act of 1951, which made refusal to participate in a drill a misdemeanor subject to a year in jail or a fine of $500 or both. But the group was surprised to find they did not go to prison. According to an observer, Judge Bushel stressed that he did not intend to "make martyrs" of them. He could not understand the motivation of the non-religious defendants, he said. He concluded his opinion by praising Dorothy Day's work in the Catholic Worker movement, expressing his wish that "she hadn't pleaded guilty. I would have found a way of acquitting her," he said. "I know a way to do it. . . . The next time you come before me — if you do — plead not guilty."[49] The affair was duly noted by the *New York Times*, the *New York World Telegram*, and many other secular and religious publications. Writers for the *Chicago Tribune*, the *Pittsburgh Post Gazette, Harper's*, the *Progressive*, the *Nation*, and Murray Kempton in the New York *Post* approved the demonstrators' actions. *Catholic News*, the New York diocesan paper, criticized the Catholic Workers for disobeying the Church tradition of obedience to duly constituted authority, and the St. Louis *Catholic Register* filled two pages denouncing the demonstrators for disobeying the laws of state and theology.[50]

Commonweal was apparently the sole Catholic publication (besides the *Catholic Worker*, of course) that defended the pacifists. It identified two major issues: freedom of conscience — "how far may the State go toward compelling an individual to cooperate in what he believes to be wrong?" — and constitutional procedure — "to what extent may the Bill of Rights be suspended and the police power invoked against free speech and free assembly during a *mock* emergency?" The article concluded that Dorothy Day "has witnessed to the uncomfortable, the not 'respectable,' truths of Christianity. The example of her life rebukes most of us for our complacency." If "a woman like Dorothy Day" could be imprisoned in America for "bearing witness to the Gospel as she believed it must be witnessed to," *Commonweal* declared, "then a terrible thing has happened to our country."[51]

Meanwhile, the FBI had compiled pages of clippings on this act of civil disobedience. Although the pacifists had violated no federal laws, the Bureau tried to persuade the Justice Department to prosecute them on the basis of their seditious leaflet, "The Only Thing We Have to Fear," which had advocated nonregistration for the draft. The Attorney General's lengthy response pointed out that "advocacy" was a protected First Amendment right. The leaflet's line concerning the draft was "stated as part of a list of seven modes of conduct" and therefore was not the main point of the demonstration. "We feel," the brief concluded, "that it would be impractical to attempt to build a case based on a single phrase."[52] This was Hoover's third unsuccessful attempt to interest the federal government in prosecuting the Catholic Worker movement for sedition. (Thereafter, the FBI seems to have become less concerned with the Day and the movement; as Ellsberg has put it, the Bureau had "bigger fish to fry."[53])

For the next several years, Day, Hennacy, and other Catholic Workers continued to protest the air-raid drills, for which they were jailed. Before they repeated their demonstration in 1956, Day commented on the testing of the hydrogen bomb in a prominent editorial in the June issue of her paper. She wrote that this new weapon was more disturbing than "utter atheism," for the bomb was the ultimate result of equating God with country.[54] In court, Day told the judge that she had been writing about pacifism and social justice for twenty-four years in the *Catholic Worker*, and that she wanted now to offer her freedom to prove that she meant what she wrote.[55] On this occasion the demonstrators, including Day, got five days in jail.

About this time, Day was having another run-in with the law for other reasons, for which she became something of a media figure. In March 1956, she was summoned to appear before a city judge, to answer charges of being a slumlord and operating a firetrap tenement, St. Joseph's House of Hospitality (then located at 221 Chrystie Street). Fined $250, she was commanded to have the building vacated within a week. *Newsweek*, the *New York Times*, and other publications carried the story, which offered much human interest appeal. Soon after when Day was leaving the House for a second court appearance, she noticed a group of men milling about, probably waiting to check the used-clothes bin. One of them came over and pressed a check into her hand. "Here is two-fifty," he said. Not until she was sitting on the subway did she discover that his "two-fifty" was a check for the $250 fine, signed by the poet W.H. Auden. In her worry and haste, she had not immediately recognized him. Later the judge suspended the fine, saying he did not know the Catholic Worker was a charitable organization. The little drama was made much of in the *New York Times*, *Time*, and elsewhere, and it drew attention to the movement's long commitment to the poor.[56]

The 1957 air raid drill took place on July 12, and again Catholic Workers, who announced beforehand that they did not intend to comply, were arrested. They were sentenced to thirty days, and *Catholic Worker* editors, members of the War Resisters League, and the American Friends Service Committee picketed the Women's House of Detention every day until Day and the other women demonstrators were finally released. In a special edition of July 17, 1957, the *Catholic Worker's* banner headline proclaimed, "Dorothy Day Among Pacifists Jailed." The full-page article, accompanied by an Eichenberg wood engraving of an impoverished family, again quoted Day's statement that the demonstration was not only "to voice opposition to war, not only to refuse to participate in psychological warfare," but "as public penance for the atomic bombing in Japan."[57]

This time coverage included approving articles in the *Daily Worker*, the New York *Post*, the *New York Times*, the *Village Voice*, and *London Daily Express*. The *Nation* commented that the jailing of Dorothy Day was a "terrifying and inescapable comment on our society."[58] Again, the only major Catholic publication that supported the demonstrators was *Commonweal*. By 1957, nearly twenty-five years after the premiere of the *Catholic Worker*, Day was moving into her place as one of the most respected of lay Catholics. As *Commonweal* wrote, "Everyone must know that Dorothy Day, who is a Christian pacifist and the founder of the *Catholic Worker*, has long opposed the immorality of modern war and with special intensity the threat of atomic conflict." *Commonweal* confessed that it had never been able to accept Day's "full plea for pacifism," but praised her for "the purity of her intentions and the sincerity of her soul," which "glow with a true Christian light." This was "the kind of faith that truly moves mountains. Why," *Commonweal* asked, "has American justice imprisoned a conscience so clear and a life so holy?"[59]

Representatives of America's three major religions — Edward S. Skillin, editor, *Commonweal*; John C. Bennett, co-chair, *Christianity and Crisis*; Rabbi Eugene J. Lipman, Union of American Hebrew Congregations — supported the Catholic Workers in a joint letter, published in the *New York Times*. They pointed out that American society had long "cherished" the "tradition of religious freedom," which "can be violated only at the nation's peril." That Day and her associates had been jailed for thirty days for "acting within this tradition" was "a matter of great anxiety to all. We must also," their letter concluded, "maintain freedom for the kind of religious dissent witnessed to by a Dorothy Day."[60]

Thus it went every year until 1960; by then Day and Hennacy had each been imprisoned four times, and *Catholic Worker* editor Deane Mowrer three times. In 1960, 1,000 demonstrators participated, singing "We Shall Overcome" as police ordered them to take shelter. This time, police passed over Day, Hennacy, and other Catholic Workers in favor of twenty-seven others, apparently arrested at random. The press reacted supportively, with favorable coverage in *Commonweal*, the New York *Post*, the *New York World Telegram*, the *Village Voice*, and the *Nation*. The latter noted the police's lack of zeal in pursuing Day and Hennacy, "hardened criminals" who "certainly had a claim to police bus seats."[61] Soon the city abandoned what had become a useless annual game.

Dorothy Day, her supporters, and the *Catholic Worker* could claim no small part for this. But all along Day had made it clear that martyrdom was not a motive. "It was not," she asserted, "a question of obedience to the law or to duly constituted authority. Law," she went on, "must be according to right reason, and the law that made it compulsory to take shelter was a mockery." She and the others had been "trying to obey God rather than men, trying to follow a higher obedience." They did not wish at all to "act in a spirit of defiance and rebellion."[62] Neither was clarification of legal issues for their own sake a motive. Day, Hennacy, and the Catholic Workers had decided in advance to plead guilty rather that rely upon the technicalities that lawyers could doubtless dredge up. "We felt that we were not morally guilty," Hennacy wrote, "but in the sense of a clear cut case of civil disobedience, we did not wish to becloud the issues with legal terms."[63] This was especially true of Dorothy Day. "I had thought to plead not guilty with the others to show our solidarity with them," Ammon Hennacy wrote, "but Dorothy being a better basic radical than I am persuaded me to plead guilty on the anarchist principle of 'we did it once and we will do it again; and no legal quibbling.' "[64]

Responding to continual criticism from some *Catholic Worker* readers and local radio commentators, Day clarified that the Catholic Workers were spending no funds for legal defense. They had pleaded guilty "against the protest of the lawyers" who were defending the non-Catholic Worker pacifists. And she and her associates "were prepared to take the penalty of our civil disobedience."[65] Emulating her, later anti-Vietnam War protestors would also take such a position of responsible dissent.

Nevertheless, some observers remained critical. The New York diocesan paper, *Catholic News*, wrote that Catholic Workers had been presumptuous in their "private interpretation" when the Church had always advocated obedience to authority, supported just wars, and kept chaplains in all armies, just or unjust.[66] And in a reply to a letter Day had sent her, Eleanor Roosevelt said she was "at a loss to know why you are opposed to cooperating with the compulsory air raid drill. Such measures are, after all, meant for your own safety."[67]

In the July-August 1957 *Catholic Worker*, Day acknowledged that some of the movement's old supporters were complaining about what they viewed as an increasing emphasis on pacifism. They charged, "Too much stuff about war and preparation for war, and the duty of building up resistance." Actually, the *Catholic Worker* had printed articles on peace topics all along. What these readers objected to was the *Catholic Worker*'s stress on civil disobedience and direct action to further pacifism. These were radical techniques indeed.

But generally, support seemed to be growing for the points that Day and the Catholic Workers, through actions and through articles, had helped to make. Later, during the Vietnam crisis, peace activists would remember with gratitude and respect the contribution of Day, her followers, and the *Catholic Worker*, in sustaining the anti-war movement in the Fifties—and in the Forties and Thirties. For Day and her colleagues had courageously met the major moral challenges of their age. As Day explained in her article, in Peter Maurin's day, "the problem was unemployment," which directed the *Catholic Worker* to emphasize labor problems. Now, she said, "we still need to build up the vision of a new social order wherein justice dwells, and try to work for it here and now." And she pledged the *Catholic Worker* to "the work of nonviolent resistance to our militarist state." Thus, fundamental issues for the paper remained the threat of war in general; and the buildup of armaments, especially nuclear, which threatened unparalleled destruction.

In her article, Day also mentioned that she had been often asked why she did not equally object to the Soviet Union's buildup of weapons. She replied that she did indeed object, but that personalism precluded the expenditure of energy in useless name-calling. "We believe in taking the beam out of our own eye, we believe in loving our enemy," she wrote, "and not contributing to the sum total of hatred and fear of him already in the world."[68] Indeed, she often pledged "to try to write of all the good which is happening."[69] And so she focused on agreement and cooperation, emphasizing, for example, Christianity and Communism's common goals. "There are many areas on which Catholics and Communists can work together," she repeated in an article in which she invoked the quotations of "Peter Maurin, the founder of the Catholic Worker movement."[70] This represented the first time a prominent, respected Catholic had publicly departed from the Church's stereotypical anti-Communism.

It was easier for her to express such conciliatory opinions after the *Catholic Worker*'s first decade, when she had established some distance from her leftist past. Now that the Catholic Worker movement had gained a measure of acceptance, to expend energy in denouncing outside forms and processes seemed a wasteful use of time. And although during her youth she had rejected the radical movements of Socialism, the I.W.W., and Communism on account of a certain lack of love in their natures, she could still glimpse some goodness there. She viewed Communists as members of the Mystical Body of Christ. "Perhaps," she wrote, "if we thought of how Karl Marx was called 'Papa Marx' by all the children on the street, if we knew and remembered how he told fairy stories to his children, how he suffered hunger and poverty and pain, how he sat by the body of his dead child and had no money for coffin or funeral, perhaps such thoughts as these would make us love him and his followers." She also saw a redeeming humanity in Lenin. And when others denigrated Communist women such as Ana Pauker and Ella Reeve Bloor, Day responded that "we have many a woman in politics or in the trade union field in this country who is just as hard, bold, brazen and ruthless." Day did not make such statements because she whole-heartedly embraced Communism. She certainly perceived its shortcomings. But she saw capitalism's just as clearly. "The Communist believes in force, in espionage," she sorrowed. But "so do the press and the pulpit of the Christian churches." She lamented that the Communist "does not believe in God, he does not see Christ in his neighbor." But "Nor do we, in the pulpit of the Christian churches." She lamented that the Communist "does not believe in God, he does not see Christ in his neighbor." But "Nor do we, in the poor, the lame, the halt, the blind, the prodigal, the sinner, the harlot; nor in those of another race."[71] Nevertheless, many Americans did not appreciate the intricacies of her views on Communism, especially as they nervously watched Fidel Castro's Cuban revolution, which the *Catholic Worker* interpreted favorably.

Writers like William Worthy of the Baltimore *Afro-American*, David Dellinger, peace activist and editor of *Liberation* magazine, and Ed Turner of the *Catholic Worker*, strongly backed the revolution. In a guest article in the *Catholic Worker*, Worthy, a former Nieman Fellow in journalism at Harvard, observed that "the struggle of eighteen million Negroes for equality and justice in the United States will have little meaning if, ninety miles south of our border, six million Cubans are denied the freedom to run their country according to twentieth-century concepts of true independence and to set a beacon example for the rest of the exploited countries of Latin America."[72] Worthy's article was a catalyst. It coincided with Cardinal Spellman's late July 1960 speech at the Eucharistic Congress in Munich in which he asserted that Communism was "the most dangerous threat since 1939." A gust of angry letters and articles blustered into the *Catholic Worker* office on the Lower East Side. In St. Paul, the August 11, 1960 issue of the ultra-conservative, non-mainstream Catholic *Wanderer* complained bitterly that Worthy's piece "might well have been featured in the Communist [*Daily*] *Worker* rather than the *Catholic Worker*," and was "in effect, a clarion call for a complete sell-out of Latin America, in first place, to the Soviet world conspiracy. Unfortunately," the *Wanderer* continued, "the *Catholic Worker* has become only too notorious over the years for its maudlin proclivities where anarchic beatnikism and outright Communist issues are involved." The *Wanderer* deemed it "shocking indeed that such open and continually defiant fraternization with Communist aims and objectives should be permitted to go unchecked under the Catholic banner."[73] A month later, Ammon Hennacy took the *Wanderer* editor to task for printing an article which said, "It is rumored that Dorothy Day is a communicant."[74]

Letters from irate subscribers rained on the *Catholic Worker* office; and there were plenty of letters from puzzled supporters. "You cannot blame people for suspecting you of Communist leanings as long as you print such stuff," wrote Paul Hallett of the *Register*, a national Catholic paper. He did not think the *Catholic Worker* editors were "undercover Reds," but as long as they defended "an admitted Communist and persecutor of the Church like Castro," they could not expect to be regarded as "bona fide Catholic editors." He added, "I think it is incumbent on your friends who do not agree with you to explain some of the facts of international life to you."[75] Cornelia and Irving Sussman wrote, "Because we love you, we are sick at heart over the CW's undiscriminating cheers for anything Cuba does. This is a very one-sided Pacifism."[76]

Dorothy Day answered in an editorial in the July-August 1961 issue. "It is hard," she began, "to say that the place of the *Catholic Worker* is with the poor," without "finding ourselves on the side of the persecutors of the Church." And the Catholic Church, she declared, sometimes deserved persecution. Pointing out his Catholicism, she remarked that "Fidel Castro says he is not persecuting Christ, but Churchmen who have betrayed him." American Catholics might not persecute clergy, but had they really lived up to Christ's teachings? She compared the violence done to the poor by the materialistic spirit of many Americans, and the violence of Castro which was aimed at helping the poor. "We are certainly not Marxist socialists nor do we believe in violent revolution," she concluded. "Yet we do believe that it is better to revolt, to fight, as Castro did with his handful of men. . . . than to do nothing." But Day was not advocating violence: "We reaffirm our belief in the ultimate victory of good over evil, of love over hatred and we believe that the trials which beset us in the world today are for the perfecting of our faith which is more precious than gold."[77] For her part, she believed that the Catholic as well as the secular press, had "mismanaged" the news on Cuba, by not accurately reporting the many positive signs of Catholicism there.[78]

Still the letters flowed in. The high tide of feeling was reminiscent of that of the early World War II years. Thomas Merton commended Day for her stand, adding that some readers "may get quite hot about the fact that you want to point out that Castro may have had good intentions and in actual fact has been less wicked than our mass media want him to have been. People who are scared and upset," he noted, "use a very simple logic, and they think that if you defend Castro as a human being you are defending all the crimes that have ever been committed by Communism anywhere and they will feel that you are threatening them."[79] His analysis was quite accurate. One cancelling subscriber wrote, "I am retching from reading your articles on Cuba. I told Dorothy long ago that it is all right to shout from the roof tops—but not to scream."[80] Another reader inquired, "Are you, perchance, blindly opening your columns to a purveyor of Cuban government propaganda? Permitting the publication of anti-American epistles which deliver the between-line message, 'See, Fidel isn't such a bad guy, after all?' "[81] Another reader observed sarcastically, " 'After all, Castro is a Catholic.' Well, well, how do you like that? And what has happened in Cuba is not the Marxist brand; and it is all very religious, really, and it is all, after all, in the name of the poor."[82]

Again and again, Day responded. To those who saw a conflict in her present position, who accused her of giving up her pacifism, she wrote: "What nonsense. We are as unalterably opposed to armed resistance and armed revolt from the admittedly intolerable conditions all through Latin America as we ever were. No one," she went on, "expects that Fidel will become another Martin of Tours or Ignatius and lay down his arms. But we pray the grace of God will grow in him and that with a better social order . . . the Church will be free to function."[83]

In the fall of 1962, Day decided to visit Cuba as a journalist, to report firsthand about social and religious conditions there. To secure permission to visit the island, she wrote to the State Department and also to the Czechoslovakian

Embassy, which was representing Cuba in Washington, D.C.[84] On September fifth she sailed from Jersey City on a Spanish line vessel.

She had no interview with any of the revolutionary leaders, although she did hear Castro speak. He reminded her of someone very familiar. "And will it be shocking to our readers," she wrote, "to learn that as I heard him speak . . . the sound of his voice, his manner of oratory, his constant repetitions, reminded me of Peter Maurin?"[85] Whether or not calculated to win acceptance from skeptical readers, such personal characterization had always been Day's forte. And personal experiences and evocative descriptions invigorated the many Cuban reports she sent to the *Catholic Worker* and to other publications, such as *Liberation*.[86] Some of the paper's criticism was now extinguished. Many favorable letters came in and circulation remained stable. Day concluded that much remained for her to write about Cuba. Although Catholic Workers remained pacifists opposed to all state control, she wrote, they remained "mightily interested" in Castro's island. This was "because the zeal and enthusiasm of the young in Cuba increase our hope for man — that he can undergo a great transformation, that he can be converted to a heartwarming zeal for the common good."[87] However, to dispel any doubts lingering among her detractors, she stressed her unwavering pacifism. It did not permit her to approve everything she saw in Cuba. She hated the "arms buildup" there, she wrote, "as I hate it in my own country, the waste of intelligence, the waste of resources." She regretted that "Incredible sums are poured into destruction that should be used for schools, hospitals, and the development of new and better institutions." She also hated the sight of women "proudly bearing arms."[88]

By Christmas, Day was back at Peter Maurin Farm — but soon away again, traveling to myriad speaking engagements. Meanwhile, Pope John XXIII's opening of the Second Vatican Council in October 1962 had brought a new sense of hope to the Catholic Church. Among other changes, the Council was stressing a new role of lay participation. This, of course, was something that Day, Maurin, and their followers had practiced for decades. Now many American Catholics were beginning to realize it. Day was increasingly in demand as a lecturer at meetings and conferences all around the country. In May 1963, the thirtieth anniverasry of the *Catholic Worker*, she was in Rome, where friends had paid for her to join a delegation of fifty women making a pilgrimage for peace.[89]

American Catholics were extraordinarily optimistic during the time of Vatican II, confident that they stood on the threshold of a major renewal. But this euphoria would soon dissipate when the Vietnam conflict produced a previously unglimpsed core of Catholic radicalism in this country. The war spawned a showdown between patriotic Catholics like Cardinal Spellman, who wholeheartedly backed the United States military, and those like Day and the Catholic Workers, who found inspiration in Christ's Sermon on the Mount admonition to be peacemakers. Traditional Catholics were shocked by the sight of priests and nuns picketing the Pentagon, drenching draft board files with blood, and encouraging men to defy the government by burning their draft cards. When it was all over, the American Catholic Church had undergone a major change in its outlook on war, due in no small way to the pacifist witness of those such as Dorothy Day and her *Catholic Worker*.

At first, pacifist groups did not pay much attention to the guerilla skirmishes that were occurring in Southeast Asia. Diminished by the McCarthy era's redbaiting and stifling anti-intellectualism, pacifists were laboring to awaken the public conscience to the immorality of nuclear warfare. As early as 1954, Dorothy Day had published in the *Catholic Worker* a lengthy, comprehensive analysis of Vietnam and Western imperialism, in which she had warned against United States involvement. "Sooner or later," she had cautioned, "we are going to be forced to be facing the ultimate issues. To recognize it is not Christianity and freedom we are defending, but our possessions."[90] But Catholic Workers,

Figure 11. Dorothy Day, early Sixties. (Photo by Ed Lettau, courtesy Dorothy Day-Catholic Worker Collection, Marquette University)

and most American pacifists, did not really begin to oppose the conflict until 1961-62, when the American military became more dramatically involved.

With the United States again fighting a war, the *Catholic Worker* jumped into the vanguard of the anti-Vietnam War movement, where it exercised an energetic leadership. By now the paper's pacifism had developed a firm moral and intellectual foundation which was much more than an emotional response.[91] In contrast to the World War II years, the Sixties and Seventies found Catholic Workers united on the question of pacifism. According to Thomas Cornell, *Catholic Worker* associate editor and activist in the Sixties, "There was no dissent. Everyone [in the Catholic Worker community] was horrified at the Vietnam War."[92]

In 1963, when Congress again approved the extension of conscription until 1967, the *Catholic Worker* intensified its denunciation of the draft, urging noncompliance:

> Our objections to the draft . . . are moral. Involuntary servitude violates the natural rights of sons of God. It interferes with a man's right to choose his vocation, to marry, to learn, to work at a meaningful job of his own choosing. It violates the right of the individual in a democracy. It is repugnant to Christianity since it violates a man's liberty at the very stage of his life when free choices for his future are most important to him.[93]

On August 7, 1964, Congress passed the Gulf of Tonkin Resolution, signifying the growing United States involvement in Vietnam. As Catholic Worker Houses across the country began to demonstrate and propagandize against the war, circulation of the paper consistently grew, rising from 64,000 in 1962 to 74,000 in 1963 and 77,000 in 1964.

The *Catholic Worker* had become the first Catholic publication to advocate civil disobedience as a legitimate form of anti-war protest.[94] As expected, its editors did not stop at editorializing now; they practiced civil disobedience, from withholding war taxes to draft card burning, with Dorothy Day's urging and blessing. In November 1962 Thomas Cornell, a Fairfield University graduate who had become an associate editor of the *Catholic Worker* that fall, led twenty-five men in burning their draft cards at a rally in Washington Square during the Second World-Wide General Strike for Peace. Cornell later burned another draft card before a national television audience, after which he was interviewed by NBC.[95] It was an act he would repeat several times, and for which in 1968 he served six months in jail.

On August 31, 1965, President Lyndon Johnson signed into law a bill that provided jail terms of up to five years and fines of up to $10,000 for those who willfully burned or otherwise mutilated draft cards.[96] "This means, of course," wrote Cornell in the September 1965 *Catholic Worker*, "that we must have a public draft-card burning soon."[97] First to make such a gesture was twenty-two-year-old David Miller, a Catholic Worker from Le Moyne College in Syracuse, New York. For burning his draft card on October 15, 1965, Miller became the first pacifist to be prosecuted for such civil disobedience, a matter of great pride to Dorothy Day. She viewed jail time as a sign of witness, as a badge of honor. In

1968, when the Rev. Daniel Berrigan said Mass at St. Joseph's House of Hospitality a few weeks after he was freed on bail for the Catonsville, Maryland, draft board raid, Dorothy Day spoke. Rising slowly, majestically from her chair, she told the assembly, "There is only one way to end this insane war. Pack the jails with our men!" She gazed about her and repeated, "Pack the jails!"[98]

But neither Day nor the *Catholic Worker* ever countenanced violence in direct action demonstrations. Of the Berrigans' draft board raids, Day remarked: "These things are not ours [to do]."[99] Shortly after the Catonsville Nine action, she told Patricia McNeal that Father Daniel Berrigan "isn't a Catholic Worker, he came to us and stole our young men away" to engage in similar sabotage activities.[100] In an interview in 1971, she told Dwight Macdonald exactly why her philosophy precluded such actions, which she viewed largely as vandalism. "The violent spirit" might "only be directed against inanimate objects now," she said, "but it could lead to the real thing. Bombings are the next step—and when it comes to bombs you can't control it, no matter what your intentions, you can't be sure there isn't a late worker or a cleaning woman around." Of the extreme elements of the Catholic Left, she remarked: "Those priests and sisters! I admire their courage and dedication but not their arrogance. Of course," she went on, "we're against any kind of violence, including psychological." If such a viewpoint "cuts us off from the young, we'll just have to accept it." But she didn't think it had; St. Joseph's was "swarming with them."[101]

And so Catholic Workers, who continued to play a prominent role in the growing anti-Vietnam War demonstrations, confined themselves to nonviolent gestures. The *Catholic Worker* publicized these incidents of direct action, which ranged from picketing to income tax withholding to draft card burning.

Then on November 9, 1965, twenty-two-year-old Roger LaPorte sat cross-legged in front of the United Nations building and held a match to his gasoline-soaked clothes. Although a United Nations guard called the fire department immediately and then doused the flames, LaPorte was burned over ninety percent of his body. En route to the hospital, he told the ambulance attendants, "I am a Catholic Worker. I am anti-war—all wars. I did this as a religious action." About thirty hours later, he died in Bellevue Hospital.[102]

LaPorte's action shocked and bewildered his Catholic Worker colleagues. Cornell thought that LaPorte had perhaps intended to take on himself the violence and suffering he saw all around him.[103] In a statement, Catholic Workers commented:

> He was trying to say to the American people that we must turn away from violence in Vietnam, and he was trying to say something about the violence that is eroding our own society here in the United States and our city of New York. And so he made this sacrifice attempting to absorb this violence and hatred personally, deflecting it from others by taking it voluntarily to himself.
>
> At the same time, we strongly urge people committed to peace to employ other means in expressing their commitment . . . bearing witness and working nonviolently to build a decent, nonviolent society, a society of conscience.[104]

The events of the fall of 1965 brought many reporters to St. Joseph's. There were articles in the *New York Times* and many other publications, both secular and religious. Some observers blamed Dorothy Day for the tragedy. A Falls Church, Virginia, group known as the Emerging Catholic Laymen broadcast their opinion that "She has sown cockle amongst the wheat. Now she is reaping some strange fruit indeed! Since Miller and LaPorte were both disciples of the Catholic Worker movement," the broadcast continued, "can it disclaim its influence on these young men to break the law of the land and the law of God?" It concluded with a rejection of Catholic Worker pacifism, because "it gives aid and comfort to the enemy."[105] And a priest writing in *Our Sunday Visitor* called Day an "apostle of pious oversimplification." He charged that the *Catholic Worker* "often distorted beyond recognition" the position of the Popes, adding:

> When Dorothy's mind is made up, such as on the question of pacifism, she and her cohorts act very irresponsibly. . . . For the nation to see a 'Catholic march on Washington,' or a 'Catholic peace fellowship' that is affiliated with far left organizations, destroys not only the prestige but the very position of the Church. These people seem to want the Church respected, but they deny it the very things which cause it to be respected.
>
> The influence of the *Catholic Worker* on the minds of the young and unstable, the unformed and the uninformed, such as the late Roger LaPorte, has done much harm. The tendency of the *Catholic Worker* has been to resist authority, to oppose the free world's commitment in Vietnam, to sabotage the drills against a possible air-raid attack in New York City, to want to be called 'Catholic,' yet not want any direction from responsible authority.[106]

Such articles seemed to ignore Pope John XXIII's 1963 encyclical, *Pacem in Terris*, which many understood to be a mandate for pacifism in a nuclear age. Influenced as well by an important Vatican II schema, "The Constitution of the Church in the Modern World," which called for clearer government recognition of the rights of conscientious objectors, the American Catholic Church began to develop an unprecedented division over the Vietnam War. On the side of Pope Paul VI, who in 1965 had criticized the United States involvement in Vietnam, were leading Catholic clergy, such as Thomas Merton, the Rev. John McKenzie, the Rev. Robert Drinan, and the Berrigans, along with the liberal Catholic press—*Commonweal*, *Jubilee*, the *Critic*, the *National Catholic Reporter*. They renounced the Vietnam War as one of the most immoral acts in American history. Opposing them were the conservative publications such as the *Wanderer* and the *Brooklyn Tablet*, most of the bishops, and most of the parishioners.[107] The American Catholic bishops were avid supporters of United States involvement in Vietnam almost to the very end. Not until November of 1971 did they condemn the war as unjust.[108]

In 1968 John Deedy commented on how the American Catholic press repeatedly "equivocated on the moral responsibilities and implications of Vietnam." He concluded that on these issues, "the liberal voice in the Catholic press is a lonely one," for "the bulk of support is historically on the side of authority."[109]

The *Catholic Worker*, however, continued to exercise editorial leadership in its uncompromising advocacy of pacifism, for which it encountered more hostility from the conservative press. Nevertheless, subscriptions to the paper poured in as the movement's sincerity and utter commitment to pacifism became more and more apparent. Circulation rose from 77,000 in 1965 to 85,000 in 1966 and 89,000 in 1967.

In February 1965, President Johnson ordered the bombing of North Vietnam, and in 1966, air strikes against non-military targets—industry and transportation. By 1967, nearly 500,000 Americans were in Vietnam, at a total monthly cost of about two billion dollars. The *Catholic Worker* was ready. In February 1965 it printed a definitive statement of its position on the war, signed by Day, A.J. Muste, the Berrigans, and other activists, scholars, and theologians. They opposed American military involvement in Vietnam and elsewhere because it "suppressed the aspirations of the people for political independence and economic freedom." They also pointed out that war in Vietnam increased "the threat of nuclear catastrophe and death by chemical and biological warfare." Considered nearly two decades later, the *Catholic Worker*'s statement seems remarkably prescient. Just a few years after it was published, President Richard Nixon came to the brink of visiting nuclear destruction on North Vietnam; and the American military's widespread use of Agent Orange and other chemical defoliants not only devastated the Vietnamese countryside, but endangered the chromosomes of all exposed. The *Catholic Worker* statement ended with a pledge to refuse service in the armed forces, and to eschew any participation "in the manufacture or transportation of military equipment" or in "military research and weapons development. We shall encourage," it concluded, "the development of other nonviolent acts, including acts which involve civil disobedience, in order to stop the flow of American soldiers and munitions to Vietnam."[110] Readers were invited to sign the declaration and mail it to the *Catholic Worker* office, but warned that by so doing they risked prosecution for civil disobedience.

In June, in an open letter to President Johnson on the front page of the *Catholic Worker*, Lewis Mumford wrote, "We are ashamed of your actions, and revolted by your dishonest excuses and pretexts."[111]

Besides the strength and consistency of its witness to pacifism, the *Catholic Worker*'s credibility was also based on its sponsorship of two peace organizations, the American Pax Association and the Catholic Peace Fellowship. The formation of the American Pax Association was announced in the October 1962 *Catholic Worker*. Sponsored by prominent American Catholics (including Dorothy Day, Thomas Merton, Karl Stern, Gordon Zahn, Helen Iswolsky, and Arthur Sheehan), Pax was somewhat similar to the first American PAX (which Catholic Workers organized during the Thirties) and also affiliated with the same British Pax group. In its first year it attracted about a hundred members. Its director was Eileen Egan, a long-time colleague of Dorothy Day's. Taking a moderate stand, disdaining direct action and civil disobedience, Pax appealed especially to Catholics who wanted peace but were not necessarily committed to total pacifism. Throughout the Sixties, Pax lobbied for peace within the Catholic Church, employing its conferences and propaganda, which included a semi-scholarly quarterly, *Peace*. (In 1971, Pax reorganized as the American affiliate of Pax Christi, the Catholic Church's official international peace association.)[112]

The Catholic Peace Fellowship was founded in the summer of 1964 by the priests Daniel and Philip Berrigan and three former *Catholic Worker* editors— Thomas Cornell, James Forest, and Martin J. Corbin. Its sponsors included Dorothy Day, John Deedy of *Commonweal*, Gordon Zahn, Thomas Merton, and Msgr. Paul Hanly Furfey. Formed in the spirit of Vatican II, which "turned the Church to the world," the Catholic Peace Fellowship became the only Catholic peace group that was institutionally connected to non-Catholics, namely the primarily Protestant, ecumenical Fellowship of Reconciliation. The Catholic Peace Fellowship emphasized the pacifist traditions of the Catholic Church, participated in direct, nonviolent anti-war protests, organized study conferences, and counseled conscientious objectors. By the end of its first year, according to Forest, it had eight hundred members.[113]

Then, of course, there was the spirited and confidence-inspiring role of Dorothy Day during the Vietnam years. Hers was an utterly sincere and winning performance for the Catholic Worker way. In September 1965, she went to Rome to observe the proceedings of the Vatican Council, where she made a ten-day fast for peace. In preparation, she planned the July-August (1965) issue of the *Catholic Worker* around the theme, "The Council and the Bomb" (after the lead story by James W. Douglass). Articles and letters urged the bishops to grapple with the question of the morality of modern war. Funds from the Catholic Worker movement and Pax paid for an airmail copy for every bishop in the world—an unprecedented lay effort to reach the teaching church. Day returned to Rome in October 1967 as a member of the Third World Congress for the Lay Apostolate, where she attended workshops on peace. She was one of two Americans (the other was an astronaut) chosen to receive communion personally from Pope Paul VI.

On November 6, 1965, back in New York, she and A.J. Muste spoke at a rally in front of the Federal Court House at which Catholic Workers Thomas Cornell, James Wilson, Roy Lisker, and two other pacifists burned their draft cards. Hecklers hooted "Moscow Mary!" and "Burn yourselves, not your cards!" as Day addressed the crowd. She had been a pacifist since 1917, and now she said:

> I speak today as one who is old, and who must endorse the courage of the young who themselves are willing to give up their freedom. I speak as one . . . whose whole lifetime has seen the cruelty and hysteria of war in the last half-century . . . . I wish to place myself beside A.J. Muste, to show my solidarity of purpose with these young men, and to point out that we, too, are breaking the law, committing civil disobedience.[114]

But the police did not choose to arrest the two venerable pacifists. Cornell recalled that "No one attacked Dorothy because of her position and her age." She was "mother of us all."[115]

In such personal experiences as these, Day continued to spread the gospel of pacifism. She was equally if not more effective in her journalism, throughout the Vietnam conflict eloquently making her points, over and over. She had several things to say about Cardinal Spellman's 1966 visit to Vietnam as the personal guest of General Westmoreland. There, a senior officer told the Cardinal, who customarily made a Christmas tour of American military bases overseas, "We hardly count it a war if you don't come."[116] On Christmas Day, the Cardinal addressed the troops. He told them he believed "This war in Vietnam is . . . a war for civilization." Although the war had been "thrust upon us," he said, "we cannot yield to tyranny. . . . We do hope and pray, through the valor, the dedication, the service of our men and women of our armed forces, we shall soon have the victory for which all of us in Vietnam and all over the world are praying and hoping; for less than a victory is inconceivable."[117]

The Catholic Peace Fellowship was quick to organize a series of demonstrations and picketings to make it clear that Cardinal Spellman did not speak for all American Catholics. And Dorothy Day, in the January 1967 issue of the *Catholic Worker*, explained why. Adroitly, without directly criticizing the Cardinal, she analyzed the situation, creatively using repetition to emphasize her points. "It is not just Vietnam," she wrote, "it is South Africa, it is Nigeria, the Congo, Indonesia, all of Latin America. It is not just the pictures of all the women and children who have been burnt alive in Vietnam or the men who have been tortured, and died. It is not just the headless victims of war in Colombia." And it was not "just the words of Cardinal Spellman," but instead "the fact that whether we like it or not, we are Americans. It is indeed our country, right or wrong," she wrote, because "We are the nation the most powerful, the most armed and we are supplying arms and money to the rest of the world where we are not ourselves fighting. We are eating while there is famine in the world." Day had "often thought" Cardinal Spellman's Christmas visits to the American troops "all over the world, Europe, Korea, Vietnam," were "a brave thing to do. But oh, God," she asked, "what are all these Americans, so-called Christians, doing all over the world so far from our own shores?" Recalling the Cardinal's remarks, she pointed out that "Words are as strong and powerful as bombs, as napalm. How much the government counts on those words, pays for those words to exalt our own way of life, to build up fear of the enemy. Deliver us, Lord, from the *fear* of the enemy."[118]

But Dorothy Day did not confine herself only to this theme. Throughout the Sixties and Seventies, the *Catholic Worker* continued to remonstrate against racism, anti-Semitism, and social injustices, strongly backing the civil rights movement, just as it always had.[119] In fact, in April 1957, when Day visited an interracial farming commune near Americus, Georgia, she had been unsuccessfully shot at by vigilantes.[120] Throughout the stormy Sixties, letters to Day poured in from prominent personalities and activists, as well as the young. "Dear Dorothy, I often think of you, and what you meant to only one person like myself," wrote Karl Stern. "God bless you and your work," said Phyllis McGinley. Allen Ginsberg, the radical poet, sent his regards.[121] And when Ignazio Silone was in New York in late October 1967, he looked up Day and the Catholic Workers.[122]

Naturally, there were many letters from the Berrigans, who saw Day as their mother and teacher. Theirs was a long and inspiring association.[123] In 1981, Father Daniel Berrigan wrote, "I am grateful beyond words for the grace of this woman's life, for her sensible, unflinching rightness of mind, her long and lonely truth, her journey to the heart of things. I think of her as one who simply helped us, in a time of self-inflicted blindness, to see."[124] Day considered the brother priests "marvelous men. Imagine," she said, "the time they've spent in jail!"[125]

And there was much correspondence from Thomas Merton. Well known because of his best-selling autobiography, *The Seven-Storey Mountain*, the Trappist monk had written many volumes of essays and poetry. In the early Sixties, he emerged as a prominent *Catholic Worker* contributor. Many of his most penetrating essays on peace topics appeared there first.[126] Merton's "The Root of War" in the October 1961 issue[127] was significant in shaping the pacifist thought of Father Daniel Berrigan.[128] To Dorothy Day Merton wrote, "I can imagine the CW would be a place where really sincere people come to the end of the line, that is to say they seek there the last resort of truth and hope to be able to do something, and see how helpless they are. . . . And at CW one at least can and doubtless must face it. . . ."[129]

And there were many letters and much support for Dorothy Day from the young. Abbie Hoffman called her "the first hippie," a characterization which pleased her. In her uncompromising adherence to pacifism, to civil rights, she was after all addressing some of the most profound concerns of the youthful rebels.[130] Throughout, she admonished them to go ahead and demonstrate for their convictions—but always to use nonviolent means of protest. For to the end she remained an old-fashioned radical who adhered to the traditional forms even while she tried to change them. In doing so, she helped make that previously rare species, Catholic pacifists, more common and accepted than ever before. Only one American Catholic conscientious objector had stood to be counted during World War I; in World War II, two hundred sprang up, most of them associated with the Catholic Worker movement. By Vietnam's conclusion, for the first time in American history, "substantial numbers" of Catholics had come to question the morality of an American war.[131] This was due in no small way to the witness of Day and her *Catholic Worker*.

After the last American troops left South Vietnam on March 29, 1973, the *Catholic Worker* did not suddenly abandon the topic of pacifism. Articles on that subject by writers such as Gordon Zahn, Daniel Ellsberg, Eileen Egan, Lewis Mumford and Father Daniel Berrigan continued to be a staple.[132]

Meanwhile, the *Catholic Worker* often ran at least one article each month throughout the Seventies outlining the farm workers' plight and urging support for them through the boycotting of various farm produce. In a prominent, front-page article in the March-April 1973 issue, Dorothy Day wrote: "This Union of Farm Workers stands closer to an ideal asociation of men than any other in the history of the American labor movement. Who knows— it may leaven all the rest."[133]

Four months later, an increasingly frail Dorothy Day, almost seventy-six, picketed with Chavez and the U.F.W. in Fresno, California. She was arrested and jailed briefly with one hundred and forty-eight others, including thirty nuns and two priests.[134] Later, Cesar Chavez would eulogize Day with these words: "It makes us very proud that Dorothy's last trip to jail took place . . . with the farm workers."[135]

In the early Seventies, Dorothy Day and the Catholic Worker movement also made headlines when the Internal Revenue Service demanded from her nearly $300,000 in fines, penalties, and unpaid income tax for the last six years. Since registration as a nonprofit charitable organization violated the movement's personalist principles, Day had never filled out such an application. The absurdity of the matter did not escape the *New York Times*, which in an editorial entitled "Imagination, Please," commented: "Surely the I.R.S. must have genuine frauds to investigate."[136] Eventually, the I.R.S. dropped the matter.[137] The entire affair emphasized the ever-present contrast between the Catholic Worker movement's personalist simplicity and the circuitous bureaucracy of modern government—which in 1980 sent the *Catholic Worker* a series of instructive cartoons to print for the 1981 filing season.[138]

Dorothy Day and the *Catholic Worker* were also prominent in 1972 news, for Day's seventy-fifth birthday on November 8 was celebrated by the media. *America* devoted its November 11, 1972, issue to her, writing that "if one had to choose a single individual to symbolize the best in the aspiration and action of the American Catholic community during the last forty years, that one person would surely be Dorothy Day."[139] *Commonweal* called her "American Catholicism's Reigning First Lady."[140] Also, that was the year that Notre Dame University presented her with its Laetare Medal as an outstanding American Catholic. Reporters jammed St. Joseph's House of Hospitality, eager for interviews. And for Day's eightieth birthday, New York's Terence Cardinal Cooke personally delivered a message of greetings from Pope Paul VI.

As usual, Day was annoyed by all the attention, not willing to be dismissed as a "saint." Also, age had visited its infirmities upon her. Though her hair, wound as usual in braids around her head, had long been snow-white, now her alabaster skin seemed paper-thin. Her dark-colored eyeglass frames accented her appearance of frailty. But she remained keenly interested in all around her. At seventy-six, one visitor found her "warm, wanting to know about you and your background." She would often tell stories of her long life.[141] With a smile, she sometimes remarked that she was retired. As she wrote in 1975, she was "leaving everything to our generous crowd of young people who do the editing and getting out of the *Catholic Worker*, seeing visitors, doing the work of the Houses of Hospitality, and performing in truth all the works of mercy."[142] Still, Day's name remained atop the mast as editor and publisher, and the important decisions were still left to her.[143]

On August 6, 1976, Dorothy Day made her last speaking appearance before a large audience, at the Catholic Eucharistic Congress in Philadelphia. Well into her seventy-ninth year and extremely weak, for the first time she had to read the words of a speech. She spoke briefly but movingly of what had occurred on that day some thirty-one years earlier: the dropping of the first atomic bomb on Hiroshima. She told of the convictions she had held for the past fifty years.[144] That night, she suffered a mild heart attack, the first of three. After that, she became fairly confined, rising early to pray for several hours as had been her custom, reading and attending a 5:30 Mass in the chapel of Maryhouse, the New York Catholic Worker House for women on Third Street. Suffering from what was diagnosed as congestive heart disease, she slackened her pace a great deal in her final years, although she remained mentally alert.[145] To Father Hugo, she wrote that she was too exhausted to finish her new book, *All Is Grace*: "Please pray for me."[146] On another occasion she acknowledged, "My life has become one of physical weakness."[147] In her July-August 1979 column, Day commented, "Visitors are too much for me. Not even strength enough to answer letters."[148]

In her final months, Day seemed more detached from the world's problems. She found contentment in prayer and in the company of her daughter.[149] Often bedridden now, Day still wrote her monthly column. "The easiest way for me to write my piece this month is just to follow my diary for the last month," she explained in the June 1975 issue.[150] The columns of Day's last few years were not nearly as well written as those of her prime; they were spiritual reflections, and chatty reports of her reading—still impressive—and of the deaths of old friends. More and more, her columns were accompanied by reprints of her earlier masterpieces.

From Maryhouse on the afternoon of November 29, 1980, Dorothy Day spoke to her old friend Eileen Egan on the telephone about the plight of the southern Italian earthquake victims, whose sufferings she had watched on television. With compassion in her voice, she inquired what was being done for them. Relieved when Egan explained that medicine, food, and blankets were being provided, Day remarked with characteristic practicality that "blankets could be used to make tents."[151] A few hours later, just as the old ecclesiastical year was ebbing away and the Vigil Mass for the First Sunday of Advent was starting in the nearby Church of the Nativity, with her daughter Tamar at her bedside, Dorothy Day died peacefully.

ADE BETHUNE

VIII: Mightier than the Sword

The Catholic Worker family held her wake in Maryhouse. She lay in a plain pine coffin graced by a single red rose. On the wall above hung a cross fashioned out of two sturdy twigs.

They came in twos and threes; others alone, making their way through the Lower East Side. For two days the poor whom she had served came to kneel by her side.

On December 2, hundreds waited in the nearby Church of the Nativity to share her funeral Mass. At the head of the procession a young Catholic Worker carried a huge white candle, made from candle stubs contributed by all the neighborhood churches. Terence Cardinal Cooke of New York blessed her coffin, then members of the Catholic Worker family carried it to the nave. The church's interior was fittingly modest, with linoleum floors, unpainted cement-block walls, and water marks on the ceiling. Among those present were Cesar Chavez, I.F. Stone, Michael Harrington, Edward Guinan, and Father Daniel Berrigan. The requiem was sung joyously, with thanks for Day's long and inspiring life.[1] Abbie Hoffman commented that Day was as close "as this Jewish boy is going to get to a saint."[2]

Day was buried on Staten Island in a grassy meadow overlooking the Atlantic, not far from where she had once lived, given birth to her daughter, and been baptized a Catholic. She would have smiled at the irony of the Archdiocese of New York picking up the tab for the opening of her grave. For it had been Dorothy Day in the Fifties who had aroused the ire of Cardinal Spellman when she had supported local gravediggers in their bitter strike against the Archdiocese.[3]

Dorothy Day's dealings with the Catholic Church paralleled in many ways Christ's relationship with the religious hierarchy of His age. In fulfilling Church law, she ultimately relied on conscience and emerged as probably the greatest lay influence on the Roman Catholic Church in this century. Her stature called forth a strong secular response. Prominent obituaries appeared in such leading media as the *New York Times*, the *Washington Post*, *Time*, and *Newsweek*. Her recognition among diocesan papers was widespread. And even the *Wanderer*, the arch-conservative Catholic paper which had previously attacked Day and her *Catholic Worker*, gave her a grudging respect, remarking that "the individuals she directly touched for the most part were better off precisely because she and Maurin tried to be better."[4]

169

Figure 12. Dorothy Day at about age 75. (Courtesy Dorothy Day-Catholic Worker Collection, Marquette University)

Every year since her death, tributes to the witness of Dorothy Day's life and work have multiplied. Perhaps the most accurate, however, was expressed nearly twenty years ago by a Catholic Worker who said: "Those who adopt the Catholic Worker [movement] completely are few. Those who have been untouched by it are fewer."[5] Catholic Workers never constituted a mass movement, nor has the *Catholic Worker*'s circulation ever exceeded that of a major daily newspaper. Yet like the roots of a tree, the movement's ideas have reached fertile and influential soil.

Catholic Workers have diffused their philosophy in extensive publications. Looming large among them is Michael Harrington's *The Other America*. Many others came to the *Catholic Worker* (like Harrington), stayed a few years, then left, inspired by some or all of the ideas they had encountered. Others, who never actively joined, nevertheless transmitted aspects of Catholic Worker philosophy they had absorbed from the paper through their books and journalism, as well as in politics and personal activism. Catholic Worker ideas inform the work of Arthur Sheehan and James F. Powers; John Cort, Edward Skillin, John Cogley, and James O'Gara of *Commonweal*; peace activists and authors Gordon

Zahn, James W. Douglass, and Robert Ellsberg; Thomas Cornell of the Catholic Peace Fellowship; Eileen Egan of Pax Christi; James Forest of the International Fellowship of Reconciliation; the Revs. Daniel and Philip Berrigan; and Eugene McCarthy and Abigail McCarthy. Skillin recently summed up the influence of Day and the *Catholic Worker* on such persons, leaders in broader political, social, and journalistic spheres. "Dorothy always served as an inspiration," he said, "reminding me of our duty as Christians toward our needy brothers and sisters. She spoke quietly but with a conviction that was overpowering. Because of her I developed a different point of view on what should be the social message of Catholicism.

"I shall remember Dorothy," he added, "for her personal courage, her patience with the outcasts of society, her love of others, and her undeniable eloquence. One cannot measure the gratitude he should feel for having known a saint."[6]

Several significant offshoot publications have been inspired by the Catholic Worker movement and its paper. Prominent examples in the area of social justice include *Liturgy and Sociology*, founded in 1936 by *Catholic Worker* editor Dorothy Weston and her husband Thomas Coddington; the first *Christian Front*, begun in 1936 by Richard Deverall and Norman McKenna; *Work*, founded in 1943 by Edward Marciniak as the official publication of the Catholic Labor Alliance of Chicago; *Today*, a social action magazine for young Catholics, started by John Cogley and associates in 1946; and *Integrity*, begun by Carol Jackson, Dorothy Dohen, and Edward Willock in 1946. Also, the publications of the many Houses of Hospitality around the country have helped spread Catholic Worker ideals. In this context, one must also cite the writings of Dorothy Day herself, both her books and her articles in such publications as *Commonweal, Sign, Blackfriars, Jubilee, Preservation of the Faith, Ave Maria, Liberation,* and the *New Republic.* Such writings have helped focus attention on the movement and its *Catholic Worker* so that while only a few hundred have actively participated in the work throughout the years, thousands more came to know and be inspired by Dorothy Day and her ideals.

Organizations with a direct debt to the example of Catholic Worker activism include the Association of Catholic Trade Unionists, founded in 1937 by John Cort and associates; the Association of Catholic Conscientious Objectors; Pax Christi; and the Catholic Peace Fellowship. The far-reaching effects of such Catholic Worker-inspired groups and publications defy ordinary measure. In seeking to pinpoint the impact of Dorothy Day and her *Catholic Worker*, one recalls her favorite quotation from William James. Indeed like "the capillary oozing of water," the personal example of Day and her followers, in journalism and other activism, has dissolved some of the "hardest monuments" of human pride.

One of the most rocky has been the position of the Roman Catholic Church on issues of war and peace. Long before it was even considered possible to be both a Catholic and a pacifist, Dorothy Day was, as the *National Catholic Reporter* wrote in 1981, "plucking the U.S. church's peace and justice base string, sounding that lonely note." And as predicted, the decade of the Eighties has seen "a significant portion of the U.S. Catholic community, directly and indirectly, peaceably and through sabotage, alone and with others, willingly and unwillingly say 'no' to U.S. militarism and the nuclear-dominated national security mentality."[7]

But though a social radical, Day was a fervent Catholic traditionalist who never criticized the Church's teachings, only its failure to live up to them. Her personal integrity and obedience to Catholic authority also helped win her the eventual support of some of the hierarchy, allowing her to continue publication uninterrupted. And the wheel has turned. Several dramatic recent events signify a shift in Catholic opinion on issues of war and peace. In 1981, Bishop Leroy Matthiesen of Amarillo, Texas, protested the planned production of the neutron bomb, and urged nuclear-weapons workers in his diocese to consider resigning from their jobs in favor of peaceful pursuits. Also that year, Archbishop Raymond Hunthausen of Seattle announced he would withhold one-half of his federal income tax in protest against military spending. In 1982, in a pastoral statement marking the eight hundredth anniversary of the birth of St. Francis, the Archbishop of San Francisco, John R. Quinn, told his flock that "nuclear weapons and the arms race are essentially evil" and that " 'just' nuclear war is a contradiction in terms."

Carrying even more weight was Pope John Paul II's February 1981 pilgrimage to Hiroshima and Nagasaki, where he called for Christians to make "audacious gestures" to reverse the arms race. "Let us pledge ourselves to peace through justice," the Pope explicitly addressed world heads of state. "Let us promise our fellow human beings that we will work untiringly for disarmament and the banishing of all nuclear weapons."[8] On November 12, 1983, the pontiff called on the scientists of the world to abandon their "laboratories and factories of death" and replace them with "laboratories of life." While he stopped just short of advising all military researchers to resign their jobs, his speech strongly implied that such endeavors should be abandoned.[9] A month later in his Christmas message, the Pope urged world leaders to spend less on arms and instead to turn their eyes to the "unspeakable sorrow" of the world's starving children.

The most drastic departure from the traditional Catholic view on questions of war and peace, however, has been seen among the United States bishops. In 1965, as the Vietnam War raged, Dorothy Day confessed that she was "afraid" the bishops were "guilty of a feeling of nationalism. We are, after all, all of us Americans," she went on, "and we are traditionally not a peace church."[10] But in May 1983 the American bishops indicated a historic shift in their thinking when they issued their pastoral letter, "The Challenge of Peace: God's Promise and Our Response." In a two hundred and thirty-eight to nine vote, the bishops overwhelmingly approved the final draft, which places American Catholics in opposition to nearly forty years of U.S. nuclear weapons policies. Declaring nuclear weapons to be a moral issue, the bishops stated, "We do not perceive any situation in which the deliberate initiation of nuclear warfare, on however restricted a scale, can be morally justified."[11] Furthermore, they gave the position of pacifism a greater measure of respect than ever before, endorsing it as an acceptable moral and political choice for Catholics. In a special section entitled "The Value of Nonviolence," the bishops singled out the Catholic Worker leader's contribution with these words: "The nonviolent witness of such figures as Dorothy Day and Martin Luther King has had a profound impact upon the life of the church in the United States."[12]

In the first year following the pastoral's issue, both diocesan and non-diocesan peace groups as well as interfaith organizations studied and debated it as intensely as they would study holy Scripture. "Not since the new liturgy was introduced in the mid-Sixties," observed the *National Catholic Reporter*, "has there been such an avalanche of books, pamphlets, manuals, study guides, tapes and films aimed at every conceivable audience from nursery schools to nursing homes." In Iowa, sixteen Protestant and Catholic religious leaders, including the bishops of Sioux City, Des Moines, and Davenport, together issued a pastoral message on peace in December 1983. Essentially it was a shortened version of the U.S. bishops' pastoral. That month, the National Catholic Educational Association distributed a special issue of its publication *Momentum*, offering in-depth features on teaching the pastoral letter in schools—even military academies—and bringing it more fully into the curriculum. The six dioceses in Illinois declared January 1984 "Peace Month," and distributed a two hundred and forty-page packet of teaching materials on the pastoral to every parish. In early 1984, the Diocese of Rockville Centre, N.Y., organized a five-month program of workshops, speakers, packets of information for clergy, and a major diocesan event to mark the first anniversary of the pastoral. And the Milwaukee archdiocese was working to establish Pax Christi chapters in at least forty parishes.[13]

It is premature to try to gauge the comprehensive impact of the bishops' pastoral letter. It has certainly invigorated the Catholic peace movement, which today seems burgeoning everywhere. And whenever the roots of contemporary concern for peace and social justice are traced—whether by the bishops and clergy, by Catholics, or by non-Catholics—those roots invariably lead to the nourishing center, Dorothy Day. Through her *Catholic Worker*, she sustained such ideals during complacent times. Day and her colleagues were the single unbroken pacifist link in the United States over the past five decades, as they remain. Father Daniel Berrigan recently summarized the peace movement's debt to her. "Without Dorothy," he wrote, "without that exemplary patience, courage, moral modesty, without this woman pounding at the locked door behind which the powerful mock the powerless with games of triage, without her, the resistance we offered would have been simply unthinkable. She urged our consciences off the beaten track; she made the impossible (in our case) probable, and then actual."[14] Today as the *National Catholic Reporter* has written, we are truly "witnessing the flowering of the [Catholic] Worker movement's peace message."[15]

But Day's impact stretches far beyond the peace movement. As the philosopher J.M. Cameron told a national television audience the year of her death, she and her Catholic Worker movement are "central to any understanding of

American Catholicism at its best." He judged Day and her associates as having "done more to preserve the balance and sanity of American Catholicism than anything else."[16] On the occasion of the *Catholic Worker*'s fiftieth birthday in May 1983, an article in the Catholic mainstream monthly, the *St. Anthony Messenger*, characterized Dorothy Day as "a beloved, fundamental, essential part of the Catholic experience for generations of Americans." "Part of coming to terms with being a Catholic in today's world," it added, "is in fact coming to terms with Dorothy Day."[17]

And as David J. O'Brien has observed, Dorothy Day has surpassed all in commanding "wide and respected attention" from those outside the Catholic Church. Furthermore, "none has matched her stature" in the regard of Catholics outside the United States. And within the American Church, only a select few have become so nationally prominent; but "millions came to admire her witness, to be proud of her work, and to stand in awe of her dedication, her persistence, and her profound religious faith."[18] Through the luminous example of her life — her writing, her speaking, her activism — Dorothy Day exerted a profound influence not only on her Church but on the several generations of Americans whose thinking on social issues she repeatedly challenged.

Many hoped that Dorothy Day would live long enough to receive a Nobel Peace Prize, and to celebrate, in 1983, the fiftieth anniversary of her singular paper. The *Catholic Worker* is a most impressive legacy. What place should be assigned to it in the history of American journalism? Instructive comparisons can be made with other types of ideological publications — the turn-of-the-century muckrakers', the radical political press, the small, iconoclastic opinion journals, and the religious press. On the basis of its social reform activism, especially on behalf of labor, the *Catholic Worker* might, for example, be classified with the Socialist *Appeal to Reason* of Girard, Kansas (1895-1922), for which Eugene Debs was chief editorial writer; the muckraking *American Magazine* (1906-1908), started by Lincoln Steffens and other defectors from *McClure's Magazine*; the Communist *Daily Worker* (1924–); Max Eastman's brilliant *Masses* (1910-1920), for which Dorothy Day wrote as a young woman; the New York daily *PM* (1940-49), which supported liberalism, organized labor, and Jews and Negroes at a time when the New York press took a far less activist view; the *Guardian* (1948–), a prominent voice for the Old and then the New Left; Dwight Macdonald's *Politics* (1944-1949); and *I. F. Stone's Weekly* (1953-1971), which provided stringent criticism of the U.S. government and defense of civil liberty. Like Day, Stone single-mindedly challenged the powers-that-be.

Two major, long-lived opinion journals, the *Nation* and the *New Republic*, also merit comparison to the *Catholic Worker*. The more editorially consistent of the two is the *Nation*, which began in 1865 as an essentially single-person organ edited by Edwin L. Godkin. It continued to have strong editors in Oswald Garrison Villard (1918-1933), Freda Kirchwey (1937-1955), and Carey McWilliams (1955-1976). The *Nation* is the classic example of the small American opinion journal, devoted to thoughtful commentary on politics, literature, and the arts. Its stellar contributors have included William Dean Howells, Henry James, Bertrand Russell, Leon Trotsky, Lewis Mumford, Carl, Mark, and Irita Van Doren, André Malraux, and Reinhold Niebuhr. The *Nation* has hewed to a consistently liberal line, defending civil rights, exposing injustices and corruption, and, especially during the Villard years, espousing pacifism.[19] Like the *Catholic Worker*, it has often found itself a lonely voice raised in protest.

A companion liberal magazine, the *New Republic*, was founded in 1914. It, too, has sharply criticized social, political, and economic abuses and embraced civil liberties. The *New Republic* exerted influence during the Wilsonian years with the writings of editor Herbert Croly (1914-1930) and Walter Lippmann.[20] Other contributors have included Rebecca West, Jane Addams, William Faulkner, Malcolm Cowley, and Mary McCarthy. After the Croly and Lippmann years the *New Republic* became less single-minded in editing and less consistent in editorial policy; for example, opposing the Vietnam War while it had supported American efforts in both world wars. Nevertheless, the *New Republic* helped sustain some reform ideals over the years.

Among religious publications, the *Catholic Worker* might be compared with the Quaker activist A.J. Muste's *Liberation*, an intellectual, Protestant ecumenical voice for peace and social justice (1956-1977); and today, with the Protestant ecumenical magazines *Christian Century* and *Christianity and Crisis*, which take a liberal, intellectual viewpoint on issues of peace and social justice. Their radical, evangelical counterparts are *The Other Side* (1965–) and *Sojourners* (1971–). Like the *Catholic Worker*, both magazines are inspired by a Biblical base.[21] "We feel a deep kinship with the *Catholic Worker*," the associate editor of *Sojourners*, Lindsay McLaughlin, recently remarked. "Our magazine has been heavily influenced by the *Worker*, which introduced us to Catholic spirituality."[22]

The *Catholic Worker* should also be compared with the two leading liberal Catholic publications, *America* and *Commonweal*. *America*, a quality weekly of social, political, and literary comment, was founded by Jesuits in 1904. It has never enjoyed a mass circulation, but it articulated opinions that were later popularized through such publications as the Catholic family weekly *Our Sunday Visitor* and the growing chain of diocesan newspapers.[23] While liberal, in the past its editorial voice has been fairly predictable: During the Spanish Civil War, it supported Franco; as World War II approached, it advocated isolationism, although expressing doubt about the possibility of "just war" under modern conditions of combat. After Pearl Harbor, *America* viewed the war as a crusade against godless Nazism, which Catholics should patriotically support. It has continued to offer more nonconformist opinion, although during the Vietnam War it was hawkish.[24]

America's lay counterpart as a Catholic opinion-maker is *Commonweal*. Established as an independent journal in 1924, it also seeks to offer sophisticated social, political, and literary comment. As it grew, it became bolder in opposing mainstream Catholic positions. For example, it joined the *Catholic Worker* in expressing neutrality during the Spanish Civil War, which increased staff tensions considerably. By 1941, a column, "The Forum," had been introduced to allow expression of alternate editorial opinions on the question of war. Editors Philip Burnham and Edward Skillin, joined by others, urged that the United States remain out of the second world war; they advocated a diplomatic solution. C.G. Paulding, William M. Agar, and others on the staff tried to persuade *Commnweal* readers to support American involvement in the conflict. Pearl Harbor resolved the dilemma; all editors urged Catholics to support the war.

Thus the *Catholic Worker* remained as the only publication articulating a clear-cut anti-war ideology both before and after Pearl Harbor.[25] *Commonweal* took a position closer to the *Catholic Worker*'s during the Vietnam conflict, when in October 1967 it joined Dorothy Day's paper in advocating civil disobedience as a form of war protest.[26]

Nevertheless, among the three publications, the *Catholic Worker*'s positions were consistently the least compromising. Many of the opinions that Dorothy Day and her followers first expounded in the *Catholic Worker* were eventually adopted by *Commonweal*, sometimes by *America*, and sometimes ultimately by the Catholic Church, making the *Catholic Worker* a voice of conscience.

And yet in some respects the *Catholic Worker* resembles the *Wanderer*, the extremely conservative St. Paul, Minnesota, publication that has criticized it fairly regularly since the Thirties. The *Catholic Worker* shares the *Wanderer*'s traditional Catholic viewpoint on doctrine and dogma—the deference for the Pope, clergy, and religious; the reverent observance of traditional liturgy; the stress on the sacraments and the devout observance of the Church seasons; the emulation of the lives of the saints and of Mary, the mother of Christ. In these regards, the *Catholic Worker* also resembles, to varying degrees, the many diocesan papers and the middle-of-the-road Catholic family publications such as the *St. Anthony Messenger*, *Catholic Digest*, and the *Liguorian*.

But to this traditional Catholicism, the *Catholic Worker* adds an extreme radicalism in many things secular. The result is a publication which deserves a prominent place in American history. A remarkable achievement in advocacy, the *Catholic Worker*'s ideological commitments have never overshadowed its goal of presenting quality journalism. Substance has never been stressed at the expense of style—a hallmark of Dorothy Day's singular devotion to her craft as well as to her ideals. To the end of her life, she was the final authority at the *Worker*, guiding its content and tone. Her determined leadership as chief writer, editor, and publisher gave the paper consistency and continuity through even those periods in American history most hostile to its message. More striking than its survival at a penny a copy (supplemented by donations) for more than half a century, is the *Catholic Worker*'s unusual editorial consistency. From the start of the paper during the Great Depression, when circulation peaked at 190,000, through the Spanish Civil War and World War II, when subscriptions plummeted to 50,500 and Catholic Workers selling the paper were sometimes beaten in the streets, and then during the McCarthy era, the Korean War and Vietnam, Day maintained the *Catholic Worker*'s commitment to peace and social justice activism. Such an editorial viewpoint represents the first fruitful journalistic union of Catholic theological traditionalism with social radicalism. But most important of all, the *Catholic Worker's* impact on American consciences seems to have far surpassed that of other small, ideological publications, both religious and secular.

What will become of the Catholic Worker movement and its paper without Dorothy Day? In the first years after her death, many often raised this question. So far, both the movement and the paper seem to be flourishing. "There has been a renaissance of both interest and participation in our work," says Catherine Morris, a Los Angeles Catholic Worker for the past eleven years.[27] St. Joseph's House and Maryhouse in New York, and the several dozen Catholic Worker Houses of Hospitality and farming communes are continuing. Indeed, on the day of Dorothy Day's death, Michael Kirwan was opening a House of Hospitality in Washington, D.C. (which was joined, exactly a year later, by

FRITZ EICHENBERG © 1982

THE CHRIST OF THE HOMELESS 1982

a Maryhouse for homeless women in the nation's capital). By 1983, Houses of Hospitality had opened in at least four more cities.[28]

In July of 1983, nearly two hundred Catholic Workers from all over the country gathered at a seminary in New Jersey, for a four-day retreat. *Catholic Worker* editor Peggy Scherer wrote that they left "with the knowledge that the task we are given is to try to continue to learn from and live out the teachings of the Gospel, as Dorothy Day and Peter Maurin did. As long as our houses, our farms, and all our other works are needed," she added, "and provide the opportunity to put our faith into action, with love, we trust they will continue."[29] One of the tasks they may face, however, is "demythologizing" Dorothy Day. While some Catholic Workers would no doubt agree with the many American Catholics who would nominate Day for sainthood, others approve the view expressed by the Los Angeles House in its *Catholic Agitator* that "a Dorothy Day cult movement would create a concomitant myth that once there was a 'Golden Age' of the Catholic Worker movement, a glorious past overshadowing the paltry present."[30]

Some mythologizing in the *Catholic Worker* seems inevitable. Confronted with the demise of their leader, the paper's editors assert their respect for the past, emphasizing a reassuring continuity. Today's *Catholic Worker* often consoles readers with the assurance that Dorothy Day's spirit lives. Its writers sprinkle their articles with fond references to her. And outstanding articles from the publication's past, especially by Day, are regularly reprinted. Combining several issues, *Catholic Worker* editors have cut down to eight issues a year, in order to save time for other pressing tasks. But otherwise they have succeeded in publishing a quality paper of familiar scope and design. For as editor Scherer has remarked, "I wouldn't feel free to change the paper in any way at all. After all, that's five decades of history."[31] Able contributors are in ample supply, among them Scherer, who has produced many perceptive pieces on Central America in recent years; Robert Ellsberg, a versatile writer whose essays, profiles, and analyses are equally astute; and columnist Deane Mowrer, whose appreciation of nature and conversational style are reminiscent of Dorothy Day's.

Can the paper sustain the glorious, vigorous quality it knew under Dorothy Day's exacting editorship? Probably only if someone of Day's stature and unusual gifts emerges: someone who can contribute excellent journalism and inspire others to do so, someone who can be intimately involved in the movement, yet focus the requisite energy on the *Catholic Worker*. It is still too early to tell. And of course no one will ever match Dorothy Day's unique constellation of talents. But her associates hardly worry about such things. On the occasion of the *Catholic Worker*'s fiftieth anniversary, Scherer remarked, "We miss Dorothy, of course." But she pointed out that the Gospel is "still here, just as it was for her."[32] Catholic Workers know that in some form or another, her — and their — work will endure. For as Dorothy Day wrote in *The Long Loneliness*: "We have all known the long loneliness and we have learned that the only solution is love and that love comes with community. . . . It all happened while we sat there talking, and it is still going on."

Appendix

The Circulation of the *Catholic Worker*, 1933-1983

The circulation of *The Catholic Worker* is difficult to pinpoint. Occasionally — especially in its early years — the paper has reported its circulation, but it has not usually specified how many copies included in these figures have constituted bundle orders to churches and other organizations. In 1960, when postal authorities required all publications to print their circulation annually in the Statement of Ownership, Management, and Circulation (SOMC), the *Catholic Worker* began to total its circulation more exactly. Unless otherwise specified, the SOMC's reported here are figures for the total distribution (excluding copies printed for office use, left over, unaccounted for, or spoiled after printing) of the issue nearest to the filing date.

The *Ayer Directory of Publications* also provides some circulation figures for various years. Finally, some letters in the Catholic Worker Papers refer to circulation totals; but especially with these sources, the data may indicate the total press run more likely than firm subscriber circulation.

DATE	CIRCULATION	SOURCE
May 1933	2,500	*CW*, April 1934, p. 2.
November 1933	20,000	*CW*, November 1933, p. 1.
April 1934	30,000	*CW*, April 1934, p. 2.
May 1934	35,000	*CW*, May 1934, p.1.
December 1934	40,000	*CW*, December 1934, p. 1.
February 1935	50,000	*CW*, February 1935, p. 1.
March 1935	65,000	*CW*, March 1935, p. 1
April 1935	65,000	*CW*, April 1935, p. 1.
May 1935	110,000	*CW*, May 1935, p. 1.

July 1935	110,000	Letter from Dorothy Day to Police Commissioner Valentine, New York City, July 1935, CW Papers.
April 1936	115,000	*CW*, April 1936, p. 1.
1936	150,000	Dorothy Day, *The Long Loneliness*, p. 207.
May 1938	190,000	*CW*, May 1945, p. 2.
November 1939	130,000	*CW*, November 1939, p. 4.
June 20, 1940	over 120,000	Dorothy Day, appeal, June 20, 1940, CW Papers.
May 1941	75,000	*CW*, May 1941, p. 5.
June 1941	75,000	*CW*, June 1941, p. 1.
December 12, 1941	75,000	Dorothy Day, circular to C.W. Houses, December 12, 1941, CW Papers.
January 1942	75,000	*CW*, January 1942, p. 1.
April 1942	75,000	*CW*, April 1942, p. 4.
December 1942	55,000	*CW*, December 1942, p. 3.
January 1943	55,000	*CW*, January 1943, p. 4.
November 1944	50,500	*CW*, April 1948, p. 3.
March 1945	60,000	*CW*, April 1948, p. 3.
May 1945	50,500	*CW*, May 1945, p. 2.
April 1948	73,000 (11,000 extra)	*CW*, April 1948, p. 3.
1948	60,000	*Ayer* (publisher's estimate), p. 661.
November 1949	60,000	*CW*, November 1949, p. 1.
1949	60,000	*Ayer* (publisher's report), p. 664.
May 1950	65,000	*CW*, May 1950, p. 3.
October 1950	63,000	*CW*, October 1950, p. 1.
1950	63,000	*Ayer* (publisher's report), p. 660.
January 28, 1951	63,000	Letter from Dorothy Day to Msgr. Gaffney, January 28, 1951 ("Feast of St. Thomas Aquinas"), CW Papers.
1951	63,000	*Ayer* (estimate), p. 661.
1952	60,000	*Ayer* (publisher's report), p. 667.
1953	58,000	*Ayer* (publisher's report), p. 670.
1954	58,000	*Ayer* (publisher's report), p. 674.
August 5, 1955	65,000	Letter from Ammon Hennacy to Irene Keating, August 5, 1955, CW Papers.
1955	60,000	*Ayer* (publisher's report), p. 678.
1956	60,000	*Ayer* (estimate), p. 690.
1958	60,000	*Ayer* (publisher's report), p. 696.
March 1959	63,000	*CW*, March 1959, p. 1.
1959	60,000	*Ayer* (estimate), p. 702.
September 27, 1960	65,000	Letter from Ammon Hennacy to Mr. Duffy, September 27, 1960, CW Papers.

November 1960	65,000 (annual avg.)	*CW*, November 1960, p. 2 (SOMC).
1960	62,000	*Ayer* (publisher's report), p. 702.
December 1961	61,500 (annual avg.)	*CW*, December 1961, p. 7 (SOMC).
1961	62,000	*Ayer* (publisher's report), p. 707.
November 1962	64,000 (annual avg.)	*CW*, November 1962, p. 3 (SOMC).
1962	62,000	*Ayer* (estimate), p. 707.
November 1963	74,000	*CW*, November 1963, p. 2 (SOMC).
April 1964	74,000	Dorothy Day, *On Pilgrimage: The Sixties*, p. 167.
September 1964	79,000	*CW*, September 1964, p. 8.
November 1964	77,000	*CW*, November 1964, p. 6 (SOMC).
1964	70,000	*Ayer* (publisher's report), p. 713.
November 1965	77,000	*CW*, November 1965, p. 7 (SOMC).
1965	70,000	*Ayer* (estimate), p. 723.
December 1966	85,000	*CW*, December 1966, p. 2 (SOMC).
November 1967	89,000	*CW*, November 1967, p. 3 (SOMC).
1967	89,000	*Ayer* (publisher's report), p. 730.
December 1968	82,000	*CW*, December 1968, p. 2 (SOMC).
1968	89,000	*Ayer* (estimate), p. 730.
Oct.-Nov. 1969	86,000	*CW*, October-November 1969, p. 6 (SOMC).
Oct.-Nov. 1970	82,000	*CW*, October-November 1970, p. 7 (SOMC).
1970	76,000	*Ayer* (publisher's estimate), p. 740.
Oct.-Nov. 1971	87,000	*CW*, October-November 1971, p. 6 (SOMC).
Oct.-Nov. 1972	82,000	*CW*, October-November 1972, p. 6 (SOMC).
Oct.-Nov. 1973	82,500	*CW*, October-November 1973, p. 7 (SOMC).
1973	80,000	*Ayer* (publisher's estimate), p. 590.
December 1974	83,500	*CW*, December 1974, p. 6 (SOMC).
1974	80,000	*Ayer* (publisher's estimate), p. 606.
December 1975	88,500	*CW*, December 1975, p. 7 (SOMC).
1975	79,000	*Ayer* (publisher's estimate), p. 616.
December 1976	91,500	*CW*, December 1976, p. 7 (SOMC).
1976	79,000	*Ayer* (publisher's estimate), p. 621.
December 1977	91,000	*CW*, December 1977, p. 6 (SOMC).
1977	90,000	*Ayer* (publisher's estimate), p. 620.
December 1978	95,000	*CW*, December 1978, p. 6 (SOMC).
1978	90,000	*Ayer* (estimate), p. 602.

December 1979	94,900	*CW*, December 1979, p. 8 (SOMC).
December 1980	94,900	*CW*, December 1980, p. 12 (SOMC).
December 1981	97,700	*CW*, December 1981, p. 8 (SOMC).
December 1982	101,000	*CW*, December 1982, p. 6 (SOMC).
December 1983	103,500	*CW*, December 1983, p. 4 (SOMC).

Notes

I: The Catholic Worker Movement

1. "Parade in Moscow Show of Strength," *New York Times*, May 2, 1933, p. 3.

2. Frederick T. Birchall, "Hitler Will Draft Youth for Labor; 1,000,000 Hail Him," *New York Times*, May 2, 1933, p. 13.

3. "May Day is Quiet Throughout the World; 50,000 Parade Here," *New York Times*, May 2, 1933, p. 3.

4. Dorothy Day, *Loaves and Fishes* (N.Y.: Harper and Row, 1963), p. 18.

5. "To Our Readers," *Catholic Worker* (hereinafter cited as *CW*), May 1933, p. 4.

6. "Filling a Need," *CW*, May 1933, p. 4.

7. Colman McCarthy, "Colman McCarthy on Dorothy Day," *New Republic*, Feb. 24, 1973, p. 32.

8. Kenneth L. Woodward and Eloise Salholz, "The End of a Pilgrimage," *Newsweek*, Dec. 15, 1980, p. 75.

9. Michael Harrington, *The Other America: Poverty in the United States* (N.Y.: Macmillan, 1962).

10. Thomas D. Frary, "The Ecclesiology of Dorothy Day," Ph.D. dissertation, Marquette University, 1972; Thomas D. Frary, " 'Thy Kingdom Come'—The Theology of Dorothy Day," *America*, Nov. 11, 1972, pp. 385-387.

11. David J. O'Brien, "The Pilgrimage of Dorothy Day," *Commonweal*, Dec. 19, 1980, p. 711; *American Catholics and Social Reform: The New Deal Years* (N.Y.: Oxford University Press, 1968), p. 192.

12. Linda Bamber, "A Saint's Life," *Nation*, Sept. 11, 1982, p. 212.

13. Woodward and Salholz, "The End of a Pilgrimage," p. 75.

14. F.G. Friedmann, "Dorothy Day und der 'Catholic Worker,' " *Stimmen der Zeit*, March 1980, pp. 195-200.

15. From an interview with NBC's "Meet the Press," July 10, 1983. Reprinted in "Interview with Petra Kelly," *Catholic Agitator*, Oct. 1983, p. 4.

16. Letter from Nina Polcyn Moore (Catholic Worker and close friend of Dorothy Day), Sauk Centre, Minn., to Nancy L. Roberts, Dec. 19, 1981.

17. Alden Whitman, "Dorothy Day, Outspoken Catholic Activist, Dies at 83," *New York Times*, Nov. 30, 1980, section 1, p. 45; Alden Whitman, "Dorothy Day, Catholic Activist, 83, Dies," *New York Times*, Dec. 1, 1980, p. D-12.

18. "Dorothy Day Dies," *Washington Post*, Dec. 1, 1980, p. 1.

19. Dorothy Day, *On Pilgrimage: The Sixties* (N.Y.: Curtis Books, 1972), p. 15.

20. Day, *Loaves and Fishes*, p. 131.

21. Dwight Macdonald, "Profiles: The Foolish Things of the World—I," *New Yorker*, Oct. 4, 1952, p. 37.

22. Bruce Cook, "Dorothy Day and the Catholic Worker," *U.S. Catholic*, March 1966, pp. 6-7.

23. Day, *Loaves and Fishes*, p. 132.

24. Bruce Cook, "The Real Dorothy Day," *U.S. Catholic*, April 1966, p. 29.

25. Reprinted in Peter Maurin, "What the Catholic Worker Believes," *The Green Revolution* (Fresno, Calif. Academy Guild Press, 1949), pp. 76-77.

26. Robert Ellsberg, ed., *By Little and By Little: The Selected Writings of Dorothy Day* (N.Y.: Alfred A. Knopf, 1983), p. xxx.

27. Anthony Novitsky, "The Ideological Development of Peter Maurin's Green Revolution," Ph.D. dissertation, State University of New York at Buffalo, 1976, pp. 331-345.

28. Peter Maurin, "A Letter to John Strachey and His Readers," *CW*, April 1935, p. 8; William D. Miller, *A Harsh and Dreadful Love: Dorothy Day and the Catholic Worker Movement* (hereinafter cited as *Love*) (N.Y.: Liveright, 1973), p. 5. The introduction (pp. 3-16) outlines the origins of the movement and was helpful in preparing this chapter.

29. Letter from Stanley Vishnewski to Julie Kernan, March 24, 1964, The Dorothy Day-Catholic Worker Collection, Memorial Library Archives, Marquette University, Milwaukee (hereinafter cited as "CW Papers").

30. Miller, *Love*, p. 7.

31. Nikolai Berdyaev, *The Meaning of History* (N.Y.: Charles Scribner's Sons, 1936), p. 17.

32. "New Heaven/New Earth," 60-min. videotape cassette interview of Dorothy Day by Herbert Jessup, broadcast by WCUB-TV, Boston (1974), CW Papers.

33. Tom Cain, "Personalism — The One-Man Revolution," *CW*, Feb. 1956, p. 1.

34. "Going to the Roots," *CW*, May 1978, p. 7.

35. Dorothy Day, *The Long Loneliness: The Autobiography of Dorothy Day* (Garden City, N.Y.: Image Books Edition, 1959), p. 41. (Original edition: N.Y.: Harper and Row, 1952.)

36. Dorothy Day, *From Union Square to Rome* (N.Y.: Arno Press, 1978; reprint of the 1938 Preservation of the Faith Press edition), p. 8.

37. Day, *The Long Loneliness*, p. 41.

38. Fyodor Dostoevsky, *The Brothers Karamazov* (N.Y.: Airmont Publishing Co., Inc., 1966), p. 56.

39. "Personalism and Communitarianism," *CW*, Oct. 1936, p. 8.

40. See, for example, Geoffrey Gneuhs, "Chesterton's Distributism: 'Something Elvish'," *CW*, Dec. 1983, pp. 1,8.

41. The Rev. Benedict Brady, "The Mystical Body of Christ,"*CW*, March 1935, p. 4.

42. Dorothy Day, "Poverty and the Christian Commitment," Talk given at the Social Action Forum, New York University, Nov. 12, 1965, CW Papers, Cassette II.

43. Brady, "The Mystical Body of Christ," p. 4.

44. Letter to Congress and President Franklin Roosevelt, n.d., CW Papers.

45. "Catholic Worker Positions, *CW*, Sept. 1954, p. 5.

46. J. Michael McCloskey, "The Catholic Worker Movement," *CW*, May 1956, p. 5.

47. "Catholic Worker Positions," p. 5.

48. Miller, *Love*, p. 97; Dorothy Day, *House of Hospitality* (N.Y.: Sheed and Ward, 1939), p. 60.

49. Marc H. Ellis, *A Year at the Catholic Worker* (N.Y.: Paulist Press, 1978), p. 52.

50. Personal interview, Milwaukee, Nov. 4, 1981.

51. Dorothy Day, "Why Poverty?" *CW*, Jan. 1946, p. 3.

52. Dorothy Day, "Poverty," *CW*, July-Aug. 1979, p. 2.

53. Day, *Loaves and Fishes*, p. 82.

54. Stanley Vishnewski, "Days of Action," unpublished manuscript, circa 1966, CW Papers, p. 13.

55. Day, *Loaves and Fishes*, p. viii.

56. Ammon Hennacy, *Autobiography of a Catholic Anarchist* (Glen Gardner, N.J.: Libertarian Press, 1954), p. 317. (Reissued as *The Book of Ammon*, N.Y.: Catholic Worker Books, 1965.)

57. Robert Ludlow, "A Re-evaluation," *CW*, June 1955, p. 1.

58. Day, "Poverty and the Christian Commitment," Cassette II.

59. Ibid.

60. Dorothy Day, "Catholic Worker Positions," in *Peace and Nonviolence*, ed. Edward Guinan (N.Y.: Paulist Press, 1973), p. 54.

61. For names and addresses of current Houses of Hospitality, see: "Houses of Hospitality," *CW*, May, 1982, pp. 7,8.

62. Arthur Sheehan, "Farming Communes," *CW*, Sept. 1942, p. 8.

63. Ellis, *A Year at the Catholic Worker*, pp. 36-37.

64. Dorothy Day, "An Appeal," March 19, 1971, CW Papers.

65. Ibid.

66. Ellis, *A Year at the Catholic Worker*, pp. 82-83.

67. Dorothy Day, "Idea for a Farm Commune," *CW*, Jan. 1939, p. 8.

68. For addresses of currrent farming communes, see: "Houses of Hospitality," pp. 7,8.

69. Dorothy Day, "On Pilgrimage," *CW*, May 1964, p. 1.

70. Dorothy Day, "Aims and Purposes," *CW*, Feb. 1940, p. 7.

71. "Going to the Roots," p. 6.

72. Miller, *Love*, p. 71.

73. The history of the *Chicago Catholic Worker*, which was edited by John Cogley, James O'Gara (present editor of *Commonweal*) and others, is detailed in Francis J. Sicius, "The Chicago Catholic Worker Movement, 1936 to the Present," Ph.D. Dissertation, Loyola University (Chicago), 1979.

II: Dorothy Day and Peter Maurin

1. John Leo LeBrun makes similar points in "The Role of the Catholic Worker Movement in American Pacifism, 1933-1972," Ph.D. dissertation, Case Western Reserve University, 1973.

2. Dorothy Day, *On Pilgrimage* (N.Y.: Catholic Worker Books, 1948), p. 31; Miller, *Love*, p. 36. The latter, along with his *Dorothy Day: A Biography* (N.Y.: Harper and Row, 1982), are the best sources for the details of Day's life.

3. Day, *From Union Square to Rome*, p. 49; Judith Nies, *Seven Women* (N.Y.: Viking Press, 1977), p. 183.

4. Day, *On Pilgrimage*, p. 47.

5. Day, *From Union Square to Rome*, p. 23.

6. Day, *The Long Loneliness*, pp. 23-24, 33.

7. Day, *From Union Square to Rome*, p. 20.

8. Ibid., p. 32.

9. Ibid., p. 25.

10. Day, *Loaves and Fishes*, p. 7.

11. Ibid., p. 7.

12. Day, *The Long Loneliness*, p. 35.

13. Ibid., pp. 35,36.

14. William D. Miller, "All Was Grace," *America*, Dec. 13, 1980, p. 382.

15. Day, *From Union Square to Rome*, p. 44.

16. Day, Ibid.; Day, *The Long Loneliness*, p. 47. However, William D. Miller's search of back issues of the campus newspaper and magazine in the University of Illinois archives revealed no signed pieces by Day (letter from Miller to Nancy L. Roberts, Feb. 5, 1984).

17. Simons Prohme died before she was thirty of encephalitis, attended in her final days by Anna Louise Strong (Nies, *Seven Women*, p. 184).

18. Day, *The Long Loneliness*, p. 44.

19. Ibid., p. 43.

20. Ibid., p. 41.

21. Ibid., p. 48.

22. Ibid., p. 50.

23. Day described her journalistic life in two *Call* stories: "Girl Reporter, with Three Cents in Purse, Braves Night Court Lawyers," Nov. 11, 1916, p. 2; "Hunting a 'Story', " Nov. 21, 1916, p. 3.

24. Day, *The Long Loneliness*, p. 60.

25. James Forest, "No Longer Alone: The Catholic Peace Movement," in *American Catholics and Vietnam*, ed. Thomas E. Quigley (Grand Rapids, Mich.: William B. Eerdmans Publishing Co., 1968), p. 142.

26. James Forest, "Dorothy Day: Witness to the Kingdom," *Catholic Agitator*, Nov. 1981, p. 3.

27. Day, *The Long Loneliness*, p. 63.

28. Laurence Leamer, *The Paper Revolutionaries* (N.Y.: Simon and Schuster, 1972), p. 17.

29. Day, *The Long Loneliness*, p. 66.

30. Floyd Dell, *Homecoming* (N.Y.: Farrar & Rinehart, 1933), p. 296.

31. Day, *On Pilgrimage: The Sixties*, p. 303.

32. Ammon Hennacy, *The One-Man Revolution in America* (Salt Lake City, Ut.: Ammon Hennacy Publications, 1970), p. 290.

33. Day, *The Long Loneliness*, p. 66.

34. Hennacy, *The One-Man Revolution in America*, p. 290; Dwight Macdonald, "Profiles: The Foolish Things of the World — II," *New Yorker*, Oct. 11, 1952, p. 40.

35. Day, *On Pilgrimage: The Sixties*, p. 305.

36. For a description of the *Masses* trial, see "The Story of the Trial," *Liberator*, June 1918, pp. 7-18.

37. Day, *The Long Loneliness*, p. 85.

38. Ibid., pp. 84-93.

39. Malcolm Cowley, *The Exile's Return (A Literary Odyssey of the 1920s)* (N.Y.: Viking Press, 1951), p. 69.

40. Dorothy Day, "Max Bodenheim," *CW*, March 1954, p. 7.

41. Day, *From Union Square to Rome*, p. 88.

42. Day, *The Long Loneliness*, pp. 81-82.

43. Miller, "All Was Grace," p. 383.

44. Miller, *Love*, p. 50.

45. Ellis, *A Year at the Catholic Worker*, pp. 51-52.

46. Harrington, *Fragments of the Century* (N.Y.: Simon and Schuster, 1972), p. 20.

47. Day, *The Long Loneliness*, p. 110.

48. Harrington, *Fragments of the Century*, p. 20.

49. Quoted by Wes Michaelson and Jim Wallis, "Interview — Dorothy Day: Exalting Those of Low Degree," *Sojourners*, Dec. 1976, p. 16.

50. Dorothy Day, "The Book of the Month," *Masses*, Nov.-Dec. 1917, p. 31.

51. Day, *The Long Loneliness*, p. 91.

52. Miller, *Dorothy Day: A Biography*, pp. 143,144.

53. Nies, *Seven Women*, p. 185.

54. Day, *The Long Loneliness*, pp. 98-102.

55. Ibid., p. 116.

56. Dorothy Day, "On Pilgrimage," *CW*, Oct.-Nov. 1976, p. 4.

57. Day, *The Long Loneliness*, pp. 130, 132.

58. Dorothy Day, "Having a Baby," *New Masses*, June 1928, pp. 5-6.

59. Day, *The Long Loneliness*, p. 135.

60. Ibid., pp. 135,136,141,143.

61. Ibid., p. 136.

62. Ibid, p. 145.

63. Jeff Dietrich and Susan Pollack, "An Interview with Dorothy Day," *Catholic Agitator*, Dec. 1971, p. 1.

64. Day, *The Long Loneliness*, pp. 160-161.

65. Ibid., p. 161.

66. Ibid., p. 9.

67. Dorothy Day, "Introduction" to Peter Maurin, *The Green Revolution*, p. i.

68. Day, *The Long Loneliness*, p. 165.

69. Dorothy Day, *House of Hospitality* (N.Y.: Sheed and Ward, 1939), p. xv; Day, *The Long Loneliness*, pp. 193-197.

70. "Peter Maurin," *Commonweal*, May 27, 1949, p. 164.

71. "Poor Man," *Time*, May 30, 1949, p. 54.

72. Arthur Sheehan, *Peter Maurin, Gay Believer* (Garden City, N.Y.: Hanover House, 1959), p. 19. This biography is especially valuable for details of Maurin's early life. A recent biography by Marc H. Ellis, *Peter Maurin: Prophet in the Twentieth Century* (N.Y.: Paulist Press, 1981) focuses on Maurin's thought. Also, Day made many references to Maurin in her writings, especially *Loaves and Fishes*; and Miller's *A Harsh and Dreadful Love* includes a chapter which provides helpful background on Maurin.

73. Miller, *Love*, p. 17.

74. Sheehan, *Peter Maurin: Gay Believer*, p. 25.

75. Ibid., pp. 50-51.

76. Miller, *Love*, pp. 26-27.

77. Sheehan, *Peter Maurin: Gay Believer*, p. 67.

78. Ellis, *Peter Maurin: Prophet in the Twentieth Century*, p. 29.

79. Peter Maurin, "Scholars and Bourgeois" (Easy Essay) in *The Green Revolution*, p. 27.

80. Day, *Loaves and Fishes*, p. 94.

81. Day, *On Pilgrimage*, pp. 83,84; Miller, *Love*, p. 19.

82. Day, *Loaves and Fishes*, p. 9.

83. Richard Deverall, "The Way It Was: 2," *Social Order*, June 1961, p. 262.

84. *Easy Essays* (Fresno, Calif.: Academy Guild Press, 1961; and Chicago: Franciscan Herald Press, 1977) was intended by Dorothy Day and the editors of the *Catholic Worker* to be the "ultimate and authoritative edition." It attempts to present the essence of Maurin's thought, "in the versions he left at his death, with some of the repetitions and the more ephemeral essays which had to do with Hitlerism, the NRA, etc., deleted." (Long out of print is a slightly different edition, also entitled *Easy Essays*, published in 1936 by Sheed and Ward, N.Y.) Hereinafter, references are to the 1977 edition.

85. Peter Maurin, "Blowing the Dynamite," in *Easy Essays* (1977 ed.), p. 3.

86. Day, *House of Hospitality*, p. xviii.

87. Personal interview, Milwaukee, Nov. 5, 1981.

88. Frank Gorgen, personal interview, Milwaukee, Nov. 4, 1981.

89. Personal interview, Newport, R.I., April 26, 1983.

90. Cook, "Dorothy Day and the Catholic Worker," p. 9.

91. Day, *The Long Loneliness*, p. 165.

92. Dorothy Day, "Introduction" to *The Green Revolution*, p. i.

93. Day, *House of Hospitality*, p. xxviii.

94. Day, quoted in *Catholics in Conversation*, ed. Donald McDonald (Philadelphia: J.B. Lippincott, 1960), p. 103.

III: "Read the *Catholic Worker* Daily!"

1. Day, *The Long Loneliness*, p. 169; Day, *Loaves and Fishes*, p. 15.

2. Day, *The Long Loneliness*, p. 169.

3. Ibid., p. 170; Day, *House of Hospitality*, p. xxviii.

4. Day, *Loaves and Fishes*, p. 15; Day, *The Long Loneliness*, p. 170.

5. Day, *Loaves and Fishes*, p. 20.

6. Peter Maurin, "Maurin's Program," *CW*, June-July 1933, p. 4.

7. Day, *Loaves and Fishes*, p. 22.

8. Ibid., p. 20.

9. Day, *House of Hospitality*, p. xviii.

10. Peter Maurin, "Journalism," *CW*, Jan. 1945, p. 1 (included in *The Green Revolution*, pp. 129-130).

11. Everette Dennis and William Rivers, *Other Voices: The New Journalism in America* (San Francisco: Canfield Press, 1974), p. 8.

12. Ibid., pp. 7,53.

13. Dorothy Day, "Technique of Action," *CW*, Dec. 1933, p. 2.

14. Dorothy Day, "Day After Day," *CW*, Sept. 1942, p. 1.

15. Letter from Dorothy Day to MacAlan Gardner, Sacramento, Calif., Sept. 30, 1935, CW Papers.

16. Dorothy Day, "An Answer to Some Charges against the *Catholic Worker*, privately published, 1937, CW Papers (reprint of an open letter in the *Brooklyn Tablet*, 1935).

17. Michael Schudson, *Discovering the News: A Social History of American Newspapers* (N.Y.: Basic Books, Inc., 1978), pp. 5-6, 120-122.

18. Dennis and Rivers, *Other Voices*, p. 2.

19. Carey McWilliams, "Is Muckraking Coming Back?," *Columbia Journalism Review*, Fall 1970, p. 8.

20. Dorothy Day, "Spreading the Good News," *CW*, July-Aug., 1944, p. 2.

21. Personal interview, Newport, R.I., April 26, 1983.

22. Letter from Dorothy Day to Msgr. Arthur J. Scanlan, N.Y., N.Y., March 16, 1934, CW Papers. (Also see editorial, "The Family vs. Capitalism," *CW*, Jan. 1936, p. 4.)

23. Personal interview, Milwaukee, Nov. 5, 1981.

24. Letter from Dorothy Day to Miss Sheridan, May 2, 1934, CW Papers.

25. Letter from the editors to Edmond B. Butler, N.Y., N.Y., Jan. 22, 1935, CW Papers.

26. Telephone interview, Jan. 11, 1984.

27. Dorothy Day, "On Pilgrimage," *CW*, June 1975, pp. 1-2.

28. Letter from the editors to Frank A. Hall, Director, N.C.W.C. News Service, Washington, D.C., Aug. 21, 1934, CW Papers.

29. Day, *House of Hospitality*, p. xxxi.

30. Letter from Dorothy Day to the Rev. J. Fitzsimons, St. Joseph's College, Lancashire, England, Dec. 1934, CW Papers; letter from Ammon Hennacy to the Rev. Magree, Oct. 4, 1960, CW Papers.

31. Telephone interview, N.Y.,N.Y., Jan. 11, 1984.

32. Letter from Martin J. Corbin to Betty Gannett, Executive Editor of *Political Affairs*, July 27, 1964, CW Papers; letter from Martin J. Corbin to Donald J. Thorman, Publisher, *National Catholic Reporter*, June 16, 1966, CW Papers.

33. Day, *House of Hospitality*, pp. 241-242; "Thank You, St. Joseph!" (editorial), *CW*, March 1934, p. 4; Dwight Macdonald, "Profiles: The Foolish Things of the World—II," p. 44; Day, *Loaves and Fishes*, p. 87.

34. "Going to the Roots," *CW*, May 1978, p. 7; Dorothy Day, "This Money Is Not Ours," *CW*, Sept. 1960, p. 1.

35. Dorothy Day, "Catholic Worker Appeal," *CW*, May 1944, p. 8.

36. Richard Deverall, "The Way It Was: 3," *Social Order*, Sept. 1961, p. 303.

37. Dorothy Day, "Fall Appeal 1977," CW Papers.

38. Letter from Anne McKeon to Dorothy Day, Sept. 16, 1967, CW Papers.

39. Letter from Mrs. P.F. Morrison to Dorothy Day, Nov. 21, 1944, CW Papers.

40. Day, *Loaves and Fishes*, p. 87.

41. Day, *House of Hospitality*, p. 86.

42. Dorothy Day, "On Pilgrimage," *CW*, June 1975, p. 2.

43. Day, *House of Hospitality*, p. xxxi.

44. Personal interview, Milwaukee, Nov. 6, 1981.

45. Day, *Loaves and Fishes*, p. 208.

46. Vishnewski, "Days of Action," p. 220.

47. Ellis, *A Year at the Catholic Worker*, p. 100.

48. Katharine Temple, "Our Computer Dilemma," *CW*, Dec. 1983, p. 2.

49. Ibid., p. 7.

50. Telephone interview, Jan. 10, 1984.

51. Letter from Donald Brown (*Catholic Worker* subscriber and friend of Day's, with whom she sometimes stayed while traveling), Corning, N.Y., to Nancy L. Roberts, May 15, 1981.

52. Letter from Dorothy Day to MacAlan Gardner, Sacramento, Calif., Sept. 30, 1935, CW Papers.

53. Dorothy Day, 'The Apostolate of Letter Writing," *Preservation of the Faith*, April 1941, pp. 17-19.

54. Vishnewski, "Days of Action," p. 223.

55. Letter from Day to Gardner, Ibid.

56. Letter from Dorothy Day to Dan J. Connolly, Keansburg, N.J., Oct. 13, 1934, CW Papers.

57. See, for example, letter from the editors to G.K. Chesterton, May 22, 1934, CW Papers.

58. Letter from Dorothy Day to the Rev. Schneeweiss, May 22, 1934, CW Papers.

59. Letter from the editors to the Rt. Rev. Msgr. Leo J. Fink, Allentown, Pa., May 3, 1934, CW Papers.

60. Vishnewski, "Days of Action," p. 222.

61. Day, *House of Hospitality*, p. 90.

62. Letter from the editors to the Rev. J.A. McGuire, C.S.S.R., Dec. 28, 1933, CW Papers.

63. Letter from the editors to the Rev. Crane, July 25, 1934, CW Papers.

64. Miller, *Love*, pp. 72, 104; see circulation chart in Appendix.

65. Day, *The Long Loneliness*, p. 178; Day, *On Pilgrimage: The Sixties*, p. 313; Vishnewski, "Days of Action," p. 223.

66. Day, *On Pilgrimage: The Sixties*, p. 313.

67. Day, *House of Hospitality*, pp. 25-26.

68. Raymond A. Schroth, "Dorothy Day," *America*, Oct. 19, 1968, p. 357.

69. Quoted by Robert Ellsberg in "Fritz Eichenberg: An Undimmed Sense of Wonder," *CW*, Oct.-Nov., 1981, p. 4.

70. Letter from Ruth Kilpack, editor, *Friends Journal*, to Nancy L. Roberts, Sept. 1981.

71. Letter from Ausim Pardue to Dorothy Day, May 31, 1949, CW Papers.

72. Letter from Del Eberhardt, Pastor, Clearlake Eastshore M.E. Community Church to Dorothy Day, May 2, 1945, CW Papers.

73. Letter from Wunnakyawhtin U Ohn Ghine to Dorothy Day, Nov. 1, 1958, CW Papers.

74. For example: Letter from Erwin Knoll, editor, *The Progressive*, to Nancy L. Roberts, Aug. 24, 1981; letter from Dean Peerman, executive editor, *Christian Century*, to Nancy L. Roberts, July 3, 1980.

75. Letter from Aldous Huxley to Dorothy Day, *CW*, Jan. 1945, p. 6.

76. Miller, *Love*, p. 74.

77. Letter from B.E. Sloane to Dorothy Day, Feb. 1, 1963, CW Papers.

78. Letter from Mrs. W.G. Never to Dorothy Day, Oct. 10, 1944, CW Papers.

79. Letter from David Wigton to the *Catholic Worker*, Aug. 26, 1968, CW Papers.

80. Day, *Loaves and Fishes*, p. 131.

81. John Brunini, "A Catholic Paper vs. Communism," *Commonweal*, Nov. 24, 1933, p. 97.

82. Peter Maurin, "Maurin's Program," p. 4.

83. "Report on Progress," *CW*, May 1935; also see Ammon Hennacy, *Autobiography of a Catholic Anarchist*, p. 205.

84. Day, *Loaves and Fishes*, p. 159; also see letter from Magda Friedman at Alfred A. Knopf, Publishers, to Dorothy Day, April 17, 1951, CW Papers.

85. Letter from Carlos Allen, N.Y.,N.Y., to Dorothy Day, Dec. 4, 1959, CW Papers.

86. Robert Coles and Jon Erikson, *A Spectacle Unto the World: The Catholic Worker Movement* (N.Y.: Viking Press, 1973), p. 55.

87. Day, *Loaves and Fishes*, p. 82.

88. "Catholic Worker Celebrates 3rd Birthday; A Restatement of C.W. Aims and Ideals," *CW*, May 1936, pp. 1,6; "Aims and Purposes," *CW*, May 1983, p. 12. Also see J. Michael McCloskey, "The Catholic Worker Movement," *CW*, May 1957, pp. 4-5; Dorothy Day,
"Letter to Our Readers at the Beginning of Our Fifteenth Year," *CW*, May 1947, pp. 1-4; "Catholic Worker Positions," *CW*, May 1975, p. 4; "Going to the Roots," *CW*, May 1978, pp. 6-7.

89. Day, "Technique of Agitation," p. 2.

90. *CW*, Dec. 1942, p. 3.

91. *CW*, Jan. 1936, p. 5; May 1950, p. 1; Feb. 1958, p. 1; April 1935, p. 1; and May 1935, p. 1.

92. Dorothy Day, "The Opium of the People?," *CW*, July 1937, p. 4.

93. Letter from Ade Bethune, Newport, R.I., to Nancy L. Roberts, Sept. 26, 1983. (Ade Bethune's papers are collected at the College of St. Catherine, St. Paul.)

94. Personal interview, Newport, R.I., April 26, 1983.

95. Ade Bethune, "Livelihood through Community Vocations," unpublished manuscript, Spring 1983, CW Papers.

96. Ade Bethune, "C.W. Artist Explains Her Pictures," *CW*, Sept. 1938, p. 8.

97. Day, *The Long Loneliness*, p. 217.

98. Letter from Ade Bethune, Newport, R.I., to Nancy L. Roberts, Sept. 26, 1983; personal interview, Newport, R.I., April 26, 1983.

99. Ellsberg, "Fritz Eichenberg: An Undimmed Sense of Wonder," p. 4.

100. Personal interview, Peace Dale, R.I., Jan. 12, 1983.

101. Letter from Mother Theresa of Calcutta to Dorothy Day, *CW*, Oct.-Nov. 1972, p. 6.

102. James Forest, "Thomas Merton and the Catholic Worker—Ten Years After," *CW*, Dec. 1978, pp. 4-6.

103. "Prof. Jacques Maritain Writes Characteristically to Peter Maurin," *CW*, Dec. 1934, p. 8.

104. See letter from Martin J. Corbin to I.F. Stone, Aug. 31, 1964, CW Papers.

105. Dorothy Day, diary entry, Dec. 16, 1966, CW Papers.

106. Personal interviews, Milwaukee, Nov. 6, 1981; Waterbury, Ct., May 15, 1983.

107. Letter from Dorothy Day to Anthony F. Schomburg, Detroit, April 26, 1934, CW Papers.

108. Letter from Dorothy Day to Mary Jo Weiler, Aug. 14, 1935, CW Papers.

IV: The Journalist

1. Day, *The Long Loneliness*, p. 91.

2. Dorothy Day, "On Pilgrimage," *CW*, June 1975, p. 1.

3. Vishnewski, "Days of Action," p. 171.

4. Personal interview, Milwaukee, Nov. 6, 1981.

5. Personal interview, Milwaukee, Nov. 5, 1981.

6. Letter from Dorothy Day to Dr. Anscome, Jan. 17, 1967, CW Papers.

7. Ibid.

8. Letter from Dorothy Day to William D. Miller, Oct. 8, 1974, CW Papers.

9. Day, *On Pilgrimage*, p. 145.

10. Dorothy Day, "Newsletter," Jan. 1973, CW Papers.

11. Letter from Dorothy Day to William D. Miller, June 25, 1970, CW Papers.

12. Vishnewski, "Days of Action," p. 172.

13. Letter from Day to Dr. Anscome, Jan. 17, 1967, CW Papers.

14. Day, *On Pilgrimage*, p. 175.

15. John W.C. Johnstone, Edward J. Slawski, and William W. Bowman, *The News People: A Sociological Portrait of American Journalists and Their Work* (Urbana, Ill.: University of Illinois Press, 1976).

16. Day, "Technique of Action," *CW*, Dec. 1933, p. 2.

17. Johnstone, et. al., *The News People*, pp. 174-175, 178, 171.

18. Robert S. Fortner, "The Depths of Depression: Sin and Salvation As Seen by the Radical Press, 1930-1939," paper presented to Association for Education in Journalism and Mass Communication, annual convention, Corvallis, Oregon, Aug. 1983, p. 7.

19. Some examples from the *Call* include:
"Mr. J.D. Rockefeller, 26 Broadway: Here's a Family Living on Dog Food," Nov. 13, 1916, p. 1, "High Prices Compel Housewife to Use Cornmeal for Flour in Bread," Nov. 15, 1916, p. 2, "The Short and Simple Annals of the Poor Are Slow Starvation," Nov. 16, 1916, p. 1, "East Side Home Is Cold and Dreary, Because Machine Takes Tailor's Job," Nov. 26, 1916, p. 4, "Dying Man Unable to Carve Turkey If Family Had One, but It Hasn't; Another Home Has a Famished Brood," Nov. 30, 1916, p. 2, " 'Doctor Said It was Malnutrition; One Baby 'Batty,' Another On Way,' " Dec. 1, 1916, pp. 1,2, "Can't Preach Sermon About Benny Leonard," Dec. 3, 1916, p. 2, "Plucky Girl on Picket Line Braves Knives of Scabs and 'Guerillas,' " Feb. 1, 1917, p. 3, "Mrs. Byrne, in Collapse, Is Pardoned by Whitman," Feb. 2, 1917, pp. 1,2, "Mrs. Byrne Too Weak to Eat After Ordeal at Workhouse," Feb. 3, 1917, pp. 1,2, "7,000 Could Live on Sum Astor Baby Requires," Feb. 4, 1917, p. 7, "Mrs. Byrne Well When Sentenced Says Physician," Feb. 4, 1917, p. 4, "Mrs. Byrne Tells Her First Story of Life During Hunger Strike," Feb. 6, 1917, p. 1, "Blackwells Island Gray, Dead, Desolate, Declares Mrs. Byrne," Feb. 8, 1917, p. 3, "Mrs. Sanger Put Near Maniac," Feb. 12, 1917, p. 5, "Here's a Home In Which Girls May Bury Past Woes," Feb. 15, 1917, p. 1, "What! Bread Crumbs Go to Waste! Won't Poor Ever Learn?," Feb. 17, 1917, p. 1, "Prices Going Up, Up, Up, Up, Up, Up! Famine Threatens!," Feb. 20, 1917, pp. 1,2, "East Side Women, Starving, Will Keep Children from School," Feb. 21, 1917, p. 2, "This Is Just the Simple Story of Poor Wolfe Lustig," Feb. 25, 1917, p. 3, "Nothing to Pawn But Her Body; Police Take That," Feb. 27, 1917, p. 1, "Girl on $12 a Week Sneers At Anne Morgan's Idea of Ease and Comfort on $15," March 4, 1917, p. 1, "Peace Pilgrims Find Common People Don't Favor War's Madness," April 2, 1917, p. 1, "Delaware Workers Emphatically Shout: 'We Don't Want War!,' " April 3, 1917, p. 2, "Europe's Moloch Claims Old Man's Son; He Comes To America and Starves," April 19, 1917, p. 3.

20. Dorothy Day, "A Coney Island Picture," *Liberator*, April 1918, p. 46.

21. Dorothy Day, "South Street," *Masses*, Nov.-Dec. 1917, p. 26.

22. For example, Dorothy Day, "The Book of the Month" (a review of *Doing My Bit for Ireland* by Margaret Skinnider, The Century Co., *Masses*, Aug. 1917, pp. 37-38, "Mary, Mary Quite Contrary" (review of *I, Mary MacLane*, Frederick A. Stokes Co.), *Masses*, Aug. 1917, p. 38, "Un-Modern Love" (review of *Helen of Four Gates* by An Ex-Mill Girl, E.P. Dutton & Co.), *Masses*, Sept. 1917, pp. 31-32, "Thousand and One Nights" (review of *Limehouse Nights* by Thomas Burke, Robert M. McBride & Co.), *Masses*, Oct. 1917, p. 30, "The Book of the Month"

(review of *King Coal* by Upton Sinclair, Macmillan Co.), *Masses*, Nov.-Dec. 1917, p. 31, "Marching Men" (review of *Marching Men* by Sherwood Anderson, John Lane Co.), *Masses*, Nov.-Dec. 1917, pp. 31-32, "Marching Men" (review of *Marching Men* by Sherwood Anderson, John Lane Co.), *Liberator*, March 1918, pp. 34-35.

23. For example: Dorothy Day, "Dance Hall Life of City Is Revealed," Feb. 3, 1924, pp. 1,2; "Dance Halls Flooded By Drink, Dope," Feb. 4, 1924, pp. 1,3; "Hangers-On Scramble to Gain Dance Hall Girls, Then Offer Them Whisky, Dope Smokes, Feb. 5, 1924, pp. 1,4; "Danceland Girls Make Only 4 Cents But Manager Explains That It 'Isn't a Rough Joint,'" Feb. 6, 1924, pp. 1,4; "Too Drunk to Dance, Some Swagger, Boast and Quarrel During Dance Hall Orgies, Feb. 7, 1924, pp. 1,4; "Woman With Knife Chases Dance Hall Girl Through Streets After Cafe Clash," Feb. 8, 1924, pp. 1,5; "Girl Supplements Wages As Store Clerk by Work At Dance Hall at Night," Feb. 9, 1924, p. 2; "Dance Hall Girl Wakes Up In Strange Room After Night of Carousing in Cabarets," Feb. 10, 1924, p. 1.

24. "Women to Ask Regulation of Dance Halls," New Orleans *Item*, Feb. 12, 1924, p. 2; "Women Thank Item for Dance Hall Expose," New Orleans *Item*, Feb. 26, 1924, p. 9.

25. "Women Crowd Fashionable Gaming Halls," Feb. 24, 1924, pp. 1,4; "The Thrills of 1924," Feb. 25, 1924, p. 5, Feb. 26, 1924, p. 13, Feb. 27, 1924, p. 5. Feb. 28, 1924, p. 12.

26. "Boxers Seem Fine Fellows By Comparison after Sleek Sheiks Mincing at Cabarets," New Orleans *Item*, Feb. 12, 1924, p. 10.

27. Day, *On Pilgrimage*, p. 145.

28. Day, "The Apostolate of Letter Writing," p. 17.

29. Ibid., pp. 17-19; letter from Donald Brown, Corning, N.Y., to Nancy L. Roberts, May 15, 1981.

30. Dorothy Day, letter to William D. Miller, Oct. 8, 1974, CW Papers.

31. Dorothy Day, "On Pilgrimage," *CW*, Feb. 1978, p. 2.

32. *CW*, April 1943, p. 5.

33. Vishnewski, "Days of Action," pp. 168-172.

34. Day, *On Pilgrimage: The Sixties*, pp. 88-89.

35. Personal interviews, Milwaukee, Nov. 5, 1981.

36. Personal interview, Milwaukee, Nov. 6, 1981.

37. Personal interview, Milwaukee, Nov. 5, 1981.

38. Personal interview, Milwaukee, Nov. 5, 1981.

39. Dorothy Day, "For These Dear Dead," *CW*, Nov. 1946, p. 2.

40. Dorothy Day, "Masked Men Plough Under Poor—Families Starve in Arkansas," *CW*, April 1936, pp. 2,7.

41. Dorothy Day, "Sharecroppers," *America*, March 7, 1936, pp. 516-517.

42. Miller, *Love*, p. 129.

43. See, for example, Dorothy Day, "Experiences of C.W. Editor In Steel Towns with C.I.O.," *CW*, Aug. 1936, pp. 1,2.

44. Mel Piehl, *Breaking Bread: The Catholic Worker and the Origin of Catholic Radicalism in America* (Philadelphia: Temple University Press, 1982) (hereinafter cited as *Breaking Bread*), p. 78.

45. Dorothy Day, "Father Kazincy, Workers' Friend, Speaks for Labor," *CW*, Aug. 1936, p. 4.

46. Dorothy Day, "Who is Guilty of 'Murders' In Chicago? (Day After Day)," *CW*, July 1937, pp. 1,7.

47. For example, "The Church and Work," *CW*, Sept. 1946, pp. 1,3,7,8.

48. *CW*, Oct. 1960, pp. 1,3.

49. *CW*, May 1954, pp. 1,6.

50. For example: "The Church and Work," *CW*, Sept. 1946, pp. 1,3,7,8; "Reflections on Work," *CW*, Nov. 1946, pp. 1,4; "Reflections on Work," *CW*, Dec. 1946, pp. 1,4; "On Distributism," *CW*, Dec. 1948, pp. 1,3; "The Pope and Peace," *CW*, Feb. 1954, pp. 1,7; "Worship of Money," *CW*, Oct. 1954, p. 8; "Distributism Is Not Dead," *CW*, July-Aug. 1956, p. 4.

51. Day, *On Pilgrimage*, p. 2.

52. Dorothy Day, "Day After Day," *CW*, Oct. 1935, p. 6.

53. Dorothy Day, "Christmas," *CW*, Dec. 1934, p. 4.

54. Day, *On Pilgrimage*, pp. 7,111.

55. Ibid., p. 175.

56. Day, *Loaves and Fishes*, pp. 37-38.

57. Dorothy Day, "Day After Day," *CW*, Feb. 1935, p. 3.

58. Day, *On Pilgrimage*, p. 10.

59. Dorothy Day, "On Pilgrimage," *CW*, Feb. 1979, p. 7.

60. Sally Cunneen made this point in "Dorothy Day: The Storyteller as Human Model," a paper presented at "The Catholic Worker and American Catholicism: Fifty Years," a conference sponsored by the History Dept., College of the Holy Cross, Worcester, Mass., May 2, 1983.

61. Rev. John J. Hugo, "Dorothy Day, Apostle of the Industrial Age," privately printed, 1980, CW Papers, p. 2.

62. Dietrich and Pollack, "An Interview with Dorothy Day," p. 2.

63. For example: Dorothy Day, "New York Call's Diet Squad Tries Life on $5 a

'Weak;' She Says Outlook Is Bright," *New York Call* (also known as the N.Y. *Leader*), Dec. 3, 1916, p. 5, "Reporter on $5 a Week Eats Farina and Cheese, and Reads Wordsworth," Dec. 6, 1916, p. 3, "Call's Diet Squad Gives Report—She Is 48 Cents to the Good," Dec. 10, 1916, p. 3, "Call's Diet Squad Fights Hard Against Solitude of Teeming City," Dec. 12, 1916, p. 2, "Call's Diet Squad Is Accused of Gluttony by Experts," Dec. 15, 1916, p. 3, " 'Man Cannot Live by Bread Alone,' and Neither Can a Normal Woman," Dec. 19, 1916, p. 2, "Call's Diet Squad Officially Reports System Won't Work," Dec. 27, 1916, p. 2.

64. Ellsberg, *By Little and By Little: The Selected Writings of Dorothy Day*, p. xv.

65. Dorothy Day, diary entry, Jan. 1963, CW Papers.

66. Quoted by Ade Bethune, personal interview, Newport, R.I., April 26, 1983.

67. Day, "For These Dear Dead," p. 6.

68. Dorothy Day, diary entry, June 1960, CW Papers.

69. Dorothy Day, "Day After Day," Sept. 1939, p. 4.

70. Day, *On Pilgrimage*, p. 10.

71. Day, "Who is Guilty of 'Murders' In Chicago? (Day After Day)," p. 7.

72. Dorothy Day, "Having a Baby," *New Masses*, June 1928, pp. 5-6.

73. "A Baby Is Born," *CW*, Jan. 1941, pp. 1,7.

74. Dorothy Day, "On Pilgrimage," *CW*, March 1951, p. 6.

75. Brian Terrell, "Books that Tell Worker, Day Stories," *National Catholic Reporter*, Dec. 12, 1980, p. 8.

76. Day, *On Pilgrimage*, p. 42.

77. Letter from Tom Albrecht to Dorothy Day, Dec. 25, 1941, CW Papers.

78. Letter Fom Anne McKeon to Dorothy Day, Sept. 16, 1967, CW Papers.

79. Letter from Mildred McLeod to Dorothy Day, Nov. 8, 1962, CW Papers.

80. Quoted in "Admirers Express Sadness, Gratitude," *National Catholic Reporter*, Dec. 12, 1980, p. 8.

V: The Lengthened Shadow

1. Vishnewski, "Days of Action," p. 166.

2. Eileen Egan, "Dorothy Day and the Permanent Revolution" (pamphlet), Erie, Pa.: Benet Press, 1983.

3. Letter from Deane Mowrer to Dorothy Day, March 14, 1961, CW Papers.

4. Personal interviews, Milwaukee, Nov. 5 and 6, 1981.

5. Ade Bethune, personal interview, Newport, R.I., April 26, 1983.

6. Michael Harrington, *Fragments of the Century*, p. 19.

7. Quoted by Judith Nies, *Seven Women*, pp. 196-197.

8. Personal interview, Milwaukee, Nov. 6, 1981.

9. Personal interview, Peace Dale, R.I., Jan. 12, 1983.

10. Vishnewski, "Days of Action," pp. 165-166.

11. Personal interview, Waterbury, Ct., May 15, 1983.

12. Robert Ellsberg, "Dorothy Day: Heroic Faithfulness," *Catholic Agitator*, Feb. 1981, p. 5.

13. Personal remarks, "The Catholic Worker and American Catholicism: Fifty Years," a conference sponsored by the History Dept., College of the Holy Cross, Worcester, Mass., May 2, 1983.

14. Personal remarks, Ibid.

15. Letter from Dorothy Day to William D. Miller, n.d., CW Papers.

16. Day, *Loaves and Fishes*, p. 101.

17. Day, "Farming Commune," *CW*, Feb. 1944, p. 8.

18. I am indebted to Piehl's analysis of Day and Maurin's relationship in *Breaking Bread*, especially pp. 61-70.

19. Letter from Dorothy Day to the Rev. Wilbur, May 22, 1934, CW Papers; Piehl, *Breaking Bread*, p. 62.

20. *CW*, Feb. 1947, p. 1; *CW*, Feb. 1934, p. 7; *CW*, May 1934, p. 1.

21. *CW*, July-Aug., 1933, p. 3.

22. Day, *The Long Loneliness*, pp. 269-272.

23. William Chafe, *The American Woman (Her Changing Social, Economic, and Political Roles, 1920-1970)* (N.Y.: Oxford University Press, 1972), pp. 107-109.

24. Ammon Hennacy, *The One-Man Revolution in America*, p. 290.

25. See, for example, this front-page story: "We Remind *The Daily Worker*— There Is a Religious Persecution in Russia," *CW*, March 1935, p. 1.

26. Personal interview, Milwaukee, Nov. 6, 1981.

27. Day, "Day After Day," *CW*, Sept. 1943, p. 6.

28. Day, *House of Hospitality*, p. 170. (Probably written in 1936.)

29. Personal interviews, Milwaukee, Nov. 5, 1981.

30. Day, "Un-Modern Love," *Masses*, Sept. 1917, p. 32.

31. Edmund J. Egan, interviewed by Deane Mowrer, Tivoli, N.Y., Oct. 1968, oral history tape, CW Papers.

32. Thomas Cornell, personal interview, Waterbury, Ct., May 15, 1983.

33. Nina Polcyn Moore, personal interview, Milwaukee, Nov. 5, 1981.

34. Day, *On Pilgrimage*, pp. 2, 174-175.

35. Dorothy Day, "Mystery of the Poor," *CW*, April 1964, p. 8.

36. Quoted by Lavine, "Forty Years of Works of Mercy," p. 8.

37. Day, *The Long Loneliness*, pp. 57-58.

38. C.S. Lewis, *Mere Christianity* (N.Y.: Macmillan, 1943), p. 103.

39. "Working Wives Opposed by Priest in Mill Town," *CW*, Dec. 1935, p. 8.

40. Eva Smith, "An Open Letter," *CW*, July-Aug., 1942, pp. 8-7.

41. Day, "Farming Commune," p. 8.

42. Day, *On Pilgrimage*, pp. 39-40, 174, 10.

43. Ibid., p. 61.

44. Day, "Farming Commune," p. 8.

45. Day, *On Pilgrimage*, p. 27.

46. Ibid., p. 9.

47. Thomas Cornell, personal interview, Waterbury, Ct., May 15, 1983.

48. "Dorothy's Way," *Newsweek*, Dec. 27, 1976, p. 61.

49. Dorothy Day, "The Book of the Month," *Masses*, Aug. 1917, p. 38.

50. Quoted by Lavine "Forty Years of Works of Mercy," p. 8.

51. "Dorothy's Way," p. 61.

52. Judith Gregory, "Remembering Dorothy Day," *America*, April 25, 1981, p. 346.

53. Ibid.

54. Day, *On Pilgrimage*, pp. 61, 57.

55. Day, *The Long Loneliness*, p. 57.

56. Letter from Dorothy Day to Sister Peter Claver, Sept. 8, 1975, CW Papers.

57. Robert Ludlow, "The Relationship Between Psychiatry and Catholicism," *CW*, Sept. 1952, p. 5.

58. Card issued by *Catholic Worker*, 1983; Henry James, ed., *The Letters of William James, Vol. II* (Boston: Atlantic Monthly Press, 1920), p. 90.

59. Quoted by Lavine, "Forty Years of Works of Mercy," p. 8.

60. Day, *On Pilgrimage*, p. 129.

61. Doris Grumbach, "Father Church and the Motherhood of God," *Commonweal*, Dec. 11, 1970, pp. 268-269.

62. Susan Ware, *Holding Their Own: American Women in the 1930s* (Boston: Twayne Publishers, 1982), pp. 135-136.

63. Vishnewski, "Days of Action," p. 165.

64. Ibid., p. 221.

65. Quoted by Dwight Macdonald, "Introduction," reprint edition of the *Catholic Worker* (Westport, Ct.; Greenwood, 1970), p. 12.

66. Thomas Cornell, "Tributes and Recollections," *America*, Nov. 11, 1972, p. 290; personal interview, Waterbury, Ct., May 15, 1983.

67. Personal interview, Waterbury, Ct., May 15, 1983.

68. Macdonald, "Introduction," p. 12.

69. Personal interview, Milwaukee, Nov. 5, 1981.

70. Florence Weinfurter, Nina Polcyn Moore, Mary Alice Zarrella, personal interviews, Milwaukee, Nov. 5, 1981.

71. Miller, *Love*, p. 67.

72. Day, *Loaves and Fishes*, p. 135.

73. Ibid., p. 134.

74. Day, "On Pilgrimage," *CW*, March 1966, p. 8.

75. Day, *The Long Loneliness*, p. 231; "On Pilgrimage," *CW*, May 1956, p. 7.

76. Day, "On Pilgrimage," *CW*, May 1956, p. 7; also, *Loaves and Fishes*, p. 133, *On Pilgrimage: The Sixties*, p. 91.

77. James Forest, "Dorothy Day: Witness to the Kingdom," p. 2.

78. James Forest, quoted by Lavine, "Forty Years of Works of Mercy," p. 7.

79. James Forest, quoted by Cook, "The Real Dorothy Day," p. 27.

80. Personal interviews, Milwaukee, Nov. 6, 1981; Waterbury, Ct., May 15, 1983.

81. Vishnewski, "Days of Action," p. 167.

82. Mary Alice Zarrella, "Peter Maurin," *CW*, Sept. 1982, p. 2.

83. Personal interview, Waterbury, Ct., May 15, 1983; also, Day, *The Long Loneliness*, p. 184.

84. Edmund J. Egan, interviewed by Deane Mowrer.

85. Vishnewski, "Days of Action," p. 219.

86. Thomas Cornell, personal interview, Waterbury, Ct., May 15, 1983.

87. Vishnewski, "Days of Action," p. 167.

88. Personal interview, Waterbury, Ct., May 15, 1983.

89. Forest, "Dorothy Day: Witness to the Kingdom," p. 2.

90. Day, *Loaves and Fishes*, p. 133.

91. Day, *On Pilgrimage: The Sixties*, p. 13.

92. Ibid., p. 91.

93. Letter from James Forest to Miss Forster, Nov. 22, 1961, CW Papers.

94. Personal interview, Milwaukee, Nov. 5, 1981.

95. Personal interview, Milwaukee, Nov. 5, 1981.

96. Day, *Loaves and Fishes*, p. 132.

97. Personal interview, Milwaukee, Nov. 6, 1981.

98. Ibid.

99. Personal interview, Milwaukee, Nov. 5, 1981.

100. Personal interview, Milwaukee, Nov. 5, 1981.

101. Personal interviews, Milwaukee, Nov. 6, 1981; Waterbury, Ct., May 15, 1983.

102. Edmund J. Egan, interviewed by Deane Mowrer.

103. Ellsberg, *By Little and By Little: The Selected Writings of Dorothy Day*, p. xii.

104. Personal interviews, Milwaukee, Nov. 5, 1981; Waterbury, Ct., May 15, 1983.

105. H.A. Reinhold, "The Long Loneliness of Dorothy Day," *Commonweal*, Feb. 29, 1952, p. 521.

106. Personal interview by Francis J. Sicius, June 24, 1976, CW Papers.

107. Personal interview, Milwaukee, Nov. 4, 1981.

108. Personal interview, Milwaukee, Nov. 5, 1981.

109. Day, *The Long Loneliness*, p. 266.

110. Personal interview, Milwaukee, Nov. 5, 1981.

111. Letter from Dorothy Day to Joseph Beller, N.Y. City, Sept. 24, 1934, CW Papers; also see letter from Dorothy Day to Catherine McSoley, Auburn, R.I., Oct. 16, 1934; CW Papers.

112. Letter from Dorothy Day to Joseph Beller, Sept. 24, 1934, CW Papers.

113. Thomas Cornell, personal interview, Milwaukee, Nov. 6, 1981.

114. Personal interview, Milwaukee, Nov. 5, 1981.

115. Day, *House of Hospitality*, p. 179.

116. Day, *Loaves and Fishes*, p. 122.

117. Quoted by Nina Polcyn Moore, Personal interview, Milwaukee, Nov. 5, 1981.

118. Francine du Plessix Gray, *Divine Disobedience: Profiles in Catholic Radicalism* (N.Y.: Alfred A. Knopf, 1970), p. 53.

119. Dorothy Day, "On Pilgrimage," *CW*, March 1966, p. 6.

120. Dorothy Day, "On Pilgrimage," *CW*, Dec. 1972, p. 2.

121. Forest, "Dorothy Day, Witness to the Kingdom," p. 2.

122. Day, *The Long Loneliness*, p. 148.

123. Stanley Vishnewski, "Dorothy Day, A Sign of Contradiction," *Catholic World*, Aug. 1969, p. 206.

124. Day, *Loaves and Fishes*, p. 122.

125. Letter from Dorothy Day to Msgr. Arthur J. Scanlan, March 16, 1934, CW Papers.

126. Miller, *Love*, pp. 87-88.

127. Bruce Cook, "Dorothy Day and the Catholic Worker," *U.S. Catholic*, March 1966, p. 11; John Corry, "The Style of the Catholic Left," *Harper's*, Sept. 1966, p. 59; James Forest, "Dorothy Day: Witness to the Kingdom," p. 2; Dwight Macdonald, "The Foolish Things of the World—I," p. 39; Miller, *Dorothy Day: A Biography*, p. 428.

128. Dorothy Day, "On Pilgrimage, " *CW*, Dec. 1965, p. 7.

129. Quoted by James Forest, "Dorothy Day, Witness to the Kingdom," p. 2.

130. James Forest, "There Was Always Bread," *Sojourners*, Dec. 1976, p. 12.

131. Lester P. Eliot, "The Troubles with American Catholicism," *American Mercury*, March 1935, p. 295.

132. Personal interview by Francis J. Sicius, June 24, 1976.

133. Letter from Dorothy Day to Msgr. Edward R. Gaffney, 1951, CW Papers.

134. Quoted by Dietrich and Pollack, "An Interview with Dorothy Day," p. 1.

135. Letter from Dorothy Day to Archbishop Doherty, Jan. 26, 1942, CW Papers.

136. Letter from the editors to the Rev. Wolfe, Thirties (no other date), CW Papers.

137. Reinhold, "The Long Loneliness of Dorothy Day," p. 522.

138. Day, *On Pilgrimage: The Sixties*, p. 92.

139. Quoted by Bruce Cook, "The Real Dorothy Day," pp. 30-31.

140. Dorothy Day, "The Case of Cardinal McIntyre," *CW*, July-Aug., 1964, pp. 6, 8.

141. Dorothy Day, "On Pilgrimage," *CW*, March 1960, p. 6.

142. Letter from Ammon Hennacy to John F. Kennedy, Sept. 30, 1960, CW Papers.

143. Donald R. Campion, "Of Many Things," *America*, Oct. 19, 1968, inside back cover.

144. Letter from Marge Hughes to Dorothy Day, Oct. 31, 1967, CW Papers.

145. Letters from Dorothy Day to William D. Miller, Jan. 29, 1965, May 12, 1973, CW Papers.

VI: Ominous Times, Valiant Decisions

1. Aaron Abell, *American Catholicism and Social Action: A Search for Social Justice*, 1865-1950 (Notre Dame, In.: University of Notre Dame Press, 1963), pp. 73-75.

2. Ibid., pp. 237-238.

3. Thomas T. McAvoy, C.S.C., "The Formation of the Catholic Minority," in Philip Gleason, ed., *Catholicism in America* (N.Y.: Harper and Row, 1970), p. 18.

4. O'Brien, *American Catholics and Social Reform*, pp. 29-30.

5. Philip Gleason, "American Identity and Americanization," in William Petersen, Michael Novak and Philip Gleason, eds., *Concepts of Ethnicity* (Cambridge, Mass.: Belknap Press, 1982), pp. 69-70.

6. Richard Hofstadter, *Anti-intellectualism in American Life* (N.Y.: Alfred A. Knopf, 1963), p. 136.

7. O'Brien, *American Catholics and Social Reform*, pp. 29-30.

8. Francine du Plessix Gray, "Profiles: Acts of Witness," *New Yorker*, March 14, 1970, pp. 84, 87.

9. Richard Deverall, "The Way It Was: 3," *Social Order*, Sept. 1961, p. 302.

10. Clement D. Brown, "A Reader Remembers," *CW*, Dec. 1983, p. 6.

11. Letter from Maurice J. Bonia to the *Catholic Worker*, March 27, 1936, CW Papers.

12. Personal interview, Milwaukee, Nov. 5, 1981.

13. O'Brien, *American Catholics and Social Reform*, p. 51.

14. "C.W. States Stand on Strikes," *CW*, July 1936, p. 1.

15. Quoted by Studs Terkel, *Hard Times* (N.Y.: Pantheon, 1970), p. 304.

16. Day, *House of Hospitality*, pp. 257-258.

17. Quoted in Terkel, *Hard Times*, p. 305.

18. "Catholic Worker Delegates to Attend Peace Conference," *CW*, Oct. 1933, p. 2.

19. "Pacifism," *CW*, May 1936, p. 8.

20. O'Brien, *American Catholics and Social Reform*, p. 86.

21. Robert Morton Darrow, "Catholic Political Power: A Study of the Activities of the American Catholic Church on Behalf of Franco during the Spanish Civil War, 1936-1939," Ph.D. dissertation, Columbia University, 1953; Esther J. Mac-Carthy, "The Catholic Periodical Press and Issues of War and Peace: 1914-1946," Ph.D. dissertation, Stanford University, 1977; John David Valaik, "American Catholics and the Spanish Civil War, 1931," Ph.D. dissertation, University of Rochester, 1964 and John Leo LeBrun, "The Role of the Catholic Worker Movement in American Pacifism, 1933-1972." The latter was helpful in preparing this section.

22. "The Mystical Body and Spain," *CW*, Sept. 1936, p. 4.

23. "Fascism Revealed in German Persecution," *CW*, Nov. 1936, pp. 1,2.

24. Emmanuel Mounier, "Spanish Catholic Flays Both Sides," *CW*, Dec. 1936, pp. 1, 8.

25. Personal interview, Milwaukee, Nov. 5, 1981.

26. Letter from Harry Guiltinan to the *Catholic Worker*, CW, June 1939, p. 5.

27. James Forest, "No Longer Alone: The Catholic Peace Movement," in *American Catholics and Vietnam*, ed. Quigley, p. 144.

28. Day, *Loaves and Fishes*, p. 119.

29. "Fake Headline of 'Catholic Worker' Misleads the American Workingman," *Social Justice*, July 5, 1939, p. 10.

30. Day, *On Pilgrimage: The Sixties*, p. 306.

31. Dorothy Day, "Explains C.W. Stand on Use of Force," *CW*, Sept. 1938, pp. 1, 4, 7.

32. Miller, *Love*, pp. 158-159.

33. Sheehan, *Peter Maurin: Gay Believer*, p. 199.

34. Ellis, *Peter Maurin: Prophet in the Twentieth Century*, p. 146; letter from Marc H. Ellis to Nancy L. Roberts, March 3, 1982.

35. Quoted by the Rev. Daniel Berrigan, "Introduction" to Day, *The Long Loneliness: The Autobiography of Dorothy Day* (N.Y.: Harper and Row, 1981), p. xix.

36. The Rev. John J. Hugo, "Dorothy Day: Driven by Love," homily, Dorothy Day Memorial Mass. Marquette University, Milwaukee, Nov. 5, 1981; privately printed, CW Papers.

37. MacCarthy, "The Catholic Periodical Press and Issues of War and Peace: 1914-1946," p. 164.

38. Quoted by Miller, Love, p. 166.

39. The Rev. John J. Hugo, "Weapons of the Spirit," CW, Nov. 1942, pp. 1,6,7; Dec. 1942, pp. 1,4,6; Jan. 1943, pp. 1,2,7; Feb. 1943, pp. 1,2,7; March 1943, pp. 1,2,6; April 1943, pp. 1,2. For a detailed summary of the Rev. Hugo's writings in the Catholic Worker, see LeBrun, "The Role of the Catholic Worker in American Pacifism, 1933-1972," especially pp. 116-119.

40. The Rev. John J. Hugo, "The Gospel of Peace," CW, Sept. 1943, pp. 1,7,8; Oct. 1943, p. 3; Dec. 1943, p. 3; Jan. 1944, p. 3; Feb. 1944, pp. 3,6; March 1944, pp. 1,4; April 1944, p. 3.

41. "Pacific Ifs," Time, Nov. 27, 1939, p. 51.

42. The Rev. Barry O'Toole, "Conscription," CW, Oct. 1939, p. 3; "Against Conscription," Nov. 1939, pp. 1,3; "Against Conscription," Dec. 1939, pp. 1,3; "Thou Shalt Not Kill," Jan. 1940, pp. 1,3; St. Thomas and Aggressive War," Feb. 1940, pp. 1,3,6; "Further Conditions of Just War," March 1940, p. 6; "Further Conditions of Just War," May 1940, p. 4; "Further Conditions of Just War," June 1940, pp. 2,6; "Peace-Time Conscription: A Catholic View," Oct. 1940, pp. 1,3; "A Counsel Not a Commandment," Nov. 1940, pp. 1,3,4.

43. "Is War Justifiable? War Preparations Cause Questioning," CW, April 1934, p. 5.

44. "War Gases," CW, March 1935, pp. 1,2; "War Imminent," CW, April 1936, pp. 1,5.

45. "Boycott Hearst," CW, July-Aug. 1935, p. 5; also, "Catholics Have No United Front with William R. Hearst," CW, Jan. 1936, p. 1.

46. "Conscientious Objection Duty of Christians," CW, Nov. 1935, p. 3.

47. "Denver Bishop Scores Un-American, Immoral Persecution of Jews," CW, Nov. 1933, p. 5.

48. Robert W. Ross, So It Was True: The American Protestant Press and the Nazi Persecution of the Jews (Minneapolis: University of Minnesota Press, 1980), p. 3.

49. "Catholic Church Stands Alone Today as Always—the True 'International'," CW, May 1934, pp. 1,7.

50. "Pope Pius XI Condemns Exaggerated Nationalism," CW, May 1934, p. 7; also see Day, "Who is Guilty of 'Murders' in Chicago? (Day After Day)" (1937).

51. Letter from Dorothy Day to Police Commissioner Valentine, New York, N.Y., July 1935, CW Papers.

52. "Anti-Semitism," *CW*, April 1936, p. 3.

53. " 'Social Justice' Publishes Anti-Semite Document," *CW*, Dec. 1938, pp. 1,2.

54. "Open Letter to Father Coughlin," *CW*, May 1939, p. 5.

55. Peter Maurin, "Let's Keep the Jews, for Christ's Sake," *CW*, July-Aug. 1939, p. 1.

56. Peter Maurin, "Why Pick on the Jews," *CW*, Jan. 1940, p. 2.

57. Archbishop Joseph Francis Rummel, "Prayers for Persecuted," *CW*, Dec. 1938, p. 1.

58. Bishop Gannon, "Bishop Flays Persecution in Europe," *CW*, Dec. 1938, p. 6; also see "Catholic Church Has Defended Jews During Times of Stress," *CW*, Dec. 1938, p. 7.

59. Donald S. Strong, *Organized Anti-Semitism in America: The Rise of Group Prejudice During the Decade 1930-1940* (Washington, D.C.: American Council on Public Affairs, 1941), p. 16.

60. Dorothy Day, Dec. 1938, CW Papers.

61. Miller, *Love*, p. 152.

62. Dorothy Day, "Grave Injustice Done Japanese on West Coast," *CW*, June 1942, pp. 1,3.

63. Arthur Sheehan, personal interview quoted in LeBrun, "The Role of the Catholic Worker Movement in American Pacifism, 1933-1972," p. 130.

64. "Forty-Eight Women Will Not Register," *CW*, Dec. 1942, pp. 1,3; Dorothy Day, "If Conscription Comes for Women," CW, Jan. 1943, pp. 1,4.

65. Gordon Zahn, "Leaven of Love and Justice," *America*, Nov. 11, 1972, p. 383.

66. Day, *Loaves and Fishes*, p. 60.

67. "To the Workers (An Appeal to Workers to Sacrifice for Peace)" *CW*, Oct. 1939, pp. 1,3.

68. Dorothy Day, "Fight Conscription," *CW*, Sept. 1939, p. 1.

69. "C.W. Fights Draft at Senate Hearing," *CW*, July-Aug. 1940, pp. 1,2.

70. Vishnewski, "Days of Action," p. 360.

71. Letter from Dorothy Day to the Rev. Tompkins, May 3, 1940, CW Papers.

72. Letter from Dorothy Day to the Rev. Whiterbone, "Eve of the Feast of St. James" (otherwise no date), CW Papers.

73. Dorothy Day, "Our Country Passes from Undeclared War to Declared War; We Continue Our Christian Pacifist Stand," *CW*, Jan. 1942, pp. 1,4.

74. Letter from Clarence E. Pickett to Dorothy Day, March 7, 1942, CW Papers.

75. Vishnewski, "Days of Action," pp. 367-368.

76. Personal interview, Milwaukee, Nov. 5, 1981.

77. Letter from Dorothy Day to Archbishop Doherty, Jan. 26, 1942, CW Papers.

78. Louis Lee Lock, "Forget Pearl Harbor," *CW*, Dec. 1942, p. 3.

79. Miller, *Love*, p. 176.

80. I am indebted to Robert Ellsberg's study of the Dorothy Day — Catholic Worker FBI file, as summarized in these two articles: "An Unusual History from the FBI" (I), *CW*, May 1979, pp. 3,4,5,6; and "An Unusual History from the FBI" (II), *CW*, June 1979, pp. 3,6,8. Hereinafter, these articles will be cited as "I" and "II," respectively.

81. The above quotations from the FBI Dorothy Day — Catholic Worker file are taken from Ellsberg, I, pp. 3-6.

82. Msgr. Matthew Smith, "Conscientious Objectors," *Denver-Register*, Nov. 15, 1942.

83. Quoted by Miller, *Love*, pp. 167-168.

84. Msgr. Charles Owen Rice, "Dorothy Day Would Make a Wonderful U.S. Saint," the *Catholic Bulletin* (St. Paul, Minn.), Dec. 19, 1980, p. 29.

85. "Houses of Hospitality," *CW*, Oct. 1944, p. 7.

86. Cook, "Dorothy Day and the Catholic Worker," p. 11.

87. Quoted by Day, *Loaves and Fishes*, p. 62.

88. Abigail McCarthy, *Private Faces/Public Places* (Garden City, N.Y.: Doubleday, 1972), p. 98.

89. Miller, *Love*, p. 168.

90. James Finn, *Pacifism and Politics* (N.Y.: Random House, 1967), p. 375.

91. Dorothy Day, June 1940, CW Papers.

92. Miller, *Love*, pp. 187-188.

93. Quoted by Vishnewski, "Days of Action," pp. 362-363.

94. Francis Joseph Sicius, "The Chicago Catholic Worker Movement, 1936 to the Present," p. 190; Chapter V, "Pacifism," outlines the conflict between the Chicago Catholic Workers and Dorothy Day and her followers over the question of World War II pacifism, and was helpful in preparing this section.

95. John Cogley, "Foreword" to Peter Maurin, *Easy Essays*, p. ix.

96. Personal interview, Milwaukee, Nov. 5, 1981.

97. Sicius, "The Chicago Catholic Worker Movement, 1936 to the Present," p. 198.

98. Day, *Loaves and Fishes*, p. 158

99. Dorothy Day, "Day After Day," *CW*, Sept. 1943, p. 6.

100. Dorothy Day, "And for Our Absent Brethren," *CW*, Dec. 1943, p. 2.

101. The Rev. Clarence Duffy, "Commenting on San Francisco," *CW*, May 1945, p. 1.

102. Day, "Explains CW Stand on Use of Force," p. 4.

103. Dorothy Day, "We Go on Record," *CW*, Sept. 1945, p. 1.

104. CW Papers.

105. Dorothy Day, "What Dream Did They Dream? Utopia or Suffering?," *CW*, July-Aug. 1947, p. 1.

106. Jack English, "Will They Go Again?" *CW*, March 1947, p. 1.

VII: Civil Disobedience and Divine Obedience

1. Lawrence S. Wittner, *Rebels Against War (The American Peace Movement, 1941-1960)* (N.Y.: Columbia University Press, 1969), p. 132.

2. For example: "A Petition to the President of the United States," *CW*, Jan. 1946, p. 8; "Ten Jailed C.O.'s Need Your Help," *CW*, March 1946, p. 7; "Reasons Why We Should Not Register," *CW*, July-Aug., 1948, p. 1.

3. Miller, *Love*, p. 227.

4. Piehl, *Breaking Bread*, p. 209.

5. Dorothy Day, "On Pilgrimage," *CW*, July-Aug. 1950, p. 1.

6. Robert Ludlow, "Personal Revolt," *CW*, July-Aug. 1950, p. 1.

7. Dorothy Day, "The Message of Love," *CW*, Dec. 1950, pp. 1,2.

8. Ibid., p. 2.

9. Ammon Hennacy, "Picketing," *CW*, Jan. 1951, pp. 1,7.

10. Robert Ludlow, "Labor and the War," *CW*, Jan. 1951, p. 1.

11. Robert Ludlow, "Capital Punishment," *CW*, March 1953, p. 6.

12. Miller, *Love*, p. 228.

13. Day, "The Message of Love," p. 2.

14. Robert Ludlow, "In Hope," *CW*, Nov. 1951, pp. 1,7; also see Ludlow, "Labor and the War," *CW*, Jan. 1951, pp. 1,3.

15. Letter from Dorothy Day to John Randall, June 1, 1952, CW Papers.

16. Robert Ludlow, "Freedom Assaulted," *CW*, Feb. 1951, p. 1. Also see Jack English, "The Internal Security Act Creates Police State," *CW*, Oct. 1950, pp. 1,2; "The Right to Differ—Justices Douglas and Black Dissent on the Conviction of the 11 Communists," *CW*, July-Aug. 1951, p. 2; George Patrick Michael Carlin, "McCarthyism Breeds Spiritual Paralysis," *CW*, Jan. 1954, p. 2.

17. Ludlow, "Capital Punishment," pp. 1,6.

18. Dorothy Day, "Meditations on the Death of the Rosenbergs," *CW*, July-Aug. 1953, pp. 2,6.

19. Cook, "Dorothy Day and the Catholic Worker," p. 13.

20. J.B. Matthews, "Red Plot to Trap Catholics," *National Police Gazette*, Aug. 1954, p. 37.

21. Francis E. McMahon, "A Catholic Worker," *New Republic*, Aug. 4, 1952, p. 21.

22. Quoted by Miller, *Love*, pp. 230-231.

23. Letter from Dorothy Day to Msgr. Edward R. Gaffney, 1951, CW Papers.

24. Harrington, *Fragments of the Century*, p. 69.

25. Tom Sullivan, "Chrystie Street," *CW*, Nov. 1951, p. 2.

26. Tom Sullivan, "Chrystie Street," *CW*, April 1952, p. 8.

27. Personal interviews, Waterbury, Ct., May 15, 1983.

28. Dorothy Day, "On Pilgrimage," *CW*, Jan. 1954, p. 8.

29. Ellsberg, I, p. 3.

30. Ellsberg, II, p. 3.

31. Ellsberg, I, p. 3.

32. Ellsberg, II, p. 3.

33. Personal interview, Waterbury, Ct., May 15, 1983.

34. Personal interviews, Waterbury, Ct., May 15, 1983; Milwaukee, Nov. 6, 1981.

35. Thomas Sullivan, interviewed by Francis J. Sicius, June 24, 1976, typescript in CW Papers.

36. Harrington, *Fragments of the Century*, pp. 18, 20.

37. Ibid., pp. 22-24.

38. Dorothy Day, "On Pilgrimage," *CW*, Sept. 1950, p. 1.

39. Much of the information on Hennacy's life is contained in his autobiographical *The Book of Ammon* (N.Y.: Catholic Worker Books, 1965), originally published as *The Autobiography of a Catholic Anarchist* (Glen Gardner, N.J.: Libertarian Press, 1954). Also see letter from Hennacy to Miss Imhof, Dec. 23, 1960, CW Papers.

40. Dorothy Day, "Introduction" to *The Book of Ammon*, p. vii.

41. Ammon Hennacy, "Open Letter to the Tax Collector," *CW*, Feb. 1951, p. 4.

42. Letter from Ammon Hennacy to Senator John Kennedy, Sept. 30, 1960, CW Papers.

43. "You are on Test Today," *New York Times*, June 15, 1955, p. 30.

44. Ellsberg, II, p. 6.

45. Dorothy Day, "Where Are the Poor? They Are In Prisons, Too," *CW*, July-Aug., 1955, p. 8.

46. Ammon Hennacy, "Civil Disobedience," *CW*, July-Aug. 1955, p. 7.

47. Day, "Where Are the Poor? They Are In Prisons, Too," pp. 1,8.

48. "Disarm" (handbill), n.d., CW Papers.

49. Quoted by Arthur Brown, "What Happened on June 15?" (N.Y.: Provisional Defense Committee, 1955, CW Papers), p. 10.

50. Hennacy, *The Book of Ammon*, pp. 288-289.

51. "The Rights of Non-Conformity," *Commonweal*, July 15, 1955, pp. 363-364.

52. Ellsberg, II, p. 6.

53. Ellsberg, II, p. 3.

54. Dorothy Day, "Creation," *CW*, June 1956, p. 2.

55. Ammon Hennacy, "In the Market Place," *CW*, Feb. 1957, p. 2; Hennacy, *The Book of Ammon*, p. 290.

56. "The Saint and the Poet," *Time*, March 12, 1956, pp. 89-90; Day, *Loaves and Fishes*, pp. 183-184.

57. Robert Steed, Beth Rogers, Charles McCormack, "Dorothy Day Among Pacifists Jailed," *CW*, special edition, July 17, 1957, p. 1.

58. "Pacifist Murderers," *Nation*, Aug. 3, 1957, p. 42.

59. "Silence and Shame," *Commonweal*, Sept. 20, 1957, p. 615.

60. Edward S. Skillin, John C. Bennett, Rabbi Eugene J. Lipman, "Pacifists' Dissent Backed," *New York Times*, July 30, 1957, p. 22.

61. "The Next Civil Defense Drill," *Nation*, May 14, 1960, p. 415.

62. Day, *Loaves and Fishes*, p. 160.

63. Hennacy, "Civil Disobedience," p. 7.

64. Hennacy, *The Book of Ammon*, p. 288.

65. Dorothy Day, "What Is Happening? Trial Continued Until Nov. 16," *CW*, Nov. 1955, p. 2.

66. Quoted by LeBrun, "The Role of the Catholic Worker Movement in American Pacifism, 1933-1972," pp. 177-178.

67. Letter from Eleanor Roosevelt to Dorothy Day, April 21, 1959, CW Papers.

68. Dorothy Day, "On Pilgrimage," *CW*, July-Aug. 1957, p. 2.

69. Dorothy Day, "More About Cuba," *CW*, Feb. 1963, p. 4.

70. Dorothy Day, "The Papacy and World Peace," *American Dialog*, July-Aug. 1964, p. 9.

71. Day, *On Pilgrimage*, pp. 126, 53, 146, 127.

72. William Worthy, "Cuba As I See It," *CW*, July-Aug. 1960, p. 6.

73. "The Catholic (?) Worker," *Wanderer*, Aug. 11, 1960, p. 4; also see "Reds Attempt Catholic Split," *Wanderer*, Aug. 6, 1964, p. 6.

74. Letter from Ammon Hennacy to the Rev. Rombouts, Sept. 23, 1960, CW Papers.

75. Letter from Paul Hallett to Dorothy Day and Ammon Hennacy, May 6, 1961, CW Papers.

76. Letter from Cornelia and Irving Sussman to Dorothy Day, Aug. 10, 1960, CW Papers.

77. Dorothy Day, "About Cuba," *CW*, July-Aug. 1961, pp. 2,7.

78. Dorothy Day, "Managed News," *Critic*, Aug.-Sept. 1963, pp. 53-54.

79. Letter from Thomas Merton to Dorothy Day, in Thomas Merton, *Seeds of Destruction* (N.Y.: Farrar, Straus, and Giroux, 1961), p. 253.

80. Letter from Matthew A. McKavitt to Dorothy Day, April 21, 1961, CW Papers.

81. Letter from Mary M. Brelsford to Dorothy Day, June 2, 1964, CW Papers.

82. Letter from Miguel de la Mora, Acapulco, Mexico, to Dorothy Day, Aug. 30, 1961, CW Papers.

83. Dorothy Day, "Pilgrimage to Cuba — Part I: Setting Sail," *CW*, Sept. 1962, p. 6.

84. Day, *On Pilgrimage: The Sixties*, pp. 96-97.

85. Dorothy Day, "On Pilgrimage in Cuba — Part II," CW, Oct. 1962, p. 4.

86. Dorothy Day, "Crusader in Exile," *Liberation*, Dec. 1962, pp. 20-22.

87. Day, "More About Cuba," p. 4.

88. Ibid., p. 4.

89. Miller, *Love*, p. 310.

90. Day, "Theophane Venard and Ho Chi Minh," p. 6.

91. Thomas Cornell, "Response to the Cold War," *CW*, Jan. 1963, p. 2.

92. Personal interview, Milwaukee, Nov. 6, 1981.

93. Thomas Cornell, "End the Draft," *CW*, May 1964, p. 3.

94. John Deedy, "The Catholic Press and Vietnam," in *American Catholics and Vietnam*, ed. Quigley, p. 131.

95. Edgar Forand, "Chrystie Street," *CW*, Dec. 1962, p. 8.

96. Richard Eder, "Hasty Marriages No Bar to Draft," *New York Times*, Sept. 1, 1965, p. 17.

97. Thomas Cornell, "We Declare Peace...," *CW*, Sept. 1965, p. 7.

98. Thomas Cornell, "Life and Death on the Streets of New York," *CW*, Nov. 1965, pp. 1,8; Catherine Swann, "Burning a Draft Card," *CW*, Nov. 1965, pp. 1,6; Gray, "Profiles: Acts of Witness," pp. 45, 50; Philip Berrigan, *Widen the Prison Gates: Writings from Jails* (N.Y.: Simon and Schuster, 1973), p. 76.

99. Quoted by Thomas Cornell, personal interview, Milwaukee, Nov. 6, 1981.

100. McNeal, *The American Catholic Peace Movement, 1928-1972*, p. 2.

101. Quoted by Dwight Macdonald, "Revisiting Dorothy Day," *New York Review*, Jan. 28, 1971, p. 18.

102. Cornell, "Life and Death on the Streets of New York," p. 8.

103. Personal interview, Milwaukee, Nov. 6, 1981.

104. Cornell, "Life and Death on the Streets of New York," p. 8.

105. Emerging Catholic Laymen, Inc., "Strange Fruits of the Catholic Worker" (Falls Church, Va.: broadcast Nov. 27, 1965), typescript in CW Papers.

106. Daniel Lyons, S.J., "Dorothy Day and the Catholic Worker—It Could Have Been So Different," *Our Sunday Visitor*, Jan. 16, 1966, p. 10.

107. Gray, "Profiles: Acts of Witness," p. 88.

108. Mary T. Hanna, *Catholics and American Politics* (Cambridge, Mass.: Harvard University Press, 1979), pp. 44, 40; 40-47.

109. Deedy, "The Catholic Press and Vietnam," pp. 123, 125.

110. "Declaration of Conscience," *CW*, Feb. 1965, p. 2.

111. Lewis Mumford, "Open Letter to President Johnson," *CW*, June 1965, p. 1.

112. Piehl, *Breaking Bread*, pp. 227, 229.

113. Quoted by Miller, *Love*, p. 316.

114. Quoted by Cornell, "Life and Death on the Streets of New York," p. 8.

115. Personal interview, Milwaukee, Nov. 6, 1981.

116. Spellman in Vietnam for 21st Christmas Abroad," *New York Times*, Dec. 24, 1966, p. 2.

117. John Cogley, "The Spellman Dispute," *New York Times*, Dec. 29, 1966, p. 3.

118. Dorothy Day, "In Peace Is My Bitterness Most Bitter," *CW*, Jan. 1967, pp. 1, 2.

119. See, for example: telegram to President Johnson to protest the police brutality in Selma, Alabama, 1965, *CW* Papers; Judith Gregory, "Justice and Violence in the South," *CW*, June 1961, pp. 1,5; Dorothy Day: "The Negro

Sit-Downs," *CW*, March 1960, p. 2, "Martin Luther King," *CW*, Nov. 1960, pp. 1,8, "On Pilgrimage," *CW*, July-Aug. 1963, pp. 1,2,7; Dianne Gannon, "A National Illusion," *CW*, April 1961, pp. 1,6; Felix Singer, "Report from a Freedom Rider," *CW*, July-Aug. 1961, pp. 1,6; the Rev. Philip Berrigan: "The Race Problem and the Christian Conscience," *CW*, Dec. 1961, pp. 1, 4-8, "The Liturgy and the Racial Struggle," *CW*, May 1964, pp. 4, 11, "The Black Man's Burden," *CW*, April 1965, pp. 1,7,8, "The Pathology of Racism," *CW*, Oct.-Nov. 1966, pp. 1,5; Thomas Cornell: "Alabama Freedom Walk," *CW*, June 1963, pp. 1,3, "Pope John and Integration," *CW*, June 1963, p. 3; Peter Dargis, "Reflections on Birmingham," *CW*, Oct. 1963, p. 7; Paul-Emile Cardinal Leger, "War, Racism and Mass Media," *CW*, Dec. 1965, pp. 1,7; Nicole d'Entremont, "To Selma and Back," *CW*, April 1965, pp. 1,4; Jack Cook: "The Powerless Blacks on Long Island," *CW*, July-Aug. 1967, pp. 1,6, "Rangers Riot, Strikers Suffer, Chavez: 'We Will Endure'," *CW*, June 1967, pp. 1,7,8.

120. Miller, *Dorothy Day: A Biography*, p. 441.

121. Letter from Karl Stern to Dorothy Day, March 12, 1967, Letter from Phyllis McGinley to Dorothy Day, Dec. 13, 1960, Letter from Allen Ginsberg to Dorothy Day, March 1, 1961, CW Papers.

122. Day, *On Pilgrimage: The Sixties*, pp. 324-325.

123. The Rev. Daniel Berrigan, "A Measure of Light," *CW*, Dec. 1980, p. 11.

124. The Rev. Daniel Berrigan, "Introduction" to Day, *The Long Loneliness: The Autobiography of Dorothy Day* (1981 ed.), p. xxii.

125. Quoted by Lavine, "Forty Years of Works of Mercy," p. 17.

126. James Forest, "Thomas Merton and the Catholic Worker—Ten Years After," *CW*, Dec. 1978, pp. 4-6.

127. pp. 1, 7, 8.

128. The Rev. Daniel Berrigan, "Daniel Berrigan on Thomas Merton," *Thomas Merton Life Center Newsletter* (N.Y.: Cathedral of St. John the Divine), April 1973, p. 7.

129. Letter from Thomas Merton to Dorothy Day, July 23, 1961, CW Papers.

130. Dorothy Day, "On Pilgrimage," *CW*, Feb. 1975, pp. 2,7.

131. Hanna, *Catholics and American Politics*, p. 41.

132. See, for example, Robert Calvert, "No Money for Warfare," *CW*, July-Aug. 1974, p. 1; Lewis Mumford, "The Morals of Extermination," *CW*, July-Aug. 1974, pp. 4-5; the Rev. Richard McSorley, "Letter to a Young Man Concerning War," *CW*, Sept. 1974, pp. 3,8; Eileen Egan: "Peacemaking: The Universal Mandate," *CW*, Oct.-Nov. 1974, p. 8, "Pax Christi: The Call to Be Peacemakers," *CW*, Jan. 1976, p. 6; the Rev. Daniel Berrigan: "A Question of Justice," *CW*, Feb. 1976, pp. 1,3, "Swords into Plowshares," *CW*, Oct.-Nov. 1980, pp. 1,3,4; Lowell Rheinheimer, "Seabrook: Resisting Nuclear Power," *CW*, Dec. 1976, pp. 3,6;

Dick and Evelyn Freeman, "Don't Pay War Taxes," *CW*, Feb. 1977, pp. 3,6; Daniel Ellsberg, "Racing the Arms Race," *CW*, Sept. 1977, pp. 1,3; Gordon Zahn, "The Church and the Arms Race," *CW*, May 1978, pp. 1,4, 9, 10; Robert Ellsberg, "A Dangerous Defense," *CW*, Dec. 1978, pp. 1,2; Meg Brodhead, "War Is Sweet to Those Who Have not Tried It," *CW*, Jan. 1979, p. 8; Thomas J. Gumbleton, "Salt II; A Moral Question," *CW*, Oct.-Nov. 1979, pp. 3,5; Eileen Egan, "Christian Pacifism," *CW*, Feb. 1980, pp. 1, 3, 6, 8; Robert Ellsberg, "Confessions of a Reluctant Resister," *CW*, Feb. 1980, pp. 1,5; Thomas Merton, "The Roots of War," *CW*, June 1980, pp. 5,6.

133. Dorothy Day, "Chavez, Workers Step Up Boycott," *CW*, March-April 1973, p. 4. Also see: Jan Adams, " 'Si Se Puede': A Report from the Grape Strike," *CW*, June 1973, pp. 3,7; Dorothy Day, "Grape Strikers Assaulted: Courage Faces Violence," *CW*, July-Aug. 1973, pp. 1,7; Jan Adams, "Farm Workers' Heroic Struggle," *CW*, Sept. 1973, pp. 1,6,8; Dorothy Day, "On Pilgrimage," *CW*, Sept. 1973, pp. 1,2,6; Jan Adams, "Imperial Valley Strike," *CW*, March-April 1974, pp. 1,6, "UFW March on Gallo," *CW*, March-April 1975, p. 1; Chris Hartmire, "Justice for Farmworkers," *CW*, Feb. 1976, pp. 1,6; Marian Moses, "Farmworkers, Look Forward," *CW*, Feb. 1978, pp. 1,3.

134. Dorothy Day, "On Pilgrimage," *CW*, Sept. 1973, pp. 1,2,6.

135. Cesar Chavez, "Always There," *CW*, Dec. 1980, p. 7.

136. "Imagination, Please," *New York Times*, May 24, 1972, p. 46.

137. Day, "On Pilgrimage," *CW*, Jan. 1973, p. 2.

138. Letter from Walter M. Alt, Director, Taxpayer Service Division, to Publisher, the *Catholic Worker*, Dec. 5, 1980, CW Papers.

139. "Let Us Now Praise," *America*, Nov. 11, 1972, p. 378.

140. "Honoring the Deserving," *Commonweal*, Oct. 27, 1972, p. 72.

141. Ellis, *A Year At the Catholic Worker*, p. 51.

142. Dorothy Day, "On Pilgrimage," *CW*, March-April 1975, p. 2.

143. Ellis, *A Year at the Catholic Worker*, p. 51; Peggy Scherer, personal interview, Milwaukee, Nov. 5, 1981.

144. Dorothy Day, "Bread for the Hungry," *CW*, Sept. 1976, pp. 1,5.

145. Anne Marie Kaune, "Deo Gratias," *CW*, Oct.-Nov. 1981, pp. 3,8.

146. Letter from Dorothy Day to the Rev. John J. Hugo, April 14, 1975, CW Papers.

147. Letter from Dorothy Day to Sister Peter Claver, Sept. 8, 1975, CW Papers.

148. Dorothy Day, "On Pilgrimage," *CW*, July-Aug. 1979, p. 7.

149. Miller, "All Was Grace," p. 386.

150. Dorothy Day, "On Pilgrimage," *CW*, June 1975, p. 1.

151. Egan, "Dorothy Day and the Permanent Revolution," p. 18.

VIII: Mightier than the Sword

1. Woodward and Salholz, "The End of a Pilgrimage," p. 75; Colman McCarthy, "The Final Tribute: Dorothy Day's Funeral and Her Lifetime as a Catholic Worker," *Washington Post*, Dec. 3, 1980, pp. D-1, 10.

2. "Street Saint," *Time*, Dec. 15, 1980, p. 74.

3. McCarthy, "The Final Tribute: Dorothy Day's Funeral and Her Lifetime as a Catholic Worker," p. D-10.

4. Timothy A. Mitchell, "Dorothy Day: Rest in Peace," *Wanderer*, Dec. 19, 1980, p. 4.

5. Edward Willock, quoted by James Forest in "For Those Who Sit in the Warm Sunlight," *Fellowship*, Sept. 1965, p. 16.

6. Letter from Edward Skillin to Nancy L. Roberts, Sept. 8, 1981.

7. Arthur Jones, "U.S. Catholic War Resistance Growth 'Historic'; Building on Catholic Worker Image," *National Catholic Reporter*, Oct. 30, 1981, pp. 1, 20.

8. "A Pilgrim's Witness at Hiroshima," *America*, March 14, 1981, p. 194.

9. Philip M. Boffey, "Scientists Urged by Pope to Say No to War Research," *New York Times*, Nov. 13, 1983, pp. 1, 36.

10. Day, "Poverty and the Christian Commitment," Cassette II.

11. "The Challenge of Peace: God's Promise and Our Response," section II, C-2, paragraph 1.

12. Ibid., section I, C-4, paragraph 9.

13. Robert J. McClory, "Peace pastoral gathers momentum," *National Catholic Reporter*, Feb. 10, 1984, p. 9.

14. Rev. Daniel Berrigan, "Introduction" to *The Long Loneliness: The Autobiography of Dorothy Day* (1981 ed.), p. xxiii.

15. Jones, "U.S. Catholic War Resistance Growth 'Historic'; Building on Catholic Worker Image," p. 20.

16. "Counsel for the Eighties: A Conversation with Professor J.M. Cameron," ABC broadcast, Jan. 20, 1980, 12:30 p.m., E.S.T. (Executive Producer: Sid Darion; Correspondent: Herbert Kaplow).

17. Bob Reilly, "The Catholic Worker Turns Fifty: Dorothy Day's Legacy Lives On," *St. Anthony Messenger*, May 1983, p. 17.

18. O'Brien, "The Pilgrimage of Dorothy Day," p. 711.

19. Edwin Emery and Michael Emery, *The Press and America* (Englewood Cliffs, N.J.: Prentice-Hall, 1984), pp. 218, 573-574.

20. Ibid., p. 325.

21. Robert Booth Fowler, *A New Engagement: Evangelical Political Thought, 1966-1976* (Grand Rapids, Mich.: William B. Eerdmans Publishing Co., 1982), Chapter Seven, "The Radicals," pp. 115-139.

22. Telephone interview, Feb. 22, 1984.

23. John Cogley, *Catholic America* (N.Y.: Dial Press, 1973), p. 175.

24. See, for example, "Democracy and the Vietnam Vote," *America*, Sept. 23, 1967, p. 294. I am indebted to MacCarthy, "The Catholic Periodical Press and Issues of War and Peace, 1914-1946," which was useful in preparing this section.

25. MacCarthy, "The Catholic Periodical Press and Issues of War and Peace, 1914-1946," p. 203.

26. "The Escalation of Dissent," *Commonweal*, Oct. 27, 1967, pp. 102-103.

27. Quoted in "Rebirth of a Catholic Cause," *Time*, July 4, 1983, p. 12.

28. Egan, "Dorothy Day and the Permanent Revolution," p. 20.

29. Peggy Scherer, "National CW Gathering," *CW*, Aug. 1983, pp. 2, 6.

30. Rachelle Linner, "The Gift of the Catholic Worker," *Catholic Agitator*, May 1983, p. 8.

31. Personal Interview, Milwaukee, Nov. 5, 1981.

32. Quoted by Reilly, "The Catholic Worker Turns Fifty: Dorothy Day's Legacy Lives On," p. 14.

Index

DATE DUE

Jan 31, 2014

FEB 1 2 2015

FEB 1 2 2015

SEP 1 7

FEB 1 2 2015